WALKING
WITH THE
ANZACS

The Authoritative Guide to the Australian
Battlefields of the Western Front

T0385298

MAT McLACHLAN

Fully revised and updated

hachette
AUSTRALIA

First published in Australia and New Zealand in 2007
by Hachette Australia
(An imprint of Hachette Australia Pty Limited)
Level 17, 207 Kent Street, Sydney NSW 2000
www.hachette.com.au

This edition published in 2015

National Library of Australia
Cataloguing-in-Publication data

McLachlan, Mat, author.
Walking with the Anzacs: the authoritative guide to the Australian battlefields of the
Western front/Mat McLachlan.

978 0 7336 3326 3 (paperback)

Australia. Army. Australian and New Zealand Army Corps.
World War, 1914-1918 – Battlefields – Europe - Guidebooks.
World War, 1914-1918 – Monuments – Europe - Guidebooks.
World War, 1914-1918 - Participation, Australian.
World War, 1914-1918 - Personal narratives, Australian.

940.4144

Cover design by Nanette Backhouse
Cover image of soldiers walking courtesy of Australian War Memorial (AWM E00833)
Text design and typesetting by Bookhouse, Sydney
Printed and bound in Australia by McPherson's Printing Group

Contents

List of Maps

For the men of the First AIF
'Pray God Australians in days to come
will be worthy of them.'

—CEW Bean

Acknowledgements

This book would not have been possible without the tireless work of the great historian Charles Bean. No student of the First World War can pick up a pen without first consulting Bean's magnificent twelve-volume *Official History of Australia in the War 1914–1918*. It is a masterpiece and must rank as one of the most thorough histories of a military force ever published.

I would also like to thank Matthew Kelly at Hachette Australia who has been a wonderful supporter of my writing efforts for the best part of a decade now. Without his vision and guidance this book would never have been written.

Thanks also to Peter Reynolds at KYSO Design. His great work designing the maps in this book has brought the walking tours to life.

The team at Mat McLachlan Battlefield Tours not only do a wonderful job of helping Australian travellers fulfil their dream of walking in the footsteps of the Anzacs, but they are also the nicest people you would ever want to work with. Thanks in particular to Karen Palfreyman, Todd Prees and Jane McCallum, plus the whole reservations and operations team. We are a great team and we have lots of good things to come!

Over the past decade many talented historians have been my mentors and friends. I have enjoyed sharing good conversation and cold beer with all of them, in Australia, the UK and on many foreign battlefields. We are blessed to have such a skilled group currently working in the military history field. They are the custodians of the Anzac legend, and it's in good hands. Thanks in particular to Michael Molkentin, Gary McKay, Brad Manera, Aaron Pegram, Peter Stanley, Rhys Crawley, Meleah Hampton, Peter Hart, Will Davies, Roger Lee, Tom Morgan, Peter Smith, Mike Peters and John Anderson.

Finally to my family, who have always supported this somewhat eccentric passion of mine and have always been there when I needed them. None of this would be possible without you.

Preface

It's summer at Mallee Plains in the wheat belt of New South Wales. The soil is parched and a lone fox, scrawny and patchy in his warm-weather coat, half-heartedly scratches in the dust, searching for grubs or crickets he knows he won't find. There's an old bush hall, a shed really, that stands forlornly beside the only road. It is weathered and canted and seems to groan under its own weight. It's stood here for decades, far longer than its builders would have expected, but it has begun to look as if its days are numbered. There's not much inside—a battered piano that has never been within earshot of a tuning fork, a dusty wooden roll of honour bearing names familiar to people in the district but belonging to another time, and, on the wall, a gun. This isn't a modern gun, all blued metal and polished wood, like the rifles used by farmers to keep the foxes down during lambing. This gun is old and obviously military. It's black and clunky, rusty and dusty, menacing and impotent at the same time. A brass plaque welded to the barrel casing chronicles its history in halting capital letters, diligently tapped out by hand in a French field a century ago:

GERMAN LIGHT MACHINE GUN. CAPTURED AND CLAIMED BY THE 20TH BATTALION AIF AT MONT ST QUENTIN ON THE SOMME. AUGUST 31ST 1918.

Mont St Quentin. A foreign name, mysterious. It doesn't roll easily off Australian tongues. It too is a farming community, but not one the old graziers of Mallee Plains would recognise. At Mont St Quentin they grow sugar beets and cabbages, on acreages Australians would call hobby farms. The land is as green as Mallee Plains is brown, and hilly—not in the way a New Zealander or Swiss would use the term, but hilly enough that a cross-country walk gets the heart rate up and a short stroll up a slope guarantees a good view from the top.

At the top of one of these hills is a memorial. In a land bursting with monuments to foreign armies, this one stands out. An Australian soldier, cast in bronze, with chiselled jaw and bulging biceps, stands squarely on a stone plinth. His pose is relaxed but his rifle is slung over his shoulder, within easy reach, and his stance is defiant, seeming to dare any foe to try and get past.

A van pulls up in front of the monument and a gaggle of French schoolchildren emerge. It's a grey day and most of them don't want to be here. They take a few snapshots, scribble some notes. One of the boys throws a stone at his mates. The more inquisitive peer up at the statue. 'Who is he?' they ask their teacher. 'Who is this tall man with the funny hat curled up on one side? Why is he here?'

It's a fair question. Now that the bronze Digger's comrades have all gone, the men who actually trod these fields and faced the guns, who does he represent? Is he still relevant to Australians almost a century after the last shots were fired?

He's a caricature of course, the embodiment of an ideal rather than flesh and blood, but it's an ideal worth holding on to. What went on here, the glory and tragedy, the courage and cowardice, the compassion and cruelty, should be remembered. And this is why Australians still stand in front of the Digger, staring into his

stoic face and wondering why, when they open their mouths, no
words come out. The Digger speaks of concepts close to our hearts:
courage in adversity, sticking by your mates, being Australian.
The bronze Digger stands at his post long after his last comrade
has gone and reminds us of an Australia that belongs in the past,
but is part of all of us.

How to Use
This Book

The Australian battlefields of the Western Front cover a large area, from the Belgian coast, through the Somme, to the *département* of the Aisne. As an extra complication, the Diggers didn't fight in these areas in any neat chronological order. They started in French Flanders in 1916 then moved to the Somme. In 1917 they fought in both France and Belgium. In 1918 they repulsed a strong German offensive at several places along the line, and then spearheaded the Allied advance eastwards from the Somme. In order to simplify things, I've divided the Australian battlefields into five main areas of operation: Belgium, French Flanders, the Somme, the Hindenburg Line and the Aisne. This is the simplest route to follow through the battlefields and only departs slightly from the correct chronological order.

Each of the main areas is broken up into chapters that detail each battle and discuss its objectives and outcomes, as well as its effects on the direction of the war and the men who fought in it. This is followed by a walking tour that takes the modern visitor to key sites on the battlefield and tries to give an impression of what it must have been like to walk these fields carrying a rifle and pack, with bullets whizzing overhead.

Each walking tour is followed by a list of other sites of interest in the area, plus local cemeteries of interest to Australians. I don't expect every visitor to walk *every* tour in the book; this would take weeks and is really only for those with a strong interest in the war, plenty of time on their hands and a love of strenuous exercise. For everyone else, I'd recommend you walk the three or four tours that interest you most and either drive the rest, or simply visit the remaining battlefields and spend an hour or so getting a feel for the place. Having said that, to do the memory of the Diggers justice there are a number of sites on the Western Front that should not be missed by Australian visitors. Allow three days to visit them all.

ESSENTIAL SITES

Belgium

- Ypres, including the Menin Gate and the In Flanders Fields Museum
- Polygon Wood and the 5th Division Memorial
- Messines and the nearby Toronto Avenue Cemetery (the only all-Australian cemetery in Belgium)
- Tyne Cot Cemetery near Passchendaele
- Lijssenthoek Military Cemetery near Poperinghe

French Flanders

- Fromelles, including the Australian Memorial Park, VC Corner Cemetery (the only all-Australian cemetery in France) and the new Pheasant Wood Cemetery and Museum

The Somme

- Pozières, including the 1st Division Memorial, Windmill Memorial and Pozières British Cemetery

- Near Pozières: Mouquet Farm, Thiepval Memorial to the Missing, Newfoundland Memorial Park (Beaumont-Hamel) and Lochnagar Crater (La Boisselle)
- 3rd Division Memorial, Sailly-le-Sec
- Villers-Bretonneux, including the Australian National Memorial and Victoria School
- Australian Memorial Park, Hamel
- 2nd Division Memorial, Mont St Quentin
- Vignacourt

Hindenburg Line

- Bullecourt, including the Australian Memorial Park, the Cross Memorial and the Slouch Hat Memorial
- Noreuil Australian Cemetery

The Aisne

- Montbrehain, including Calvaire Cemetery
- 4th Division Memorial, Bellenglise.

By concentrating solely on Australian actions during the war, this book runs the risk of understating the contribution of other nations. That is not my intention. This was a big war and the Australians didn't fight in isolation; at almost every step they were accompanied by brave and skilled fighters from Britain, Canada, France, New Zealand or the United States. But this book was written to record the achievements of the Australian forces. I will leave it to writers from the other countries to tell their nations' stories. Additionally, I have tried to avoid the stereotype of the incompetent British general sending the brave Aussie Digger to his death. Where British leadership was questionable, however, I haven't shied away from the fact. It's a fine line to tread, but hopefully I have succeeded.

PLACE NAMES

The names and spellings of many towns and villages in the
battlefield area have changed since the war years. This is particularly
the case in Belgium but can also be an issue in northern France.
For the sake of consistency, I have used wartime names and spellings
throughout this book, except where precise travel directions are
required. The most common changes in placenames are:

Wartime name	Modern name
Becelaere	Beselare
Dixmude	Diksmuide
Hamel	Le Hamel
Langemarck	Langemark
Lijssenthoek	Lijsenthoek
Lille	Rijsel (in Belgium only)
Messines	Mesen
Neuve-Eglise	Nieuwkerke
Nieuport	Nieuwpoort
Passchendaele	Passendale
Poperinghe	Poperinge
Ypres	Ieper

Planning Your Trip

Unlike other Australian battlefields, such as Gallipoli in Turkey or the Kokoda Track in Papua New Guinea, the battlefields of the Western Front are located very close to destinations likely to be visited by Australians on any Western Europe holiday, such as Paris and Brussels. By hiring a car and adding a few days to your itinerary, a comprehensive tour of the Australian battlefields will slot easily into your trip.

Three days is really the bare minimum of time required to do the area justice. The Australian sites are spread out. Any trip shorter than this will be conducted at breakneck speed and won't give you time to fully appreciate what you are seeing. For a three-day trip, spend one night in Ypres and one in the Somme (probably Albert). Only a couple of the shortest walking tours in this book can be completed on a three-day trip.

The more dedicated battlefield enthusiast should allocate about a week to the Australian battlefields. Five to seven days will give you time to complete more of the walks in this book, explore the battlefields in more depth and visit some of the smaller cemeteries. For a trip of this length, add a couple of nights in

Ypres and a few in the Somme, which will give you the extra time you need to explore the battlefields to the east.

If you are an enthusiastic historian, a trip of approximately two weeks will enable you to see every major Australian battlefield, complete as many walks as your fitness allows and spend time exploring off the beaten path. This is really only an option for the most dedicated student of the war, as a battlefield visit of this length can be emotionally and physically draining.

WHEN TO GO

The best time to visit northern France and Belgium is during the European summer, from June to August. The weather is pleasant, battlefield sites are accessible, days are long and the gardens in cemeteries and at memorials are in full bloom. Spring and autumn can also be good times to visit, with the added bonus that fields will be clear of crops, providing a better view of the lie of the land and unimpeded access to farm fields. Winter in this part of the world is not a pleasant time to be outdoors. If you visit the battlefields between November and February, prepare for wind, mud, rain and even snow. Still, seeing the battlefields during winter is better than never seeing them at all. The essential sites on pages 2–3 are accessible throughout the year.

GETTING THERE

The Western Front battlefields are easily accessible from Paris, Brussels and London. In Paris or Brussels, the best option is to hire a car. It is less than a two-hour drive on excellent roads to the battlefields. If coming from London, the best option is to catch the Eurostar fast train to Lille and hire a car there. Ypres (now known as Ieper, its Flemish name) is only a 30-minute drive away. You can also fly into Lille from a number of European centres.

If you are crossing the Channel by ferry, cars can also be hired in Calais.

There are some rail services to the battlefields, particularly to the big centres at Amiens and Lille, with less frequent services also calling at Ypres (Ieper) and Albert. Car hire is limited once you are in the battlefield areas, so if you are coming by train it is better to travel to Amiens or Lille and then hire a car for the short drive to the battlefields.

GETTING AROUND

The only practical way to tour the battlefields is by car. Public transport in the area is virtually non-existent and taxis will prove expensive for anything more than a short trip.

Roads in the battlefield areas receive little traffic and are easy to drive on, but a satellite navigation system is essential.

Bikes can be hired in Ypres and in the tabletop flatness of Flanders are a lovely way of visiting the battlefield sites close to town. This is not an option for touring in France, where distances are greater, or for visitors short on time.

A number of companies offer day tours of key battlefield sites. This is a good option if you are short on time or don't want to drive your own car, but bear in mind these tours will only give a basic overview of the battles and will not visit many sites of specific interest to Australians. Check with the tourist office in Ieper or Albert for departure dates and costs.

Extended tours of the Australian battlefields are becoming increasingly popular. These tours are often fully escorted from Australia, are hosted by experienced historians and specifically visit the Australian battlefields. Check with your travel agent for full details. (My own tour company, Mat McLachlan Battlefield Tours, offers tours to the Western Front throughout the year.)

WHERE TO STAY

The battlefield sites are predominantly rural and provide a range of accommodation options. Ypres is the most central base for touring the Ypres Salient, and Albert (and its surrounds) is an excellent option for exploring the Somme and the Aisne. Larger centres such as Lille and Amiens offer more accommodation but are less convenient than the smaller towns in the heart of the battlefields.

Accommodation options range from large international hotels to tiny farmstays and B&Bs. The following are a few of my favourites:

Ypres

Albion Hotel
This bright and clean hotel in converted law offices fills an accommodation gap that Ypres has had for years. It offers better rooms, facilities and services than the budget hotels in town, but is still reasonably priced. It is in a great location less than two minutes walk from the Menin Gate and the Cloth Hall, and has an excellent bar and lounge area. Highly recommended.

Albion Hotel
St. Jacobsstraat 28
8900 Ieper
Belgium
Phone: +32 (0)57 20 02 20
Fax: +32 (0)57 20 02 15
email: *info@albionhotel.be*
web: *www.albionhotel.be*

Ariane Hotel
A good choice if you are looking for a little more luxury. Nice facilities and rooms. Central location.

Ariane Hotel
Slachthuisstraat 58
8900 Ieper
Belgium
Phone: +32 (0)57 21 82 18
Fax: +32 (0)57 21 87 99
email: *info@ariane.be*
web: *www.ariane.be*

Main Street Hotel

A welcome addition to the accommodation options in Ypres, this fresh and funky boutique hotel offers six rooms, each with its own flamboyant style. Choose from rooms named 'Wild', 'Experiment', 'Glory' and more. Outstanding service, excellent amenities and a central location combine to make this the best small hotel on the Western Front. Highly recommended.

Main Street Hotel
Rijselstraat 136
8900 Ieper
Belgium
Phone: +32 (0)57 46 96 33
Fax: +32 (0)57 46 94 34
email: *info@mainstreet-hotel.be*
web: *www.mainstreet-hotel.be*

Hotel O

A bright and comfortable hotel offering a great location and excellent value. Rooms and public areas are decorated in a military theme.

Hotel O Ieper − Grote Markt
D'Hondtstraat 4
8900 Ieper
Belgium
Phone: +32 (0)57 36 23 30

Fax: +32 (0)57 36 23 31
email: *ieper@hotelhotelo.com*
web: *www.hoteloieper.com*

Messines Peace Village

An excellent hostel located in the village of Messines (Mesen), on ground fought over by Anzac troops in 1917. A great option for travellers on a budget, families and groups.

Messines Peace Village
Nieuwkerkestraat 9a
B–8957 Mesen
Belgium
Phone: +32 (0)57 22 60 40
Fax: +32 (0)57 22 60 45
email: *info@peacevillage.be*
web: *www.peacevillage.be*

Varlet Farm

For something a bit different, this family-owned working farm is a great option. Located in the heart of the Passchendaele battlefield, Varlet Farm offers cosy accommodation in an atmosphere very closely linked with the 1917 battles. Ask to see the collection of war relics found on the farm.

Varlet Farm
Wallemolenstraat 43
8920 Poelkapelle
Belgium
Phone: +32 (0)51 77 78 59
email: *info@varletfarm.com*
web: *www.varletfarm.com*

The Somme

Le Macassar (Corbie)

This art deco B&B is a gem. Finding accommodation of this standard in the heart of the battlefields comes as a real (and welcome) surprise. Individually styled rooms, period furnishings and warm service from hosts Ian and Miguel make a stay here a real pleasure.

Corbie is one of the most beautiful towns in the Somme and has a strong connection with Australians. Many Diggers remembered it as their favourite French town. It's about a 10-minute drive from the Australian National Memorial at Villers-Bretonneux and is close to Albert and the 1916 battlefields, making it one of the most convenient bases for Australian visitors in the area.

Le Macassar
8 Place de la Republique
80800 Corbie
France
Phone: +33 (0)3 22 48 40 04
email: *info@lemacassar.com*
web: *www.lemacassar.com*

Royal Picardie (Albert)

A clean and comfortable family-run hotel on the outskirts of Albert, and probably the nicest hotel in town. Albert is very central to the Australian battlefields, and the hotel is a short drive from the restaurants and cafes on the town square. The Royal Picardie also offers an excellent restaurant and bar.

Best Western Royal Picardie
138 Avenue du Général Leclerc
80300 Albert
France
Phone: +33 (0)3 22 75 37 00
Fax: +33 (0)3 22 75 60 19
email: *reservation@royalpicardie.com*
web: *www.royalpicardie.com*

Orchard Farm B&B
A delightful B&B in the heart of the Somme battlefields, operated by British couple Martin and Kate Peglar, who have been exploring the Western Front for more than 35 years. Martin is a published expert on First World War arms, and also appears regularly on television. Orchard Farm offers both B&B and self-catering accommodation.

Orchard Farm
2 rue Gaston Caron
80360 Combles
France
Phone: +33 (0)3 22 86 56 72
email: *thepeglers@orchardfarmsomme.com*
web: *www.orchardfarmsomme.com*

Hôtel de la Basilique (Albert)
A basic but comfortable hotel located in the heart of Albert, the central town for touring the Somme. It has a good restaurant and is conveniently located. Albert is a fairly charmless town, but is close to Pozières and the 1916 battlefields.

Hotel de la Basilique
3 et 5 rue Gambetta
80300 Albert
France
Phone: +33 (0)3 22 75 04 71
Fax: +33 (0)3 22 75 10 47
email: *contact@hoteldelabasilique.fr*
web: *www.hoteldelabasilique.fr*

MAPS AND RESEARCH

The Western Front battlefields are rural and most battlefield sites are unmarked, so a good map is an essential accessory for every battlefield tour. Without one the maze of French and Belgian villages will flummox even the most intrepid traveller, and it will be hard to get the most out of this book. The best map for navigating the entire Western Front region is Michelin Regional Map number 511 (Nord-Pas-de-Calais, Picardie). At a scale of 1:275 000 it is ideal for planning the best route between towns. The Regional series of maps replaced the venerable 'yellow cover' 1:200 000 series of maps in 2004.

The Michelin map is all you need for a battlefield visit but if you want a more detailed planning tool the IGN (National Geographic Institute) blue series of maps from Paris is a good choice. At a scale of 1:25 000 these maps provide excellent detail of specific battlefields but you will need to buy several to cover all the areas you wish to visit.

Michelin and IGN maps can be bought at bookshops in France, Belgium and England or online from international sites including www.stanfords.co.uk and www.amazon.com. A compass is also a handy tool for navigating the battlefields. A modern GPS navigation system (updated with maps of the battlefield areas) is also essential for finding your way around.

For a complete historic record of Australia's involvement in the First World War, see the *Official History of Australia in the War of 1914–1918*, written and edited by Charles Bean, founder of the Australian War Memorial. As the name suggests, this isn't a light read, but it is certainly the most comprehensive record of Australia's involvement in the war. Copies of the different volumes can be hard to find in bookstores but are usually in the reference sections of larger libraries. In 2003 the Australian War Memorial published the entire 12 volumes on its website, www.awm.gov.au. The Official History is too cumbersome to carry on a battlefield tour, but short sections of interest can be photocopied or downloaded and printed from the AWM website. The *Official History* was an invaluable source of information when compiling this book. Further useful reading can be found in the Select Bibliography, pages 350–351.

WHAT TO WEAR

The weather in Northern France and Belgium can be variable. Always prepare for cool weather, even in summer. A warm jumper or coat can be your best friend during a chilly evening trek back to your car. Rain can also appear out of nowhere, so carry an umbrella or waterproof jacket.

Wear sturdy boots or hiking shoes and take gumboots if the ground is muddy. A plastic garbage bag can be useful for transporting muddy shoes and helping to keep your car's interior clean.

If you intend to do some exploring off established paths, wear long trousers to protect your legs from cuts and scratches. Even after a century, barbed wire can still cause some nasty injuries.

SOUVENIRS

The former battlefields are littered with relics from the war. Although it can be tempting to bring back souvenirs, this should only be done with caution and the right attitude. Locating the site of a famous action and then taking away a cartridge case or a few shrapnel balls as a memento is a rewarding experience; walking across farm fields with your head down, picking up anything that catches your eye, is just souvenir hunting.

The types of souvenirs to be found (and that are safe to handle) include shell fragments, shrapnel balls, cartridge cases, pieces of barbed wire and assorted unidentifiable pieces of equipment.

A warning: In addition to myriad harmless relics, the battlefields of the Western Front contain a large amount of material that has the potential to injure and kill. Unexploded shells in particular are numerous and dangerous and should be left alone. All visitors to the battlefields will come across piles of unexploded shells, usually stacked at the corner of a military cemetery, waiting to be collected by bomb disposal units and destroyed. In no circumstances should these be touched. Hundreds of French and Belgian farmers have been killed handling shells since the end of the war. This, however, does not stop the insane practice by local farmers of removing the valuable copper driving band from an unexploded shell with a hammer and chisel.

Other dangerous items battlefield visitors are likely to encounter include unexploded grenades, unfired bullets and shell fuses. First World War grenades are inherently unstable. Even during the war they would often explode prematurely or malfunction in other equally undesirable ways. Today they should be viewed as highly dangerous, and should not be touched.

Unfired bullets are generally not as unstable as shells or grenades but they still should not be handled. Shell fuses (also known as 'nose cones' or 'nose caps') are safe to handle if from a detonated shell, but unsafe if from a dud. As it is difficult to tell which of these categories a fuse fits into, they are best left alone. It seems ludicrous to have to point it out, but it is also illegal to remove unexploded ordnance from the battlefield. The black market trade in these items is a growing problem and French authorities will deal harshly with anyone in possession of an undetonated bullet, grenade or shell.

There are many safe souvenirs that can be taken from the battlefield, such as shell shards, shrapnel balls and the like, without risking life and limb on unexploded ordnance. Remember: if you don't know what an object is, don't touch it.

Unless you are keen to experience small arms fire first-hand, think twice about entering woods in France and Belgium during the hunting season (November to February).

CEMETERIES

More than 330 000 Australians served in the First World War; 61 000 of them were killed, 46 000 on the Western Front. Today these men lie in 523 cemeteries across France and Belgium. Military cemeteries are the most tangible connection with the slaughter of the Western Front and seeing them should be a priority for every battlefield visitor.

The most striking aspect of the history of the Western Front cemeteries is how much they have changed. After the war, cemeteries were moved, enlarged, closed and merged. Individual graves were 'concentrated' into larger cemeteries, and small, isolated cemeteries were either closed completely and their graves moved to more accessible places or enlarged by the addition of graves from the surrounding area, sometimes ballooning from just a handful of graves to several thousand. Other cemeteries were started from scratch and grew as bodies were brought in from the battlefields. Some of these 'concentration' cemeteries are now among the largest on the Western Front.

British cemeteries are administered by the Commonwealth War Graves Commission (CWGC) and contain some common elements. With few exceptions, all headstones are identical in size and design. This reflects the ideal that all men killed in the war made an equal sacrifice, regardless of rank or social position. Each cemetery, regardless of size, features a Cross of Sacrifice made from stone and bearing a bronze sword. The size of the cross is proportional to the size of the cemetery. Many cemeteries, particularly the large ones, also have a large Stone of Remembrance, inscribed with the phrase 'Their Name Liveth for Evermore'.

All but the smallest cemeteries contain a register with a map of the cemetery and details of the burials. This should be your first port of call when seeking a particular grave. Visitors are also invited to add their names and thoughts to a visitor's book, housed with the register.

When permanent headstones replaced temporary wooden grave markers in the 1920s, the CWGC decided on a standard design. Each gravestone displays the soldier's unit badge (or country badge in the case of dominion graves, Australian included), regimental number (except for officers), rank, name, unit, date of death and age (unless withheld by the family). A standard Christian cross was included with the permission of the family. The only other religious symbol allowed was the Star of David for Jewish burials. Beneath the cross, the family was invited to add a personal inscription. These inscriptions make poignant reading and are a personal link with each buried soldier. Some families chose not to include an inscription (or could not afford it—the CWGC charged three-and-a-half pence per letter) and New Zealand did not allow personal inscriptions at all.

The CWGC also decreed that every British and Dominion man killed in the war should be commemorated by name, either on a grave or on a memorial. All unidentified bodies would be buried in graves with the inscription 'A Soldier of the Great War'. These unknown graves also carry a Christian cross and the stirring phrase suggested by Rudyard Kipling, himself a grieving parent: 'Known Unto God'. Some unknown graves carry a small amount of information that could be determined from the body, such as 'An Australian Soldier of the Great War' or 'A Corporal of the Great War'.

Occasionally graves carry more than one name, or two co-joined unit badges. This usually indicates that the soldiers' remains were so badly mangled that they could not be separated.

Often during the war a soldier would be buried in a known grave which was later lost due to shelling or further battles. Many cemeteries therefore carry special memorial headstones to soldiers 'Known to be Buried' or 'Believed to be Buried' in that cemetery. These are usually located along the cemetery wall with a nearby monument explaining the reason for the missing graves. There are no bodies buried beneath these headstones; they are memorials only. These headstones carry another poignant Kipling line: 'Their Glory Shall Not Be Blotted Out'.

Military cemeteries are organised into plots (indicated by a Roman numeral) and rows (indicated by a letter). To find a particular grave, first find the plot, then the row, then count along the graves. For example, a grave located at VI.B.24 is the 24th grave in Row B of Plot VI. The first headstone in each row will usually display the row and grave number carved into its side. Smaller cemeteries may not be separated into plots. In these, graves will simply be indicated by row and number (e.g. A.7). In cemeteries that were started during the war but then enlarged after the Armistice, the original wartime burials are traditionally designated as Plot I.

Take time when visiting a military cemetery. Wander the rows and scan the headstones for interesting unit badges or inscriptions. Each cemetery has its own character. All are sacred places.

GENERAL ADVICE

Visit the battlefields with an open mind. Try to see past the picturesque rural scenery that exists today to the carnage and destruction endured by the fighting men. The best way to do this is to get out into the field. Battles were not fought along well-trodden paths, but across the farm fields that surround the area. Farmers are remarkably tolerant of battlefield visitors. Most appreciate the significance of the area and are friendly and helpful. If you see a farmer, give him a warm greeting and ask for permission to enter his land. A few words of French or Flemish can be invaluable here, but hand gestures often suffice. Many farmers share your interest in the war and will often show you interesting relics they have found on their land. Most farmers have a large heap of scrap metal on which they dump war relics, and these can be of great interest to war visitors. You will often see old helmets, rifle parts, empty shell cases and barbed wire pickets discarded in these piles.

Always respect the rights of the landowner by not trampling crops or frightening livestock and by leaving gates as you found them—either open or closed.

RESEARCHING AN AUSTRALIAN SOLDIER

One of the most rewarding aspects of a trip to the battlefields is tracing the footsteps of a relative who fought there. Wartime placenames take on special significance if you know that a family member or friend trod the ground before you.

It used to be a challenge to research the military career of an Australian soldier, but, thanks to the internet, times have changed.

In a few mouse-clicks you can get a fairly detailed picture of the military service of an individual soldier and plan which areas of the battlefield are most significant for your visit.

The first stop for any First World War researcher should be the Australian War Memorial. The memorial's website, *www.awm. gov.au*, probably has more information available online than any other museum of its type in the world. This includes:

Roll of Honour: Details of the final resting place of all Australians killed in war.

Nominal Roll: Basic information about the military service of every First World War soldier, including date of enlistment, fate, service number and more.

Honours and Awards: Details of tens of thousands of Australians who received medals or awards in the First World War (excluding campaign and service medals).

Red Cross Wounded and Missing Enquiry Bureau files: Details the circumstances of death of more than 30 000 Australian servicemen.

Commemorative Roll: Details of Australians who died on active service with other Allied countries.

The AWM has a comprehensive Research Centre which is open to the public. They can also answer basic research questions over the phone.

For the most detailed record of an Australian soldier's war service, contact the National Archives of Australia. The National Archives holds the service records of all Australian First and Second World War soldiers. This is a personal record of a soldier's entire military career and sometimes stretches to hundreds of pages. The NAA's website, *www.naa.gov.au*, has an online search facility for service records (as well as other historic documents). Service records of all Australians who served in the First World War can be downloaded free of charge.

USEFUL WEBSITES

Australian War Memorial (*www.awm.gov.au*): The essential site for researching Australia's involvement in war.

National Archives of Australia (*www.naa.gov.au*): Stores Australian historic documents and service records of Australian soldiers.

Google Maps (*www.google.com.au/maps*): Useful for planning driving routes in the battlefield areas.

Commonwealth War Graves Commission (*www.cwgc.org*): Custodian of all Commonwealth war graves throughout the world. Online database of cemeteries and casualties.

Mat McLachlan Battlefield Tours: (*www.battlefields.com.au*): Information about my tours and books.

Somme Tourism (*www.visit-somme.co.uk*): Official tourism website of the Somme region. Use to plan your visit, accommodation, etc.

Australians on the Western Front (*www.ww1westernfront.gov.au*): Australian government site with information about the fighting in France and Belgium.

Department of Veterans Affairs (*www.dva.gov.au*): Administers Australian war graves and memorials overseas. Provides useful information about cemeteries and memorials.

Ypres (Ieper) Tourism (*www.ieper.be*): Official tourism information for Ypres.

Australian Bronze Commemorative Plaques (*www.plaques.satlink.com.au*): Since 1990 Melbourne sculptor Dr Ross Bastiaan has placed bronze plaques commemorating Australia's wartime heritage at battlefields all over the world. His website gives details about the 16 plaques at key sites in France and Belgium.

Western Front
Timeline

The term Western Front was originally coined by the Germans, who were forced to fight on two fronts: the Eastern Front against Russia and the Western Front against France, Britain and (eventually) the United States.

The Australian Imperial Force (AIF) first came to the Western Front in March 1916, following retraining and reinforcement in Egypt after the Gallipoli evacuation. By the time the AIF arrived in France, about half its members were Gallipoli veterans and half were new recruits.

The following table outlines the major battles on the Western Front and Australia's involvement in them.

☞

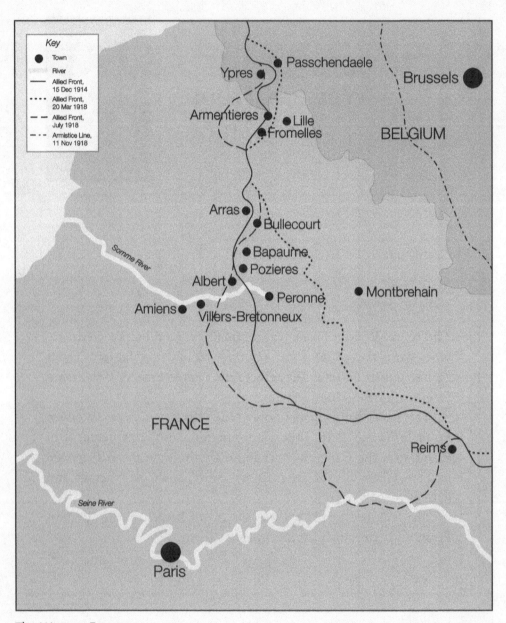

Key

● Town

River

—— Allied Front,
    15 Dec 1914

····· Allied Front,
    20 Mar 1918

– – – Allied Front,
    July 1918

–·–·– Armistice Line,
    11 Nov 1918

Passchendaele

Ypres

Brussels

Armentieres

Lille

Fromelles

BELGIUM

Arras

Bullecourt

Bapaume

Pozieres

Somme River

Albert

Peronne

Montbrehain

Amiens

Villers-Bretonneux

FRANCE

Reims

Seine River

Paris

The Western Front

1914

4 August
Germany invades neutral Belgium, prompting Britain to declare war on Germany. Her allies, France and Russia, had declared war a few days earlier. British dominions Australia, New Zealand, Canada, South Africa and India pledge their support within days and call for volunteers. Germany soon begins to advance into France.

22 August
Battle of Mons. British and German forces meet for the first time. British forces are outnumbered and begin a long retreat.

5–10 September
Battle of the Marne. British and French troops halt the German advance. The Germans give up on their plan to quickly capture France, and dig in. They must now fight the war on two fronts: the Eastern Front against Russia and the Western Front against France and Britain.

19 October–22 November
First Battle of Ypres. Germany fails in its efforts to reach the Belgian coast and digs in east of Ypres. The Ypres Salient is formed.

5 November
Turkey enters the war as a German ally.

1915

March–December
Britain launches offensives against the Germans at Neuve-Chapelle, Aubers and Festubert with high casualties and limited results.

22 April–25 May
Second Battle of Ypres. Germany renews its efforts to capture Ypres and uses poison gas for the first time in the war. British and Canadian forces stop the advance.

25 April
Gallipoli Landing. Australian, New Zealand, British and French forces land on the Gallipoli Peninsula in Turkey.

25–28 September
Battle of Loos. Britain launches a disastrous attack against German positions and loses 50 000 men without taking the German trenches.

December
Gallipoli evacuation begins.

1916

21 February–19 December
Battle of Verdun. Germany launches a massive attack against French forces in an effort to inflict high casualties and shatter French resolve. This was the longest sustained action of the war and cost the lives of more than a quarter of a million men on both sides.

March
Australian troops arrive on the Western Front and are sent to the 'Nursery' sector of French Flanders.

1 July–18 November
Battle of the Somme. British and French forces attack on a 40-kilometre front in an effort to break through the German lines. On the first day alone Britain loses almost 60 000 men. By the end of the fighting more than a million men on both sides are killed or wounded.

19–20 July
Battle of Fromelles. The Australian 5th Division attacks the German lines near the town of Fromelles in an effort to stop the Germans sending reinforcements south to the Somme. The battle is a disaster and 5533 Australians are killed or wounded in one night's fighting.

23 July–5 September
Battle of Pozières. The Australian 1st, 2nd and 4th Divisions join the Battle of the Somme by attacking the crucial village of Pozières. More

than 23 000 Australians will be killed or wounded in six weeks of fighting, the most costly battle of the war for Australia.

November

Battle of Flers. Australian troops attack German positions near Flers in atrocious weather on November 5th and 17th. Although they take some of their objectives, they are unable to hold them against German counter attacks and retire with heavy loss.

1917

March

German withdrawal. In an effort to secure a better defensive line, German forces withdraw several kilometres to the pre-constructed Hindenburg Line, an immense defensive system of deep trenches, concrete bunkers and thousands of kilometres of barbed wire. As extra protection, the Germans fortify a series of outpost villages in front of the Hindenburg Line and defend them with crack troops.

March–April

Australian troops attack the outpost villages as they advance towards the Hindenburg Line.

6 April

The United States declares war on Germany, but its army will not be ready to fight for months.

11 April

First Battle of Bullecourt. The Australian 4th Division and British 62nd Division attack the Hindenburg Line near the town of Bullecourt. Tanks, which are supposed to support the infantry, prove ineffective, breaking down before reaching the German lines or being knocked out by artillery. In spite of this the Australians succeed in breaking into the Hindenburg Line and spend a day and night of close fighting with Germans on all sides. Cut off and without support, the Australians eventually withdraw with heavy loss, including 1170 men taken prisoner, the largest number captured in a single engagement during the war.

3–17 May

Second Battle of Bullecourt. The Australian 2nd Division, supported by the 1st and 5th, renews the attack on Bullecourt and again penetrates the Hindenburg Line. Over the next two weeks the Australians resist fierce German counterattacks and eventually secure the ground. Even though the town is of little strategic value, the cost to capture it is immense. Australian casualties total more than 7400.

7–10 June

Battle of Messines. Australian, New Zealand and British troops attack Messines Ridge in Belgium. The battle is heralded by the explosion of 19 great mines and the Allied troops drive the Germans from the ridge. The attack is considered the finest of the war to date.

31 July–6 November

Third Battle of Ypres. British forces launch a massive assault on German positions in the Ypres Salient. Even though the attack begins smoothly, by October the autumn rains have turned the battlefield into a quagmire. By the time the village of Passchendaele is captured in November, more than 300 000 British troops have been killed or wounded. The effort leaves the British forces exhausted and vulnerable to a German counterattack.

20 September

Battle of Menin Road. Australian troops join the Third Battle of Ypres when the 1st and 2nd divisions attack alongside the British near Menin Road. The attack is a success and the Australians take their objectives, but at a cost of more than 5000 casualties.

26 September

Battle of Polygon Wood. The Australian 4th and 5th divisions continue the advance and capture the heavily defended Polygon Wood at a cost of 5400 men.

4 October

Battle of Broodseinde Ridge. Australian troops play their next role in the Third Battle of Ypres when the 1st, 2nd and 3rd divisions attack German positions on Broodseinde Ridge. During the advance German pillboxes prove difficult to subdue, but the Australians take all their objectives. The attack costs them more than 6500 men but is considered one of their finest victories of the war.

9–12 October
Battle of Passchendaele. With the weather having broken, the Australians join in two violent attacks on the village of Passchendaele in atrocious conditions. Inadequate artillery support, poor communication and a sea of mud contribute to a massacre. The 2nd, 3rd and 4th divisions lose more than 5000 men without capturing the town. The Canadian Corps takes over and eventually secures Passchendaele after two weeks of bitter fighting and 15 000 casualties.

1 November
After two years of lobbying, the five Australian divisions are brought together as the Australian Corps. Up to this point, each division has fought as an independent unit of the British Army.

7 November
Lenin's Bolsheviks seize control of Russia in the October Revolution. By December Russia has made peace with Germany and withdrawn from the war. With the end of fighting on the Eastern Front, Germany is free to concentrate her troops in France and transfers more than 500 000 men to the Western Front.

1918

March–April
German Spring Offensive. Bolstered by an influx of troops from the Eastern Front and keen to act decisively before US troops are ready to fight, Germany launches a massive offensive in France and Belgium. Crack assault troops attack the British line and break through at several points. The British fall back and the Germans begin a fierce drive for the Channel ports. Australian troops play a leading role in stopping the Germans well short of their objectives. Even though the Allies have suffered a major reverse, the effort has exhausted the German Army.

4–27 April

Battle of Villers-Bretonneux. In an effort to reach the crucial railhead of Amiens, German troops launch two attacks on the village of Villers-Bretonneux, 16 kilometres to the east. They capture the village but the Australian 5th Division launches a decisive counterattack on Anzac Day and regains the ground. This action halts the German Spring Offensive on this part of the front.

31 May

Lieutenant General John Monash takes command of the Australian Corps. For the first time in the war the five Australian divisions are united under an Australian commander.

4 July

Battle of Hamel. In a meticulous action devised by Monash, the Australian 4th and 11th Brigades, accompanied by 1000 American troops, capture the village of Hamel. The attack is hailed as a masterstroke and the close cooperation between infantry, tanks, artillery and aircraft is used as a template for British attacks for the rest of the war.

August–November

Advance to Victory The Allies steadily push the German line back until the reverse turns into a rout. In less than 100 days the Allies advance to the German border and the Germans sue for peace. Australian troops play a vital role, advancing against the Germans almost every day for two months.

8 August

Der Schwarze Tag On the first day of the Advance to Victory, Australian and Canadian troops spearhead an attack that pushes the Germans back more than eight kilometres in a day. The German commander later dubs this *der Schwarze Tag*, the 'Black Day' of the German Army.

31 August–2 September

Battle of Mont St Quentin. The 2nd Division attacks Mont St Quentin, a key position that has been turned into a German fortress. In three days of fighting the desperately under-strength division captures the mount, along with 2600 prisoners. The 5th Division also captures the important town of Péronne. Many consider this attack the AIF's most outstanding achievement of the war.

5 October
Battle of Montbrehain. In the last Australian action of the war, the 21st, 24th and 2nd Pioneer Battalions capture the village of Montbrehain in the *département* of the Aisne. The attack is not strategically important and costs the Australians more than 400 men, some of them Gallipoli veterans. On 6 October the AIF is sent to the rest area in the rear of the line. They are still there when the Armistice is signed five weeks later.

British Military Organisation

Unit	Size (full strength)	Commanded by
Army	150 000+ men	General
Corps	75 000+ men	Lieutenant General
Division	18 000 men	Major General
Brigade	4000 men	Brigadier General
Battalion	1000 men	Lieutenant Colonel
Company	250 men	Major or Captain
Platoon	60 men	Lieutenant
Section	15 men	Sergeant

Unit sizes are approximate and are for the period 1916–1918. By 1918 Australian forces were depleted to the point that most battalions were down to half- or quarter-strength.

Military Abbreviations

ADS	Advanced Dressing Station
AFA	Australian Field Artillery
AFC	Australian Flying Corps
AIF	Australian Imperial Force
ANZAC	Australian and New Zealand Army Corps
BEF	British Expeditionary Force
CCS	Casualty Clearing Station
CO	Commanding Officer

CSM	Company Sergeant Major
CWGC	Commonwealth War Graves Commission
GSW	Gun Shot Wound
HE	High Explosive
HQ	Headquarters
KIA	Killed in Action
MO	Medical Officer
NCO	Non-Commissioned Officer
OC	Officer Commanding
RAP	Regimental Aid Post
RFA	Royal Field Artillery
RFC	Royal Flying Corps
RSM	Regimental Sergeant Major

Common Decorations (in order of precedence)

VC	Victoria Cross
DSO	Distinguished Service Order (officers only)
DCM	Distinguished Conduct Medal (other ranks only)
MC	Military Cross (officers only)
MM	Military Medal (other ranks only)
MID	Mention in Despatches

Notes: 'Bar' indicates a decoration was awarded twice (eg: MM & Bar). During the First World War the only posthumous decorations that could be awarded were the Victoria Cross or Mention in Despatches. This explains why many men who were killed during a gallant act were seemingly overlooked for a bravery award (only receiving an MID) and why some men arguably received a posthumous VC for actions that would have warranted a lesser award had they survived.

In August 1916 it was decided that VCs would no longer be awarded for rescuing wounded.

Part I

Belgium

The fighting in Belgium during the First World War centred mostly on the strategically important town of Ypres (today known as Ieper). Only 12 kilometres north of the French border and 50 kilometres from the Belgian coast, Ypres was the gateway to the English Channel for the German Army. Access to the Channel ports would have given the Germans supply lines across sea and land, as well as bases for their powerful navy and submarine fleet. But dogged resistance by Allied forces, particularly the under-strength British Expeditionary Force, halted the German advance and forced them to dig in east of Ypres. The British defensive line, shaped like a crescent around the town, formed a 'salient', a bulge in the line that thrust out into German territory. Salients are difficult to defend. Their bulbous shape leaves the defender surrounded on three sides, and the enemy can pour fire into the confined space. With both sides desperate to dominate the ground, the Ypres Salient became a bloodbath. In an area of less than 100 square kilometres, more than a million men on both sides were killed or wounded.

Ypres was the scene of two ferocious battles in 1914 and 1915 but it is best known for the epic Third Battle, launched by the British in July 1917 in an effort to break out of the Salient. If the first two battles were hellish, the third was Armageddon: more than 400 000 British troops and 200 000 Germans were killed or wounded in four months of carnage. The British initially made good progress and the opening attacks went well, but then the weather broke. The battlefield turned to a sea of glutinous mud that clogged machinery and swallowed men. Troops were ordered to advance against machine-guns through thigh-deep mud and were cut down in waves. Wounded men who toppled off tracks sank into the mud and drowned before their mates could save them. By the time the attack was called off in November 1917, the British Army had been devastated.

Australian troops were prominent in the Ypres Salient battles throughout 1917. In June they attacked with New Zealand and British troops at Messines Ridge and pulled off a remarkable victory, at the time considered the greatest of the war. In September Australian troops played their first part in the Third Battle of Ypres, attacking along the Menin Road and then capturing the heavily defended Polygon Wood. In October they performed magnificently at Broodseinde Ridge, developing techniques that would later make them some of the toughest fighters on either side of the line. Later that month they played a central role during the carnage near the town of Passchendaele, attacking the village in atrocious weather conditions and dying in their thousands.

The Ypres Salient is one of the most important areas on the Western Front for Australian visitors. It is easy to visit, with the welcoming town of Ypres at its heart and tabletop flat countryside to explore. It is possible to see the most important sites, including Ypres, Passchendaele, Polygon Wood, Messines and Broodseinde Ridge, in one very busy day, but allow two days to do the area justice.

1

Ypres, 1917

Ypres was a First World War icon. As one of the few major Belgian towns not captured by the Germans during the war, it came to signify the defiance of the Allied forces—their unbreakable determination to withstand anything the Germans could throw at them.

Australian troops first saw Ypres in late 1916. By this time the town had been pummelled by two great battles and reduced to rubble. In spite of the storm of shells that rained down on the town it remained a major support base. Troops were billeted in the buildings still standing, and hospitals and supply bases were set up in protected corners. The town's massive ramparts proved impervious to shellfire and were home to headquarters, hospitals and supply dumps. During the horrific Third Battle of Ypres in 1917, tens of thousands of Australian troops marched through the shattered remnants of the town, past the looming shell of the Cloth Hall and into the killing fields beyond.

For regular battlefield visitors, modern Ypres is a bit like an old friend. The town that was so thoroughly pulverised has been reborn and, except for a few charmless areas on the outskirts, is an attractive and friendly town. Unlike some centres in France,

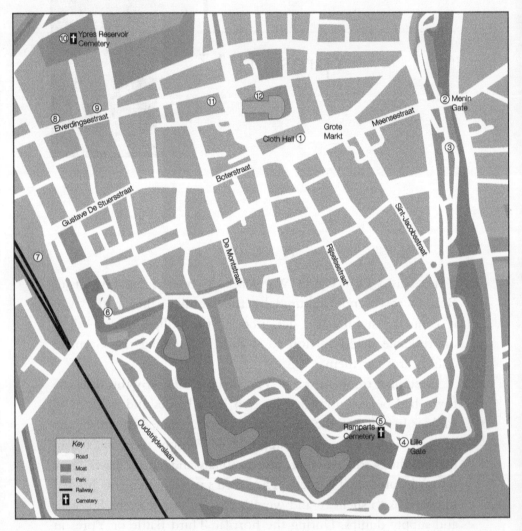

Ypres

Ypres embraces its wartime heritage. Today the town stands as a tribute to sacrifice and to the memory of an entire generation who were lost in its fields.

YPRES TOUR

Ypres is a friendly, compact town and serves as a great introduction to the Western Front. This tour visits the key wartime sites and is a fairly easy walk, with the occasional flight of steps the only real obstacle. In the warmer months it makes for a lovely evening stroll, with the Last Post ceremony at Menin Gate a fitting conclusion. The walk takes about three hours, but could occupy half a day if you linger at the cemeteries, Menin Gate, churches and In Flanders Fields Museum.

Begin your tour in the Grote Markt (Great Market), the centre of Ypres life and commerce for more than a thousand years. The buildings that surround the square are fairly faithful reproductions of the gabled structures that, until the war, had stood here for centuries. Dominating the square is the Cloth Hall [1], originally built during the 13th century and the heart of the medieval town's prosperous cloth industry. The first shells struck the Cloth Hall in 1914 and over the next four years the building was skeletonised by artillery fire. Its battered facade formed the backdrop for countless war photos. Reconstruction of the Cloth Hall began in the 1920s but was not completed until 1962. Pillars of the original building that were structurally sound were incorporated into the reconstruction. They still bear the scars from thousands of shell blasts.

On the ground floor is the Tourist Information Centre, a good starting point for planning your tour of the Salient. Next door is the outstanding In Flanders Fields Museum, named in honour of the famous John McCrae poem. As well as displaying arms and equipment, the museum cleverly uses technology to explore the human elements of war. On arrival, visitors are given an electronic wrist band encoded with the life story of a participant in the war. The bands can be scanned at terminals throughout the exhibition to reveal a sequential summary of the person's war experience, including sound and pictures. It's an innovation that adds a strong personal element to your visit. Relics from the fighting are displayed alongside audio-visual presentations, seamlessly incorporating history and technology. Allow at least two hours to do the museum justice.

After leaving the museum, walk diagonally across the square and follow Meensestraat until you reach Menin Gate [2]. As the town's easterly exit, this was the main route used by troops during the war to reach the front line. Hundreds of thousands of soldiers trudged along this road and out into the battlefields to the east; thousands fewer returned. In the war years there was no 'gate' here, simply a gap in the ramparts that was symbolically guarded by a pair of stone lions. These lions, battered and bruised, today guard the entrance to the Australian War Memorial in Canberra.

After the war Menin Gate was selected as the site to honour the thousands of missing British soldiers from the bitter fighting in the Ypres Salient. Sir Reginald Blomfield, a noted architect and designer of many cemeteries on the Western Front, suggested a design that incorporated elements of both a victory arch and mausoleum. The memorial was unveiled in 1927. Stone tablets on the interior walls record the names of 54 338 Commonwealth servicemen who have no known grave. Australian missing total 6176. Despite its imposing size, Menin Gate was not large enough to accommodate the names of all the British missing from the Salient. The monument therefore records the names of men killed up to 15 August 1917, with the remaining 34 872 names recorded on memorial panels at Tyne Cot Cemetery (see pages 96–97). Anzac troops are the exception to this rule. All Australians missing in Belgium, regardless of the date they died, are recorded on Menin Gate. New Zealand missing are recorded at Tyne Cot, Polygon Wood and Messines Ridge.

Every night at 8 pm the streets around Menin Gate are closed to traffic and crowds gather to hear volunteers from the Ypres

fire brigade play the *Last Post* in bugle chorus. It's a ritual that
has gone on here every night and in all weather since 1928. The
only pause was during the four-year German occupation in the
Second World War. The fire brigade recommenced the service
on 6 September 1944, the day the town was liberated.

With more than 6000 Australians commemorated on Menin
Gate, there are literally hundreds whose service in the war could
be considered noteworthy. There are no Australian Victoria Cross
winners recorded here, but the number of other bravery award
recipients is astounding. Three Australian soldiers honoured here
won the Distinguished Service Order (the second highest award),
22 received the Distinguished Conduct Medal (the second highest
award for non-officers), one soldier earned the Military Cross
twice (MC & Bar), two others earned both the Military Cross
and the Military Medal, 21 earned the Military Cross, four earned
the Military Medal twice (MM & Bar) and an astonishing 93
won the Military Medal.

One of the most notable Australians commemorated on Menin
Gate is Major Alexander Steele DSO, DCM (11th Battalion, died
07/10/1917). As a staff sergeant major in the 9th Battalion, Steele
landed at Gallipoli on 25 April 1915 and manned a machine-gun
in a dangerous position for four days. He was the only member
of his section not killed or wounded and was awarded the
Distinguished Conduct Medal. He was killed during preparations
for the attack on Passchendaele.

Also remembered here is Major Philip Howell-Price DSO, MC
(1st Battalion, died 04/10/1917), one of three officer brothers to
die on the Western Front. Lieutenant Colonel Owen Howell-
Price DSO, MC, commander of the 3rd Battalion, was killed
at Flers on 4 November 1916 and 2nd Lieutenant Richmond
Howell-Price MC was killed at Bullecourt on 4 May 1917. Philip
Howell-Price was Mentioned in Despatches three times at Gallipoli
and received the Distinguished Service Order for gallantry during
a trench raid in June 1916. In July 1916 he won the Military
Cross at Pozières. He was killed during the attack on Broodseinde
Ridge in October 1917.

Captain Harold Wanliss DSO (14th Battalion, died 26/09/1917) was a beloved officer who was dux of Ballarat College and an agricultural pioneer. Many who knew him (including General Monash, commander of the Australian forces) considered that, had he survived, he would have been a future candidate for prime minister. He was killed during the attack on Polygon Wood, after which his battalion commander 'cursed the day' he was not able to save Wanliss' life.

Major Gladstone Hunt MC (1st Field Ambulance, died 04/10/1917) was a doctor by profession and served in Gallipoli, France and Belgium. During the Australian advance at Thilloy in February–March 1917 he commanded an advanced dressing station for six weeks straight, organising stretcher bearers and treating wounded men under fire. For this bravery and devotion he was awarded the Military Cross. He was killed later that same year during the Battle of Broodseinde Ridge.

Lieutenant Clarence Mummery MC & Bar (8th Battalion, died 20/10/1917) was awarded the Military Cross twice in 18 months, and was unlucky not to receive a third. During the fighting at Pozières in 1916 he was the battalion's intelligence officer and was nominated for the award twice, in July and August. His commanding officers deemed that the two actions were close enough together to be considered a single event, for which he received the MC. At Polygon Wood a year later he led the battalion to the jumping off point and went forward with the attack. He was soon badly wounded in the side by a machine-gun bullet but refused to be carried to the rear. Incredibly, he led an assault on a machine-gun position and helped capture the garrison, an action that earned him a second MC. He was killed three weeks later.

One of the AIF's great young leaders is remembered on Menin Gate. Lieutenant John Lyons MC, MM, MSM (17th Battalion, died 09/10/1917) was a born leader who won the Military Medal as a sergeant at Gallipoli. He was badly wounded at Pozières in 1916 and was awarded the Meritorious Service Medal for his leadership there and at Bois-Grenier earlier in the year. During the first attack on Passchendaele in October 1917 he led a charge against Assyria House, a strongly defended pillbox. Fourteen Germans and three machine-guns were captured but Lyons was badly wounded by a shellburst. In the face of heavy German counterattacks his men were forced to leave him in the pillbox. He was never seen again. For several months after the attack his fate was unknown and, during this time, he was awarded the Military Cross.

Privates George and Theo Seabrook, aged 25 and 24, and 2nd Lieutenant William Seabrook, aged 21, were brothers who served in the 17th Battalion. All three sailed from Sydney on 25 October 1916 and fought together in France and Belgium. On 20 September, during the Battle of Menin Road, George and Theo were both killed by a single shell. William had not heard about the deaths of his brothers when he was wounded later the same night. He died the next day and is buried in Lijssenthoek Cemetery near Poperinghe. George's and Theo's names are recorded together on Menin Gate.

Climb the stairs on the left side of the memorial. Most of the panels in this area record the names of Australian missing. On the ramparts above is a bronze plaque by Melbourne sculptor Ross Bastiaan which details Australian involvement in the Third Battle of Ypres.

Walk back down the stairs, cross the road under the memorial and climb the stairs on the opposite side. These lead again to the ramparts [3], where a path meanders for about two kilometres along the eastern and southern edges of the town. The star-shaped ramparts that protect Ypres were built in the 17th century by the French architect Vauban, minister for fortifications in the court of Louis XIV. At this time Ypres was a northern outpost of the French empire and Vauban devised an intricate system of ramparts, a moat, gun platforms and artificial islands to protect it. During the First World War the sturdy ramparts proved impervious to German artillery fire, and headquarters and dressing stations were established in its casements.

Follow the path for about a kilometre until it crosses a stone bridge above a road. This is Lille Gate [4], the southern entrance to the town. Troops heading to and from the front line most often passed through Menin Gate, but it was constantly exposed to enemy shellfire, making Lille Gate a good alternative. No part of the Ypres Salient was safe, however. A road intersection not far from Lille Gate was so often targeted by German guns that it was dubbed Shrapnel Corner. Hundreds of men were killed at the spot. Beside the road beneath Lille Gate is a group of original cemetery signs from the Imperial War Graves Commission, the predecessor of the Commonwealth War Graves Commission. Battlefield pilgrims in the 1920s followed these signs to find the graves of lost sons. This is one of the few places where original signs remain.

Continue past Lille Gate to Ramparts Cemetery [5]. The cemetery was started by French troops who occupied the area in November 1914, and was used by Commonwealth troops from 1915 to 1918. The French graves were removed after the Armistice, leaving 198 Commonwealth burials. Ramparts Cemetery overlooks the moat and is shrouded by willows, making it one of the most beautiful cemeteries on the Western Front, particularly on a warm summer's evening. Eleven Australians are buried here, all of whom are identified. Among them are six men who were killed when a single shell struck the 2nd Division headquarters on 29 October 1917.

Continue along the path past the cemetery. After a short distance you will reach the remains of the first of two medieval towers, part of the original defences of the ramparts. Continue past the second tower and turn left at the intersection with another path. Follow this until you reach a small concrete structure on the edge of the path. This is one of two British pillboxes [6] that remain on the ramparts. They were built early in 1918 to defend against the German offensive that was closing in on Ypres. The Germans were eventually halted at Hellfire Corner, on the outskirts of the town.

Carry on past the pillbox and follow the path as it leads off the ramparts. Opposite the main road on your left is the Ypres railway station [7]. It remained open for most of the war and was used to supply troops, ammunition and tanks to the town during the great offensives in the Salient. Little remained of the original building after the war and the modern station bears no resemblance to its predecessor. A British tank stood in the square opposite the station between the wars, but it was removed by the occupying Germans in the Second World War and scrapped.

Follow the main road past the station and turn right onto Elverdingsestraat. This was the road most commonly used by troops as they marched into the shattered remnants of Ypres from their billets in the rear. After a short distance you will come to the Commonwealth War Graves Commission office [8] on the opposite side of the road. The team there will help locate graves and give directions to cemeteries, but this information is also readily available on the CWGC's website, www.cwgc.org.

Continue past the CWGC office until you reach a looming red building on the left. This is the Ypres prison [9], one of the few buildings in the town sturdy enough to withstand the ferocious German bombardments. Rudyard Kipling visited Ypres after the war and described the prison as a 'fine example of the resistance to shell-fire of thick walls if they are thick enough'. For this reason an advanced dressing station was established here early in the war. Men who died while receiving treatment here were buried in one of three nearby cemeteries, the largest of which was known simply as the Cemetery North of the Prison. After the war the two other cemeteries were closed and the graves consolidated into this cemetery. To avoid distasteful connotations with the word 'prison', the cemetery was renamed Ypres Reservoir Cemetery. Walk to it now by turning left into the road just past the prison.

Ypres Reservoir Cemetery [10] was begun in October 1915 and used until after the Armistice. At war's end it contained 1099 graves and was enlarged by the concentration of graves from smaller cemeteries and the gathering of isolated graves from the Ypres battlefields. Today it contains 2613 graves, of which 143 are Australian. Twenty-two of these are unidentified.

The most senior Australian soldier buried here is Major William Adams DSO, commander of the 3rd Pioneer Battalion. Adams was awarded the Distinguished Service Order in March 1917 for 'all round conspicuously useful services' and 'constant devotion to duty' since the formation of the battalion. He was killed by a shell while overseeing construction of a road near the front line on 15 October 1917 (grave I.H.43).

Also buried here is Captain Eric Kerr of the 11th Field Ambulance, one of three officer brothers to serve in the war. He had earned a medical degree with honours and had, in the words of his widow, 'every prospect of a brilliant future'. He was killed, aged 25, at Broodseinde Ridge on 4 October 1917 (grave I.C.17). His 21-year-old brother, Lieutenant Alan Kerr, had been killed in action at Pozières in July 1916. A third brother, Captain F Kerr, won the Distinguished Service Order while serving with British forces in the Royal Army Medical Corps.

Two English brothers lie side by side in Row B of Plot V: Captain Henry Knott of the 9th Battalion Northumberland Fusiliers and Major James Knott of the 10th Battalion West Yorkshire Regiment. Henry died of wounds in Ypres in September 1915. What is unusual is that James was killed on 1 July 1916 at the Somme village of Fricourt, more than 120 kilometres away. Their father, Sir James Knott, was a major benefactor of St George's Memorial Church in Ypres and lobbied the CWGC to have James's grave moved next to his brother's in Ypres. Respected war historian Paul Reed called this a 'most rare, if not unique, occurrence'. Their headstones carry identical inscriptions: 'Devoted in life, in death not divided'.

Leave the cemetery and return to the street that passes the prison. Turn left and carry on until you reach a small church on the right-hand side of the street. This is St George's Memorial Church [11], constructed in the 1920s to serve the families of English war grave workers living in Ypres and battlefield pilgrims from the United Kingdom. Construction of the church was largely funded by donations, and many families placed memorial plaques on the pews and walls to commemorate sons killed in the war. This huge collection of commemorative plaques is the main drawcard for most visitors, although services are still regularly held here.

Australian visitors should look for the plaque placed here by the RSL in 1953 with its rather broad commemoration of all Australian men and women killed in the two world wars. Individual memorials remember Australians Lance Corporal George Downton who was killed in April 1917 and Lieutenant Humphrey Watson who died at Broodseinde Ridge in October 1917. The family of Driver Joseph Green chose eloquent words to remember him: 'To the glory of God and in grateful remembrance of Driver Joseph Green, 25th Machine Gun Company, and his comrades of the Australian Commonwealth Forces who fell in Flanders'. In the late 1990s a plaque was unveiled commemorating Lieutenant Frank Scott and his raiding party of the 10th Battalion who were killed in the raid on Celtic Wood in October 1917 (see page 98).

Leave the church and turn right at the first street. The impressive St Martin's Cathedral **[12]** on the other side of the street is hard to miss. Aside from the Cloth Hall, the cathedral was the most prominent building in pre-war Ypres. Like nearly every structure in the town, it was reduced to rubble by the end of the war. In the opening year of the war the cloisters of the cathedral were used to billet troops, but that ended on 12 August 1915 when German shelling destroyed the cloisters and killed 20 British soldiers. The cathedral has been rebuilt in a similar style to the original 13th-century building, although the spire was squat and square-topped before the war, unlike the magnificent needle-point spire on the tower today. Monuments and stained glass windows inside the cathedral commemorate Ypres' wartime heritage.

After visiting the cathedral, return to the Grote Markt through an archway in the side of the Cloth Hall.

OTHER SITES OF INTEREST

Hellfire Corner

This intersection on the Menin Road, not far from Menin Gate, was a prime target for German artillery and was known during the war as the 'hottest spot on earth'. Hellfire Corner was an easily identifiable landmark on the main Allied thoroughfare to the front line and was pounded by the Germans day and night, in the hope of catching troops as they marched to the line. Hellfire Corner became iconic after a series of photos was released in 1917 showing transport teams furiously whipping their horses as they raced through the intersection. An original Hellfire Corner signboard, souvenired by a returning soldier but then lost, was discovered in Edinburgh in the 1990s and is now on display at the National Army Museum in London.

Directions
Hellfire Corner is easily located on the Menin Road. Leave Ypres (Ieper) and drive in the direction of Menin ('Menen'). After two kilometres you will reach a large roundabout linking several major roads. This is Hellfire Corner. Until the 1980s Hellfire Corner hadn't changed much since the war, but the modern roundabout has totally altered the intersection. Just before the roundabout is a demarcation stone marking the point where the Germans were stopped in their Spring Offensive of 1918.

Hill 60

This 60-metre hill is not a naturally occurring feature, but spoil from the nearby railway cutting, which was created in the 19th century. As one of the few elevated positions on the flat Flanders plain it was a highly prized objective for both sides and changed hands several times during the course of the war. When the fighting became too hot on top of the hill, both armies resorted to an underground war and began tunnelling and mining operations under the earth. The fighting underground was particularly grubby. The miners had often come from goldfields and coal pits and would spend months tunnelling with picks and shovels under the enemy trenches. There was constant danger from tunnel collapses and asphyxiation. Often the Germans would dig their own shafts and detonate small charges in an effort to destroy the British mines and kill the miners. Occasionally British or German miners would dig into an enemy shaft and ferocious hand-to-hand fighting would break out in the cramped tunnels. The 1st Australian Tunnelling Company spent much of 1916 and 1917 digging mines below Hill 60 and considered the work such an achievement they erected a memorial to their comrades here in 1919. Many of them still lie beneath the hill. Hill 60 was never restored after the war and the ground is still torn and battered from artillery fire and mine explosions. Several British and German pillboxes still guard the summit.

Directions

Leave Ypres (Ieper) in the direction of Menin and, after two kilometres, turn right at the roundabout towards Zillebeke. Turn left at the T-junction in Zillebeke and follow this road for about a kilometre to Hill 60. The Australian Tunnellers Memorial is located next to the entrance to the site. Bullet holes in the memorial are from fighting here in the Second World War. One of the great mines blown during the Battle of Messines and known as the 'Caterpillar' is located next to Hill 60. Take the bridge over the railway line (pausing to note the memorial to two French Resistance fighters killed here in 1944) and follow the track to the left across a field. The Caterpillar is surrounded by trees and looks deceptively like a natural pond. Its near-perfect symmetry betrays the violence that created it.

Nieuport

This seaside town was home to several bathing resorts and a golf course before the war and had been earmarked as the site for a British seaborne landing during the Third Battle of Ypres in 1917. In preparation, Australian tunnellers from the 2nd Tunnelling Company were sent to the area in July to dig mine shafts into large sand dunes beneath the German line. Anticipating the upcoming attack, the Germans launched their own attack on Nieuport on 10 July in an effort to drive the Allied troops in this sector back towards the coast. To help with the job they used a new type of gas shell for the first time, which smelled, according to a British artillery diary, 'like new mixed mustard'. Mustard gas would, of course, become one of the most feared weapons of the war.

Following the artillery barrage, the Germans attacked in strength and soon overcame the forward British positions. Men began streaming back towards the British support area but found that safety was on the far side of the wide Yser River. The first that the Australian tunnellers knew of the attack was when their tunnels were blown in by German trench mortars and no support troops arrived to dig them out. A dozen men barricaded one of the tunnels and held off the Germans until the next morning, but the Germans threw smoke bombs down the shaft and eventually forced the suffocating Australians to surrender. At the river, two Australians, Sappers Tom Burke and John Coade, were preparing to swim to safety when they realised that many of the British soldiers with them couldn't swim. Burke swam across the river holding one end of a rope and Coade held it taut while the non-swimmers used it to cross the river, then followed them. Both Australians received the Military Medal.

Many wounded men could not be moved and were left on the riverbank to be captured by the Germans. To everyone's surprise, an Australian sapper, James O'Connell, who had been burnt on the face by a flamethrower, hit in the head by shrapnel and had his hands shredded by a shellburst, stood up and began crossing the river by a rickety bridge. He crossed as far as he could on the damaged bridge and then swam the rest of the way. Hearing the cries of a British soldier struggling in the water, he leapt back in and dragged the man to safety before collapsing from exhaustion. For this unbelievable act of selflessness he was awarded the Distinguished Conduct Medal. Of two British battalions guarding Nieuport, only 80 men, including Burke, Coade and O'Connell, escaped.

Directions
Nieuport (Nieuwpoort) is about 40 kilometres north-west of Ypres (Ieper), along the N8. The town is still a popular seaside resort and has grown significantly since the war, but the sand dunes and riverbank where the tunnellers mounted their courageous resistance are still there. The main action occurred west of the village of Lombardsijde, between the east bank of the river and the village. On the way to Nieuport, visit the ominously named 'Trench of Death' at Diksmuide.

Poperinghe

This Flemish town, about 10 kilometres west of Ypres, was the major support centre for British troops in the Ypres sector. More than a million men were billeted around the town, or utilised the network of headquarters, supply dumps, hospitals and camps in the nearby hopfields at some time during the war. The town was occasionally knocked about by German shelling, but most of its restaurants and estaminets stayed in business and provided rest and refreshment to British troops. Australian troops first arrived in 'Pop' in 1916 and grew very fond of the town over the next 18 months.

The main wartime attraction in Poperinghe was Talbot House, a soldiers' rest house established by the Reverend Philip 'Tubby' Clayton, an Australian-born minister serving in the British 6th Division. A tireless and witty man, Clayton scorned rank and turned Talbot House (or 'Toc H' as it became known in army shorthand) into an 'everyman's club', open to officers and men alike. Clayton encouraged visiting soldiers to rest and relax while at Toc H, adorning the walls with humorous signs and creating a cramped chapel in the attic. It is estimated that more than 25 000 men took communion in the chapel before leaving to face the horrors of the Salient. Toc H is now a museum and Tubby Clayton's signs still hang on the walls. A tattered wartime map of the Ypres area hangs near the door; brown smears across its surface, left by a thousand muddy fingers, mark key sites on the battlefield. After the war the Toc H organisation was founded, based on the Christian principles established at Talbot House.

Directions

Poperinghe is reached by following the N38 for 10 kilometres west from Ypres (Ieper). Talbot House is in Gasthuisstraat, a street leading from the main square. Prison cells under Poperinghe's town hall, located on the main square, housed condemned men who were executed for desertion. The cells have been preserved, as has an original execution post, known to have been used in one execution and suspected of having been used in several others. Poperinghe's main square has not changed much since the war and is surrounded by buildings well known to the troops. 'Skindles', a popular officers' club, was located at 57 Gasthuisstraat, the same street as Talbot House.

Sanctuary Wood/Hill 62

Sanctuary Wood must rate as the most inappropriately named battlefield site in Flanders. While the area may have proved relatively safe for resting troops very early in the war, it soon found itself in the heart of the battlefield, and for the rest of the war only dead men would find sanctuary beneath its shattered trees. After the Armistice a small section of British trenches was preserved by the local farmer and operated as a museum for battlefield pilgrims. Descendants of the original owner still run the 'museum', but the term 'collection' would be more appropriate—there is no real order to the displays, most of which consist of rusty battlefield relics. The trenches are still there, but it is highly likely a bit of creative maintenance has altered them over the years. The museum is one of the most popular sites in the Salient for school groups, so don't expect solitude when you visit. For more peace and quiet, the Bayernwald trenches are a better option (see page 72).

Directions
From Ypres (Ieper), follow the Menin Road for three kilometres and turn right into Canadalaan, signposted to a Canadian Memorial. Sanctuary Wood is at the end of this road.

CEMETERIES NEAR YPRES

Hooge Crater Cemetery

The hamlet of Hooge was in the thick of the fighting throughout the war and possession of it seesawed between the British and Germans from October 1914 until the end of 1918. The area was devastated by shellfire, and a mine crater, blown by the British in July 1915, became the only prominent landmark in an otherwise featureless morass. Hooge Crater Cemetery was begun in October 1917 and is the perfect example of a small battlefield cemetery ballooning in size after the Armistice. At the end of the war the cemetery contained 76 graves, but after the concentration of graves from the surrounding area it reached its current size of 5922 burials. Reflecting the ferocity of the fighting in the area, 3578 of these are unidentified. Australian graves number 513, including 178 unknowns.

The most prominent Australian buried here is Private Paddy Bugden of the 31st Battalion, who won a posthumous Victoria Cross for attacking machine-gun positions and rescuing comrades during the attack on Polygon Wood, 26–28 September 1917. He was killed by shellfire, aged 20, on the 28th (grave VIII.C.5).

Also buried here is Lieutenant Frank Goodwin of the 8th Battalion, who won the Military Cross on two separate occasions (MC & Bar) in 1916. He was killed during the attack on Broodseinde Ridge on 4 October 1917 (grave XV.D.15).

Directions
Hooge Crater Cemetery is four kilometres from Ypres (Ieper) along the Menin Road. The most distinguishing design feature of the cemetery is a stylised 'crater' built near the entrance. There is a good small museum across the road from the cemetery.

Lijssenthoek Military Cemetery, Poperinghe

During the war this massive cemetery was the largest on the Western Front. It was built on the main transport lines between the rear areas of the British sector of the Ypres Salient and the front line, next to a collection of hospitals and casualty clearing stations. It was begun in 1915 and used during all the major battles around Ypres, but received most of its burials during the horrific Third Battle of Ypres in 1917. Today there are 9901 Commonwealth soldiers buried here, plus 883 soldiers from other countries, including Germany, France and the United States. Because the men buried here mostly died of wounds in military hospitals, there was usually ample opportunity to identify them, resulting in a low proportion of unknown graves. This is certainly the case with the Australian burials, all 1131 of which are identified.

The most notable Australian buried here is Major Frederick Tubb of the 7th Battalion, who had won a Victoria Cross during the fierce fighting at Lone Pine in Gallipoli. While leading his men during the Battle of Menin Road on 20 September 1917, he was wounded by a British shell. He died from his wounds later that day (grave XIX.C.5).

Also buried here is 2nd Lieutenant William Seabrook of the 17th Battalion, who died of wounds on 21 September 1917, aged 21 (grave XXIII.B.5). William Seabrook was one of three brothers killed within two days during the Battle of Menin Road. His brothers George and Theo were both killed on 20 September and have no known grave. Their names are recorded on Menin Gate.

Two senior officers are buried side by side in Lijssenthoek: Lieutenant Colonel Stan Gibbs of the 2nd Division Train,

Australian Army Service Corps and Lieutenant Colonel James Nicholas of the 5th Australian Field Ambulance. Gibbs had served at Gallipoli and was Mentioned in Despatches in January 1917. He had been instrumental in organising transport services to support the Australian attacks in the Third Battle of Ypres, but was killed when the Germans bombarded the Australian support area during the Battle of Menin Road on 20 September 1917 (grave XIX.C.3). Nicholas had also served in Gallipoli and was Mentioned in Despatches in 1917. He was killed in the same barrage as Gibbs on 20 September (grave XIX.C.4).

Directions
Lijssenthoek Cemetery is near the town of Poperinghe, 10 kilometres west of Ypres (Ieper). From Poperinghe, take the N38 south. After 800 metres turn left into Lenestraat then immediately right into Boescheepseweg. The cemetery is two kilometres along this road on the right-hand side.

Menin Road South Military Cemetery

The Menin Road was the main route to the front line used by British troops during the fighting in the Ypres Salient. Menin Road South Cemetery was begun by field ambulances in 1916 to bury wounded men who had died while being transported from the front line to hospitals in the rear. It was used until the summer of 1918 and then greatly enlarged after the Armistice. Today it contains 1657 graves; of these, 267 are Australian, including eight unknowns.

Buried here is Captain Fred Moore of the 5th Battalion, who was mortally wounded at Polygon Wood on 20 September 1917 by a German who had feigned surrender (grave I.T.4). (See **Black Watch Corner** in the Polygon Wood chapter, page 86, for the full story.)

Sergeant Thomas 'Bert' Major of the Australian Army Service Corps was a good example of the fine leadership qualities of Australian non-commissioned officers. He had landed at Gallipoli on the first day of the campaign and was adored by all the men he served with. On 21 October 1917, he was helping load ammunition on the Menin Road when a barrage of shells caught the transport company. According to witnesses, Major was wounded by two shell blasts before being killed by a third. His last words to one of his distraught men were: 'I'm all right, laddie.' After his burial the men of his company chipped in to make him an elaborate iron cross, but the Germans captured the area before it could be erected over his grave (grave III.L.22).

The high price paid by the Engineers to keep roads and rails in good repair during the Ypres fighting is well illustrated at this cemetery. They number forty of the 267 Australians buried here.

Directions
Menin Road South Military Cemetery is two kilometres from Ypres (Ieper) on the Menin Road.

Perth Cemetery (China Wall)

This frontline cemetery was started by French troops in 1914 and used until October 1917. It is unknown how the cemetery came to be called Perth, but the China Wall part comes from a nearby trench known as the Great Wall of China. The cemetery was also known to troops as Halfway House Cemetery and contained 130 graves at the end of the war. After the Armistice, Perth Cemetery was enlarged by the concentration of graves from more than 30 smaller cemeteries. Today 2791 Commonwealth soldiers are buried or commemorated here—the French graves were removed after the war. Australian graves number 147, including 19 who could not be identified.

The most notable Australian buried here is 2nd Lieutenant Fred Birks of the 6th Battalion, who won a posthumous Victoria Cross for extraordinary acts of bravery during the Battle of Menin Road on 20–21 September 1917. Birks was killed on the 21st while digging out comrades who had been buried by a shell (grave I.G.45).

Directions

From Ypres (Ieper), take the Menin Road and turn right towards Zillebeke. Perth Cemetery is one kilometre along this road on the left.

Ramparts Cemetery: see Ypres walking tour, page 37.

Sanctuary Wood Cemetery

Sanctuary Wood was so named because it was used to screen troops behind the front line early in the war. By 1915 the wood was squarely in the front line and was the scene of several bloody battles between 1915 and 1918. Three cemeteries were built in the wood in 1915 but these were almost obliterated by later fighting and most of the graves were lost. One of the cemeteries was partially reconstructed and became the basis for the modern Sanctuary Wood Cemetery. It contained 137 graves at the time of the Armistice and was enlarged to 1989 graves in the post-war years. Of these, 88 are Australian but only 35 are identified. Most of these men were killed in the Polygon Wood sector in 1917 and originally buried in isolated graves.

The most notable grave here belongs to Lieutenant Gilbert Talbot of the British Rifle Brigade, who was killed in July 1915. Talbot House in Poperinghe was named in his honour (grave I.G.1).

Directions

As for Sanctuary Wood (page 50). The cemetery is just before the museum on the right.

Ypres Reservoir Cemetery: see Ypres walking tour (page 37).

2

Battle of Messines, 7 June 1917

By 1917 the failure of the British to break through the German lines on the Somme had led them to look for other opportunities. The Ypres Salient had long been a pet favourite of the British High Command and had been earmarked for an attack since 1915.

The Salient was defined by the sickle-shaped ridges that curved around Ypres. East of the town the Broodseinde and Passchendaele ridges formed the blade of the sickle and joined with Messines Ridge south of the town to form the handle. The Germans were firmly entrenched at the top of these ridges and gazed across most of the British line on the flat Flanders plain below. If the British had any hope of breaking the German line, they had to force them from the high ground.

In preparation for the attack, 23 huge mines were dug beneath key German positions along the entire Messines front. With luck, the mines would destroy the strongest German positions and demoralise the survivors in the surrounding area. Mines had been used during previous battles, but they were a practice run compared to what was about to occur at Messines.

The attack plan was bold and called for nine divisions to advance on a 15-kilometre front and capture Messines Ridge in a single day. Seven British divisions from the IX and X Corps would attack the ridge south of Ypres, the New Zealand Division would capture the village of Messines, and the 3rd Australian Division would capture the southern shoulder of the ridge and hold the right flank of the advance. The 4th Division would support them.

The 3rd Division was the baby of the AIF, formed out of new recruits in Australia in 1916. While the older Australian divisions were being mauled on the killing fields of the Somme, the 3rd Division was training in the relative comfort of England. Not surprisingly, the veteran divisions were dismissive of the 3rd and derided its late arrival in the war by calling its men the 'neutrals'. The 3rd Division had a point to prove.

The battle began with an artillery barrage that pummelled the Germans from 1 to 7 June. The use of artillery was ingenious, with many of the guns concentrating on German artillery sites and tracks known to be used for the transport of food and supplies. At 3.10 am on 7 June, a huge bubble swelled beneath the earth on the ridge and then burst with a thunderous roar—the first mine had exploded. In the next 20 seconds, 18 more bubbles formed and burst as the rest of the mines were detonated. The thunder from the mine blasts was so loud it rattled windows in Kent and was clearly audible in London. Four of the mines were outside the area of the attack and were not detonated.

The 3rd Division set off as soon as the mines went up and found the going easy in the early stages. The Germans were so shaken by the mine blasts that many were captured without firing a shot. The only point where any resistance worthy of the name was encountered was on the right flank, where a machine-gun was holding up the advance. Private John Carroll of the 33rd Battalion leapt into the German trench and bayoneted four men, before attacking and killing the machine-gun crew. Moving on, he saw a comrade tussling with a group of Germans and joined the fight, killing another German. Over the next few days Carroll worked tirelessly, helping to consolidate the line and digging out two mates who had been buried by a shell. The 33rd's advance was fairly straightforward, but would have been much tougher if Carroll had not performed so fearlessly. He was awarded the Victoria Cross.

Further north, the 39th Battalion faced heavy machine-gun fire from a pillbox near Grey Farm. Captain Alexander Paterson stood up and used his rifle to suppress the German fire. With a small group of men he rushed the position and captured two machine-guns. He was awarded the Military Cross.

Nearby, the 38th Battalion was held up by a machine-gun that they couldn't locate. Captain Francis Fairweather edged forward with three other men until he saw smoke rising from a pillbox beside a road. Assuming this was the gun, he sneaked behind it and charged, capturing several men and the machine-gun. Fairweather was also awarded the Military Cross. He was killed in action at Bony on 29 September 1918, in one of the last Australian actions of the war.

As the Australians advanced during the second stage of the attack, the fight grew tougher. Resistance was particularly fierce at the concrete pillboxes scattered across the ridge. This was the first time the Diggers had encountered pillboxes, and the fighting around them was intense and unpleasant. Some of the pillboxes had 'loopholes' cut into the concrete which enabled the machine-guns to fire from inside, but most were simply solid concrete shelters that were only open at the back. The machine-gunners would shelter inside until the barrage had passed and then rush out, setting up their guns on top of or beside the pillbox. Attacking a pillbox was terrifying. The troops faced murderous fire from machine-guns that were protected and seemingly impervious to attack. Then suddenly, the fire would stop as the Germans realised they were surrounded and attempted to surrender. This was usually the signal for a killing spree as the attackers, half-mad from the trauma of the assault, ferociously set upon the machine-gunners.

At one pillbox the 37th Battalion was badly cut up by a machine-gun firing through a loophole. Captain Bob Grieve called up a trench mortar and a machine-gun to deal with it but saw both crews hit as they tried to advance. Ordering his men to stay down, Grieve took a bag of bombs and rushed the post, throwing bombs as he went. Taking advantage of a lull in the firing each time a bomb exploded, Grieve worked his way from shell hole to shell hole until he reached the trench behind the pillbox. He rolled two bombs through the loophole and charged into the pillbox, ready to take on the garrison. His bombs had done their work, however, and all the Germans were dead or wounded. Grieve climbed onto the parapet of the trench and called to his men to come on, but just then a shot rang out and he fell, wounded. The sniper's bullet that caught him in the shoulder almost killed him. For his bravery, Grieve was awarded the Victoria Cross. Apparently not one to blow his own trumpet, his report on the attack stated: 'The company was held up by fire from machine-guns in a concrete building. These were put out of action by the aid of Mills grenades and the company was able to get forward on to the objective allotted to us.'

The Australian advance continued until they had secured their objectives beyond the ridge. For the first time they looked out on the green fields behind the Salient, almost untouched by war. The attack was expensive for the Australians—the two divisions lost almost 6800 men between them—but had achieved a great victory. With the Germans driven from Messines Ridge, the way was now open for the great Third Battle of Ypres. The Battle of Messines was considered the greatest victory of the war to date.

The detonation of the great mines adds an interesting footnote to the battle. The unexploded mines were simply abandoned, their massive explosive charges still in place. In the ebb and flow of war their exact locations soon became vague and by war's end they had been completely lost. Opinions vary as to how many mines lie undiscovered beneath Messines—as few as one or as many as half a dozen. In any case, there's enough high explosive buried in the area to make the locals edgy. And with good reason. In 1955 a lightning strike set off a previously unknown mine, obliterating a farmer's field and no doubt putting the cows off the milk for some time.

MESSINES TOUR

This is a very long tour (about 17 kilometres), so allow at least half a day to do it justice and only attempt the entire circuit on foot if you are in good health and keen for a challenge. (Driving it is by far the best option. Roads in this area are good, so the tour can be driven in about three hours.) Note that the road into Ploegsteert Wood (known to the troops as 'Plugstreet' Wood) is closed to traffic, so this section of the tour must be made on foot. It is a rewarding walk, taking in eight cemeteries, two massive mine craters and the sites of two Victoria Cross actions.

The tour begins in Messines (Mesen) village, about 10 kilometres south of Ypres. Drive to the village and park in the main square [1]. In the centre of the square a Bastiaan plaque outlines Australia's involvement in the battle, although don't be misled; the village itself was captured by the New Zealanders. A memorial to their achievements, depicting a New Zealand soldier in his distinctive lemon-squeezer hat, was unveiled in the square on Anzac Day 2014. At the western end of the square (near the New Zealand memorial) turn right onto Ieperstraat. Turn left at the crossroads and follow the signs to Messines Ridge British Cemetery [2].

This cemetery was constructed after the Armistice, on the site of an old convent know as the Institution Royale. The convent had been destroyed early in the fighting but its extensive network of cellars was used by the Germans for shelter and defence. The cemetery was made when isolated graves from the surrounding fields were brought in, and smaller cemeteries in the area were closed. It contains 1531 burials, ranging from early fighting at Messines in October 1914 to the recapture of the village for the final time in October 1918. Most of the burials are from the bitter fighting here in 1917 and the vast majority (954 graves) are unidentified. Australian graves total 342, of which 138 are unidentified. Nearly all these men were killed in the Battle of Messines in June 1917. The cemetery also incorporates a memorial to more than 800 New Zealand soldiers who were killed in the area and have no known graves. Other memorials at Tyne Cot Cemetery and Polygon Wood also remember the New Zealand missing.

A notable Australian buried here is Major William Mundell (15th Battalion, died 19/08/1917, grave I.A.17), a Gallipoli veteran who was wounded by machine-gun fire while inspecting the front line at Messines. He died of his wounds later the same day. He was well liked by his men and a gentleman to the last: while being stretchered to the rear, he insisted that the men carrying him stop and rest during the long journey.

Another is 2nd Lieutenant Leslie Boully DCM (16th Battalion, died 05/08/1917, grave V.A.5). Boully also served at Gallipoli and won his Distinguished Conduct Medal as a sergeant at the First Battle of Bullecourt. He was killed during the consolidation that followed the Battle of Messines.

Also buried in Messines Ridge British Cemetery are two brothers, Privates George and William Platt. They served together in the 41st Battalion and were killed on the same day, 8 July 1917. They are buried side by side in graves V.C.39 and V.C.40.

Leave the cemetery and return along the main road towards the village. Turn right at the crossroads and follow this road, the N365, through Messines and turn right in front of the church, towards Ploegsteert. Turn right at the second road, signposted to the New Zealand Memorial. Follow this road for about 300 metres until you reach the memorial on your left. It is set back from the road and easy to miss if you are driving.

The New Zealand Memorial [3] is built in the middle of the sector captured by the New Zealand Division on 7 June 1917. It is a white stone obelisk surrounded by attractive gardens and a grove of trees. Inscribed on it is the poignant phrase found on many New Zealand memorials: 'From the uttermost ends of the earth'. At the bottom of the garden are two German pillboxes, captured by the New Zealanders early in the battle. The New Zealanders were well aware of the presence of the pillboxes; they had watched the Germans constructing them during the spring of 1917. The pillboxes are of a standard German design,

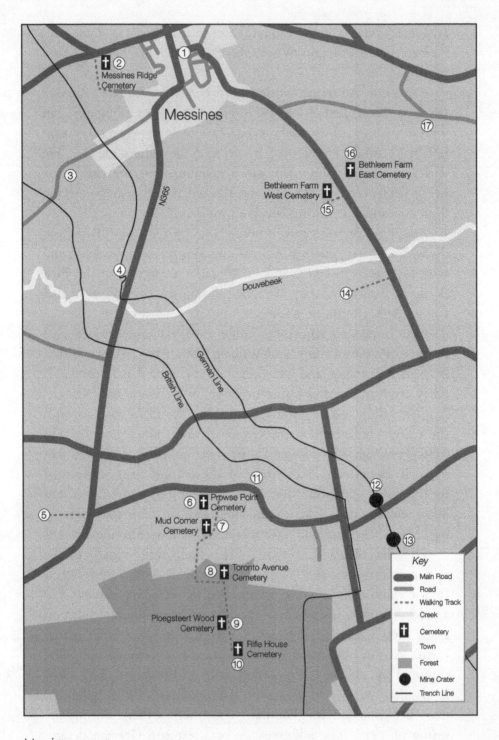

Messines

with a fire step at the rear. Machine-gun crews would shelter inside until the artillery barrage passed, then climb the rear steps to the platform and fire their machine-guns across the top of the pillbox. This plan didn't work for them on 7 June, however. The Kiwis advanced so quickly behind their barrage that they captured the German defenders before they had a chance to set up their guns. Near the pillboxes is an information panel detailing the attack in this area but, curiously, it is set up on the far side of the hedge and you have to leave the park and walk around the outside wall to read it.

For a great view of the battlefield, climb on top of one of the pillboxes and look across the valley. At the foot of the valley was the British front line. The New Zealanders advanced up the slope from directly in front of you, past your position and on into the town. The Australians advanced on their right (your left as you look across the valley) and passed south of Messines. The British IX and X Corps attacked left of the village (your right).

Leave the memorial park, follow the road back towards Messines and turn right at the intersection with the N365. This road takes you into the heart of the ground captured so magnificently by the Australian divisions. After 300 metres you will pass the Island of Ireland Peace Park, unveiled in 1998.

Follow the N365 for about 700 metres, until you reach a farm on the right side of the road, just before a small creek. This is La Petite Douve Farm [4], a German strongpoint captured early in the advance by the 40th Battalion. The Australians anticipated fierce resistance but instead were met by feeble fire from a solitary machine-gun. The German defenders were so demoralised by the shock of the mine explosions that they were happy to surrender and 'made many fruitless attempts to embrace us', reported Lieutenant Garrard of the 40th Battalion. La Petite Douve Farm has a dubious honour. This is the site of an unexploded mine. During the mine's construction in 1916, the Germans detected the presence of the British tunnellers and began counter-mining operations against them. Worried that the Germans would stumble across the mine and the whole plan would come undone, the British flooded and collapsed the shaft. The tonnes of explosive, neatly laid and ready to do its dirty work, is still there, buried below the farm. Its unnerving presence doesn't seem to bother the farmer. He has happily worked this land for years.

Continue south on the N365 past the farm. The Australian front line crossed the road just before the point where a smaller road joins it on the right, and then carried on south-east towards Ploegsteert Wood in the distance. Drive for another kilometre until you reach a large Commonwealth War Graves sign pointing to several cemeteries down a minor road to the left. Just past the sign, park your car and walk along the track to the right up a slope. Stop when you reach the top of the hill. This is Hill 63 [5], the highest point in the Ploegsteert sector. It was behind the British lines from 1914 until the German Spring Offensive in 1918 and was an important observation point for much of that time. The site was well protected from shellfire and in 1917 the 1st Australian Tunnelling Company dug a labyrinth of tunnels and chambers into the south side of the hill. This underground city was known as the Catacombs and provided shelter for up to 1500 men at a time. The tunnels collapsed decades ago and there is now no trace of them.

Return along the path to the main road, return to your car and follow the minor road as indicated by the cemetery signs. Stop at the first cemetery you come to, Prowse Point. You must leave your car here and continue this part of the tour on foot.

Prowse Point Cemetery is the first stop on a side-tour to Ploegsteert Wood, a key landmark in the Ypres Salient. For much of the war the wood was just behind the British front line and hundreds of thousands of troops found shelter among its smashed trees. Ploegsteert Wood was massive during the war and is massive today. A thorough exploration would take days. It contains many remnants of the war, including shell holes, trench lines and pillboxes, but the key attraction for visitors is the group of British cemeteries almost lost in its depths. These are some of the most peaceful on the Western Front.

Prowse Point Cemetery **[6]** was named after Brigadier General Charles Prowse DSO, commander of the British 11th Infantry Brigade. He was killed on the first day of the Battle of the Somme, 1 July 1916, and is buried in Louvencourt Military Cemetery in France. Prowse Point Cemetery was begun by the 2nd Royal Dublin Fusiliers in November 1914 and was used on and off until the German offensive in April 1918. Today the cemetery contains 224 burials, of which 13 are Australian. Several men from the 27th Battalion are buried here, including four who were killed on Christmas Day 1917 and are buried together in Plot III, Row B. They were repairing barbed wire in front of the Australian line when killed by a single shellburst. Among the New Zealand casualties buried here are several men from the Maori Pioneer Battalion.

Prowse Point is one of the few 'open' cemeteries in the Ypres Salient, meaning that it can still be used for the reinterment of bodies of Commonwealth soldiers discovered on the battlefields. A recent addition is the grave of Private Alan Mather of the 33rd Battalion, who was killed aged 37 on 8 June 1917 during the Battle of Messines. His body was not found until 2008, when a group of British archaeologists excavating the nearby Trench 122 mine crater unearthed him on the spot where he had been buried 91 years earlier by a shell blast. His personal effects included a German pickelhaube helmet, which he had presumably souvenired earlier in the war and carried with him into battle to prevent it from being stolen in the rear area. He was identified using DNA testing and was laid to rest with full honours in 2010 (grave III.C.1AA).

Leave the cemetery and follow the track to the right towards the wood. After 300 metres you will reach Mud Corner British Cemetery **[7]**. This is truly an Anzac cemetery, with all graves except one belonging to Australians or New Zealanders. The cemetery was started after the capture of Messines on 7 June 1917 and used until the following December. Most of the Australians buried in Mud Corner were killed during the Battle of Messines or soon after. Of the New Zealanders buried here, one man stands out. Private Alexander McKenzie served with the Auckland Regiment and was a veteran of both Gallipoli and the Boer War. He died on 27 June 1917, aged 47 (grave II.A.9).

Mud Corner is an excellent example of a battlefield cemetery. It was constructed very close to the front and the track that runs past it was an approach route used by British troops as they marched to the trenches in the Ploegsteert sector. It does not take too great a leap of imagination to visualise the cemetery as the troops saw it: the green fields a quagmire, the muddy track leading past crooked wooden crosses into the shattered remnants of Ploegsteert Wood. There is probably no better place in the Ypres Salient to so easily visualise the 1917 battlefield.

Leave the cemetery and continue along the track into the wood. Turn left at the T-junction and you will soon reach Toronto Avenue Cemetery [8]. In spite of its name, this cemetery has no Canadian connection and is instead a small piece of Australia. This is the only all-Australian cemetery in Belgium, one of only two on the entire Western Front (the other being VC Corner Cemetery at Fromelles in French Flanders). All 78 men buried here belonged to the 9th Brigade of the 3rd Division and were killed at Messines between 7 and 10 June 1917. The 36th Battalion erected a wooden memorial to its dead here soon after the battle, but it has long since disappeared. The most senior soldier buried in Toronto Avenue is Captain Francis Piggott of the 36th Battalion, who was killed by shellfire near La Potterie Farm on 10 June (grave at end of Row C). The only other officer in this cemetery is Lieutenant Charles Alexander, acting commander of the 9th Light Trench Mortar Battery, who was killed by a sniper on 8 June (grave A.15). Five of the soldiers buried here were teenagers, the youngest being Private Cecil Wise of the 9th Machine-Gun Company, who was only 17 when he enlisted in 1916. He was killed by a shell at Messines, less than a year later (grave C.11).

There are two more cemeteries in Ploegsteert Wood; neither has a particularly strong Australian connection but both are very picturesque. If you are short on time, return to Prowse Point Cemetery and continue the tour from point 11; otherwise, leave

Toronto Avenue Cemetery and follow the path further into the wood until you reach a cemetery on your right.

Ploegsteert Wood Cemetery **[9]** was made in 1916 when a number of small British regimental cemeteries, dating from early in the war, were amalgamated. The New Zealand Division used it again in 1917, after their capture of Messines, and it was in German hands for much of 1918. It contains 164 graves, of which only one is Australian. It is a peaceful place, set deep in the wood and shaded by lush trees.

Carry on along the path until you reach Rifle House Cemetery **[10]**, named after a strongpoint located nearby. The first burials were made here in November 1914 and the last in June 1916. There are no Australians among the 230 men buried here but there are some interesting British graves. Among them is Rifleman Robert Barnett of the 1st Battalion, Rifle Brigade, who was killed at Ploegsteert on 19 December 1914. Aged only 15, he was one of the youngest battle casualties of the First World War (grave IV.E.10).

Leave the cemetery and follow the path back to Prowse Point Cemetery. Return to your car and carry on until you reach a small wooden cross on the left **[11]**. The cross marks the assumed site of one of the legendary events of the First World War, the Christmas Truce. According to the legend, on Christmas Day 1914 British and Germans in this sector of the line laid down their arms for several hours and fraternised in no man's land. Reports are sketchy and the legend has undoubtedly grown with the passage of time, but eyewitness testimony and official accounts seem to indicate that the Christmas Truce did take place at a few locations on the British front. Suggestions as to what actually occurred vary wildly. Most accounts claim the British and Germans met in no man's land and exchanged food and photographs but the most enduring element of the legend is that the opposing troops took part in a casual football match. Whether true or not, it is appealing to believe that, for a few hours at least, human decency ruled over hatred. The cross is a private memorial, erected by a group of British Great War enthusiasts known as the Khaki Chums. The cross was dedicated in 1999. This sturdier version replaced the original in 2004.

In recent years the site's connection with the football legend has made the cross an informal shrine to English football, and supporters often drape the cross with team scarves and leave dozens of footballs at its base.

Continue along the road until you reach a house on the right with a plaque fastened to the front wall. This marks the site of a dugout that was used by one of the most popular artists of the war, cartoonist Bruce Bairnsfather. According to legend, it was here that Bairnsfather first drew the cartoons that would evolve into his famous Fragments from France series, the most famous character of which was the indefatigable 'Old Bill'. The plaque was unveiled in 2003 and was an initiative of noted Great War historians Tonie and Valmai Holt.

Carry on and turn right at the T-junction, then immediately left at the next road. After 200 metres you will reach a large crater in a field on the left [12]. This was the site of Trench 122, a German position obliterated by one of the 19 great mine explosions on 7 June 1917. Twenty thousand pounds of ammonal made a crater 65 metres wide. This crater marked the right flank of the Australian advance during the Battle of Messines. It was captured early on the day by the 33rd Battalion, but it was so exposed they had a hard time consolidating it until nightfall. The crater is on private land but the adventurous can brave an electric fence and a herd of cattle to view it.

It was in this area that Private Carroll captured a machine-gun post and rescued a comrade, earning him the Victoria Cross. John Carroll was a working man from Western Australia and went largely unnoticed in the army until his extraordinary bravery during the Battle of Messines. He was wounded twice in 1917 and sent back to Australia in August 1918. He spent the next nine years working at a timber mill in Yarloop, Western Australia, until he was badly injured in an industrial accident. He retired to Bedford Park in Perth, where he died in 1971, aged 79.

In the field on the other side of the road is another crater, known as Trench 122 Right or Factory Farm **[13]**, and created by a 40 000-pound ammonal charge. This was beyond the right flank of the Australian advance and would have provided the Germans with an excellent position to enfilade the Australian attackers. Desperate to prevent the Germans from occupying the crater, the 33rd Battalion used a team of snipers to eliminate any enemy soldier who showed his head. After half a dozen had been shot trying to reach the crater, the Germans gave up and fell back.

Return along the same road and turn right at the T-junction. Follow this road for 700 metres and turn right at another T-junction. Turn left at the next road and follow it for 350 metres. Note the farm buildings on your left. This is Grey Farm **[14]**, the German strongpoint captured by Captain Alexander Paterson in his MC-winning action. Private H Sternbeck of the 35th Battalion also captured a machine-gun in this area—a remarkable feat considering he was only 16 years old at the time.

Continue along the road for another 700 metres until you reach the intersection of a minor road to the left. This corner marks the site of the German machine-gun captured by Captain Francis Fairweather, an action that earned him the MC. Ahead and to the right is Bethleem Farm, another German strongpoint captured by Fairweather's men.

Walk along the minor road to the left and follow the grass path to Bethleem Farm West Cemetery **[15]**. The cemetery was started by men of the 3rd Division soon after they captured the farm on 7 June 1917. British units who later occupied the sector also buried their dead here. Today the cemetery contains 166 graves, of which 114 are Australian. All the Australians were killed in the Messines fighting or in the months that followed, and all but one are identified. Unusually for this area, the cemetery also contains an unidentified Commonwealth soldier from the Second World War. The only Australian officer buried in Bethleem Farm West is 2nd Lieutenant Randal Virgoe (10th Battalion, died 23/12/1917, grave F.15), who was only 20 years old when he was killed by a German trench mortar while leading a fatigue party.

Also buried here is Private William Hynes (37th Battalion, died 08/06/1917, grave A.26), who served under the name William Wilson. Official documents record his age as 22 at the time of his death but he was actually only 17, placing him among the youngest Australian casualties in Belgium.

Leave the cemetery, return to the road and take the farm track to the right after 70 metres. This leads behind the rebuilt Bethleem Farm to Bethleem Farm East Cemetery [16]. This tiny cemetery of 44 graves almost qualifies as wholly Australian; except for the grave of a private from the British Machine Gun Corps, all the graves belong to Australians. The cemetery was begun at the same time as Bethleem Farm West and mostly contains men who were killed in action between 7 and 10 June. The most senior soldier buried here is Captain William Bryan (44th Battalion, died 08/06/1917, grave A.2). The only other officers are Lieutenant Richard Walsh (44th Battalion, died 08/06/1917, grave C.1) and 2nd Lieutenant Thomas Bartley (42nd Battalion, died 10/06/1917, grave D.1). There is a special memorial along the northern wall of the cemetery and it illustrates the difficulties in identifying war dead. The memorial commemorates Private Maurice Dane (37th Battalion, died 07–09/06/1917), who was buried here but whose grave was later destroyed by shelling. After the war it was impossible to tell which of several unidentified remains belonged to Private Dane, so they were all buried as 'unknowns' and a special memorial was erected to Dane, who was 'known to be buried in this cemetery'.

Leave the cemetery, return to your car and drive on. Turn right at the next intersection. Follow this road for about 800 metres until it joins a smaller road on the left [17]. This intersection marks the site of the pillbox that disrupted the advance of the 37th Battalion during the battle and was captured single-handedly by Captain Bob Grieve in the action that earned him the Victoria Cross. The pillbox was located to the right of the main road, immediately opposite its intersection with the minor road. It was firing at the 37th Battalion along the road you have just taken and into the field beside it.

Bob Grieve was an enthusiastic cricketer and footballer who had attended Wesley College in Melbourne. After graduating he often returned to the school to watch his old football team in action, once even joining them on the field in his dinner suit and borrowed boots when they were one man short! The shoulder wound he received at Messines kept him out of the rest of the war and he returned home with one of the nurses who had attended him in 1918. He married her the same year. He ran a smallgoods business in Melbourne for many years and served in the Volunteer Defence Corps from 1942 to 1944. Bob Grieve died on 4 October 1957, aged 68.

Follow the road back the way you came and turn right at the T-junction. This road leads uphill to the town square where the tour began.

OTHER SITES OF INTEREST

Spanbroekmolen (Pool of Peace)

Spanbroekmolen was a strong German defensive position, one of 19 selected for destruction by the great mine explosions that heralded the start of the Battle of Messines. The Spanbroekmolen mine was detonated 15 seconds late, at 3.10 am on 7 June 1917. The 8th Battalion, Royal Irish Rifles had already begun its attack and was halfway across no man's land when the mine went up. Some of its men were killed by debris from the tremendous explosion.

After the war local farmers began filling in the Messines Ridge mine craters and 'Tubby' Clayton, founder of the Talbot House recreation home in Poperinghe, suggested that at least one should be preserved as a memorial. Lord Wakefield, Chairman of Castrol Oil, purchased the crater (along with several other Western Front sites) and donated it to the Toc H movement for preservation. Today the crater is known as the Pool of Peace and is one of the most visited sites in the area. Like all the remaining Messines mines it has filled with water and is surrounded by lush trees. A plaque on the lip of the crater gives details about the explosion that created it. A German blockhouse is buried in the bushes at the rear of the crater. Soldiers who first occupied the spot found the bodies of several German officers inside, with no visible signs of injury. They had been killed by the concussion from the mine explosion.

Directions
Spanbroekmolen is easily reached from Messines. Drive west on the N314 in the direction of Messines Ridge British Cemetery and turn right onto the minor road directly opposite the cemetery (Kruisstraat). Follow this road for about 2.5 kilometres until you reach Spanbroekmolen on the right. (If coming from Ypres, drive to the village of Wijtschate, follow Wijtschatestraat west and turn left onto Kruisstraat. The crater is 200 metres along this road.) On the opposite side of the road to the crater a path leads through a field to Lone Tree Cemetery, where several Irishmen killed by debris from the mine explosion are buried, along with comrades killed in other actions in the area.

BAYERNWALD TRENCHES

In 1914 a small wood known to the Allies as Croonaert Wood was captured by the Germans. The Bavarian units that occupied it referred to it as 'Bayernwald' (Bavarian Wood) and constructed a complex series of trenches and bunkers on the site. Adolf Hitler won an Iron Cross near here in 1914 and returned to the site during a tour of his old stamping grounds in 1940. For many years after the war Bayernwald was preserved as a trench museum but it closed decades ago. In 2004 the area was purchased by the local government and restored: the wood was cleared of undergrowth and the weathered trenches were re-dug based on archaeological surveys of the 1915 trench system. In my opinion, Bayernwald is the best preserved trench system in the Ypres Salient, and much less crowded than more popular sites such as Sanctuary Wood. Ten minutes spent wandering the rabbit warren layout will give you a good indication of the complexities of a Great War trench system.

Directions

The Bayernwald trenches can only be accessed by a somewhat complicated system that involves buying a ticket at the tourist office in the town of Kemmel and using an access code to open a gate at the site. To find the site, drive to the village of Wijtschate and follow Vierstraat north out of the village. Drive for one kilometre, and turn right on a road signposted to Bayernwald. Continue until you reach a parking area and information panel on your left. Park here and follow the road in front of the wood to the Bayernwald entrance.

CEMETERIES NEAR MESSINES

Berks Cemetery Extension and the Ploegsteert Memorial

Berks Cemetery Extension was begun in mid-1916 and used until the end of 1917. It was enlarged after the Armistice and now contains 876 graves, of which 180 are Australian, all identified.

Buried here is a well-loved officer, Captain Ben Brodie of the 34th Battalion, who was killed by machine-gun fire during a trench raid on 5 March 1918 (grave II.A.33).

Also buried here is 2nd Lieutenant William Parsons of the 22nd Battalion. Parsons was formerly with the 6th Light Trench Mortar Battery and, as a sergeant, was in charge of a small party that caused havoc among counterattacking Germans during the Second Battle of Bullecourt in May 1917. He was awarded the Military Medal, as were the six men under his command. He was killed on 26 March 1918, during the German Spring Offensive (grave II.A.41).

Next to Berks Cemetery Extension is Hyde Park Corner (Royal Berks) Cemetery, which contains one Australian among 83 burials. He is Major George Patterson of the 7th Brigade Australian Field Artillery, who was killed on 14 April 1917 (grave C.1).

Within the grounds of Berks Cemetery is one of the most majestic memorials on the Western Front. The Ploegsteert Memorial commemorates 11 367 British and South African servicemen who were killed in this sector and have no known grave. Although the memorial serves the southern part of the Ypres Salient, most of the area it represents is actually in northern France and includes battlefields at Hazebrouck, Merville, Bailleul, Armentières, Aubers Ridge, Fromelles (1915), Nieppe Forest and Ploegsteert Wood. The men remembered on this memorial generally did not die in major attacks, but were killed in the day-to-day occupation of trenches in the area or small set piece battles with limited objectives. The memorial was originally intended for Lille, but the French, in one of the most churlish decisions of the post-war years, complained about the number of British memorials being erected on their land. The Belgians had no such qualms and offered Ploegsteert as the site for the memorial, only two kilometres across the border.

The memorial incorporates a classical circular temple guarded by two stone lions. One lion rests serenely while the other snarls with bared teeth, representing both facets of the British Empire at the time—a kind friend, but a ferocious enemy!

Directions
Berks Cemetery Extension and the Ploegsteert Memorial are on the N365, five kilometres south of Messines.

Bethleem Farm East and Bethleem Farm West cemeteries: see Messines tour (page 60).

Kandahar Farm Cemetery, Neuve-Eglise

Kandahar Farm was close to the front line in the Messines sector for most of the war. A cemetery was started here in November 1914 and was used until the ground was lost to the Germans in April 1918. The cemetery was briefly used again when the area was recaptured by the Allies in September. Of the 443 graves, 186 are Australian, mostly belonging to men killed in the Messines area or northern France in late 1917. All the Australian graves are identified.

Buried here is Captain William Connell DCM of the 12th Battalion. As a sergeant on the day of the landing at Gallipoli, Connell was instrumental in the fight for Johnston's Jolly and was awarded the Distinguished Conduct Medal for leading an attack on a Turkish machine-gun. He died of wounds on 28 December 1917 (grave II.H.6).

Two corporals who lie here, Henry Coombes of the 39th Battalion and Robert Hill of the 4th Field Company Engineers, won the Military Medal at Messines. Coombes supervised the evacuation of wounded after all the stretcher bearers in his battalion were hit, and Hill made three dangerous journeys through the German barrage to carry barbed wire to the front line. Coombes was killed on 3 August and Hill on 8 August (graves II.F.22 and II.G.4).

Directions
Although Kandahar Farm Cemetery is officially listed as being near Neuve-Eglise (now Nieuwkerke), it is actually closer to the village of Wulvergem. From Messines, take the N314 and pass through Wulvergem in the direction of Nieuwkerke. The cemetery is on the left, one kilometre after leaving Wulvergem.

Messines Ridge British Cemetery, Mud Corner Cemetery, Ploegsteert Wood Cemetery, Prowse Point Cemetery, Rifle House Cemetery, Toronto Avenue Cemetery: see Messines tour (page 60).

3

Battle of Polygon Wood, 26 September 1917

Australians first contributed to the Third Battle of Ypres in September 1917, when they attacked along the Menin Road and at Polygon Wood. Named for its unusual shape, the wood had been the site of the Ypres rifle range before the war and even contained a racecourse. By 1917, three years of constant bombardment had reduced the wood to shattered stumps and pulverised the racecourse beyond recognition. The most prominent feature of the area was the Buttes, a rough mound that was originally the backdrop of the rifle range and had been turned by the Germans into a fortress, bristling with machine-guns and honeycombed by dugouts, tunnels and barbed wire entanglements.

The Australian 4th and 5th divisions attacked Polygon Wood along a 2000-metre front on the morning of 26 September 1917. This was the 5th Division's first major engagement since it had been mauled at Fromelles more than a year earlier and it was keen to prove its worth to its sister divisions. In this attack the 5th Division would need all the fighting spirit it could muster. To reach its objectives it would have to advance through the heart of the wood and overcome dozens of pillboxes and machine-gun emplacements before tackling the Buttes itself.

Fortunately for the 5th, a remarkable change had taken place in British tactics by the time of the attack. The powerful but imprecise artillery bombardments that had failed them so monumentally at Fromelles had been replaced by the well-orchestrated 'creeping barrage', a concentrated wall of artillery fire that would advance in stages as the troops attacked. On 26 September the coordination of the artillery approached art. It was 'the most perfect that ever protected Australian troops', and roared ahead 'like a Gippsland bushfire', according to the *Official History*. Buoyed by the sight and eager to move quickly before the Germans could react, the Australians swept through the wood. As the battalions advanced in rows, the line of men would ripple as fire from a German strongpoint found its mark, before an organised rush would overcome the position. Several pillboxes were taken by acts of individual dash and the heavy resistance expected from defenders at the Buttes never materialised: at the first sight of the advancing 53rd Battalion the Germans fled.

On the left of the attack the 4th Division advanced smoothly until, in its eagerness, it ran into shells from the British barrage. Captain Albert Jacka, who had won Australia's first Victoria Cross of the war at Gallipoli, plus the Military Cross at Pozières and another at Bullecourt, steadied the men and led them to the objective. Later in the day a German machine-gun harassed the Australians as they dug in. Sergeant John Dwyer of the 4th Machine Gun Company stole ahead of the Australian position and blasted the Germans from less than 30 metres distance, killing the crew and putting the gun out of action. Ignoring snipers who were taking pot shots at his head, Dwyer collected the German gun and brought it back to the Australian line, where he used it in conjunction with his Vickers gun to repel a German counterattack. The next day his gun was blown up by a shell, but Dwyer led his team through the German barrage to the rear, picked up a reserve gun and had it set up in the front line soon after. Dwyer showed a total 'contempt for danger' and was awarded the Victoria Cross. After the war Dwyer established a sawmilling business and later served as a Member of Parliament for the seat of Franklin in Tasmania. He still held the seat when he died in 1962, aged 72.

On the right of the attack the 31st Battalion advanced well until it ran into a group of strongly defended pillboxes. An assault party was organised and led by a young private, Paddy Bugden, a hotelkeeper from the north coast of New South Wales. He led the men in a series of ludicrously bold charges against devastating machine-gun fire. He bombed one pillbox after another and captured the lot, along with dozens of prisoners. Later in the day he single-handedly rescued a corporal who had been captured, killing three Germans in the process. Over the next two days he rescued wounded men on five occasions but was killed by shellfire on the 28th. Not surprisingly, he was awarded a posthumous Victoria Cross. Private Bugden was buried by his comrades in nearby Glencourse Wood, with an elaborate cross and a low fence around his grave. He now lies in Hooge Crater Cemetery. Paddy Bugden had joined the 31st Battalion in France in March 1917, only six months before he was killed.

Bugden's actions were typical of the raw courage that was required to overcome an obstacle like Polygon Wood. Similar actions took place throughout the wood and by late in the day all the Australian objectives had been taken. The Germans launched several counterattacks which were beaten back by the clever use of artillery and stiff Australian resistance. The Battle of Polygon Wood was a great success that gave the Allies a solid platform to launch the decisive Battle of Broodseinde Ridge two weeks later. But the price was high for the Australians: the attack cost the 5th Division 3723 officers and men, and the 4th Division 1729.

POLYGON WOOD TOUR

Today Polygon Wood is a place of pilgrimage for Australian visitors and is an essential stop on any tour of the Western Front. It meant so much to the men of the 5th Division that they placed their divisional memorial, commemorating their entire service during the war, on the Buttes.

This walk visits six pillboxes that still remain in the wood, shallow trench lines, two memorials and two cemeteries. It is relatively short and can be completed in less than two hours. There is no driving option—the wood is closed to traffic—but visitors lacking time or mobility can park their car and see the two essential sites, Buttes New British Cemetery and the 5th Division Memorial, without walking far. The wood is always muddy, even in summer, so wear appropriate clothing and walking shoes.

From Ypres (Ieper), drive to Zonnebeke. Polygon Wood is reached by following the signs to Buttes New British Cemetery and the 5th Division Memorial from the centre of the village. Park beside Polygon Wood Cemetery **[1]**. This is a good example of a battlefield cemetery, its irregular layout suggesting the urgency of burials in the frontline areas. (Due to the atrocious conditions during the Third Battle of Ypres, most of the men who were killed in the Salient in 1917 were either lost or buried in isolated graves. After the war these graves were concentrated into a handful of huge cemeteries, of which Tyne Cot is the best example. Genuine battlefield cemeteries such as Polygon Wood are rare in this part of the Ypres Salient.) Polygon Wood Cemetery was started in August 1917 and used until the following April. It was briefly used again when the Germans were driven from the area in September 1918. There are no Australians buried here but New Zealand is well represented, with 60 graves out of a total of 103. Until the 1950s there was a large German plot (clearly marked on trench maps) behind the cemetery. Anti-German sentiment after the Second World War led to the removal and reinterment of the graves, along with thousands of others from the Ypres area, in a mass plot at Langemarck German Cemetery.

Cross the road and follow the wide path to Buttes New British Cemetery **[2]**. This large cemetery was created after the war by the concentration of isolated graves from the surrounding battlefields,

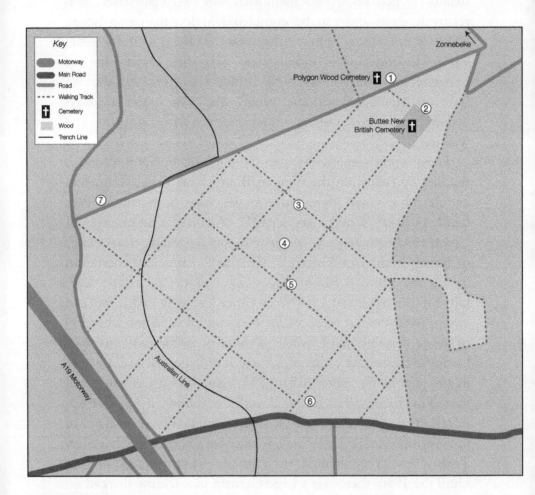

Polygon Wood

mostly of men killed in 1917. There are 564 Australians buried here and, due to the terrible fighting in this area, 407 of them are unidentified. Australian involvement in the Third Battle of Ypres is well chronicled, with casualties buried here from the Battle of Menin Road (20–21 September 1917), Battle of Polygon Wood (26–28 September 1917), Battle of Broodseinde Ridge (4 October 1917) and Battle of Passchendaele (9–12 October 1917). One of the most distinguished Australians buried in the cemetery is Lieutenant Colonel Alan Scott, who commanded the 56th Battalion (grave II.A.12). He had earned the DSO at Gallipoli and was one of the youngest battalion commanders in the AIF. After a hard fight at Polygon Wood, the 56th Battalion was relieved on 1 October. Scott remained behind to familiarise his successor with the sector and was killed by a stray bullet while standing on the Buttes. In what must rate as one of the unluckiest mishaps of the war, the bullet reportedly ricocheted from a discarded British helmet and killed both Scott and the relieving British officer, Lieutenant Colonel Dudley Turnbull.

Near the far corner of the cemetery stands a group of five headstones, designated as Row E of Plot I, that marks the resting place of the 'Westhoek Five', a group of Australian soldiers whose bodies were uncovered during nearby roadworks in 2006. The five bodies were immediately recognised as Australians, but it wasn't until DNA testing (a first for First World War remains) that three of the soldiers were able to be identified. They are Private George Storey (51st Battalion, died 30/09/1917), Private Jack Hunter (49th Battalion, died 26/09/1917) and Sergeant George Calder (51st Battalion, died 30/09/1917). They were reinterred here during a ceremony in October 2007, alongside their two comrades whose DNA was too badly decomposed to be matched. Their story was told in the ABC documentary *Lost in Flanders*.

The headstone of British private William Grant of the 20th Battalion, Manchester Regiment, features one of the most poignant personal inscriptions on the Western Front. It reads 'Sacred spot. Tread softly. A mother's love lies here.' Private Grant was killed on 8 October 1917, aged 19 (grave XXIII.D.1).

Climb the steps to the 5th Division Memorial at the top of the Buttes. From here, the outstanding position occupied by the German defenders can be well appreciated. The memorial, a stone obelisk, is the only Australian divisional memorial in Belgium and records the battle honours of the 5th Division at Fromelles, Bapaume, Beaumetz, Doignies, Louverval, Bullecourt, 3rd Battle of Ypres, Polygon Wood, Broodseinde, Battle of Amiens, Villers-Bretonneux, Morlancourt, 8th August, Vauvillers, Péronne, Hindenburg Line and Joncourt. It is not often that the disastrous attack at Fromelles is listed as a battle honour.

Behind the Buttes is a large depression that was created when Australian troops dug earth to reshape the smashed Buttes after the fighting.

At the rear of the cemetery is the Buttes New British Cemetery (New Zealand) Memorial, which records the names of 378 officers and men of the Otago and Canterbury regiments who have no known grave. They died while this sector was occupied by the New Zealand Division between September 1917 and May 1918. This is one of seven memorials in France and Belgium to the New Zealand missing.

Climb over the rear wall of the cemetery (technically against the rules of the CWGC) or leave by the gate and follow the wall to the rear of the cemetery. Walk along the wide path leading away from the cemetery, the main road through the wood. Keep walking past the intersection with a smaller track on the right. At the intersection of the next track, turn right and follow it for about 150 metres. Near here are two concrete shelters [3] that were constructed by the 4th Field Company, New Zealand Engineers in January 1918. They are low and hidden in the undergrowth and are often hard to find but persistent scrub bashing should reveal them.

Return to the main path and continue along it. Soon a large, overgrown pillbox will be visible in the trees to the right, which can be accessed via a well-worn track. This is Scott Post [4], captured by the 56th Battalion and named in honour of their commander, Lieutenant Colonel Alan Scott, who was later killed at the Buttes (see page 81). Scott Post is a two-chambered bunker that is scarred by hits from high explosive shells. According to the 56th's diary, the German defenders surrendered after a brief fight and emerged from the bunker like 'whimpering boys, holding out arms full of souvenirs'. Scott Post was used as a British headquarters in later battles.

Return to the main path and continue. At the intersection of a path on the left is the remains of a German pillbox [5], also captured by the 56th Battalion.

Turn left and follow the path past a clearing. Turn right at the next path. Follow this until you reach the remains of two German pillboxes [6] on either side of the path, just inside the southern boundary of the wood. These proved a tough obstacle for the advancing Australians before they were overcome. More than 60 Germans and a regimental commander were captured.

Turn right at the path immediately beyond the pillboxes and follow it through the woods. It is worth leaving the path and exploring the woods on either side: shell holes and shallow trenches, probably dug by the Australians before the attack, can still be found. Continue on the path until you reach the far end of the wood. On the other side of the sealed road is a small cafe [7], a good spot to sample a refreshing Belgian beer. The owner, Johan Vandewalle, is an amateur war historian and is very welcoming to Australians. Ask to see his collection of photos and relics, including a mud-encrusted British rifle, complete with fixed bayonet. It was Johan who recovered the bodies of the 'Westhoek Five' in 2006 (see page 81).

Leave the cafe and turn left onto the main road, which leads back to Polygon Wood Cemetery and your car.

OTHER SITES OF INTEREST

Battle of Menin Road, 20–21 September 1917

This battle was the AIF's first action in the Third Battle of Ypres. The Australian 1st and 2nd divisions would attack in the centre of a 13-kilometre British front and were tasked with advancing up the Westhoek Ridge and capturing Glencourse Wood and Nonne Bosschen (Nun's Wood), then advancing to the western edge of Polygon Wood. This was the first time two Australian divisions would advance side by side and the troops were enthusiastic. This was amplified by a friendly rivalry between the Australian units: the 25th Battalion was from Queensland and was keen to beat the 9th Battalion, the oldest Queensland battalion and the first to land at Gallipoli, to the objective.

The attack went smoothly, a dense artillery barrage shielding the advancing troops and dazing the German defenders until they were overcome. Pillboxes were scattered thickly all over the ridge and small groups of men peeled off from the main assault line to attack them. On the right of the Australian advance the Germans briefly resisted with a flamethrower, but the crew was quickly killed.

At one point the advance was held up by a stubbornly defended pillbox until 2nd Lieutenant Fred Birks and Corporal William Johnston of the 6th Battalion rushed towards it. Johnston was wounded in the leg by a bomb but that didn't stop Birks: he attacked the place on his own and captured the garrison. Later in the day Birks led a small party that captured another pillbox, along with an officer and 15 men. Early the next morning the 6th Battalion's line came under heavy artillery fire which buried several men. Birks stood up and began furiously digging them out, even though this left him dangerously exposed above the parapet of the trench. He was still digging when another shell burst, killing him and several other men. He was posthumously awarded the Victoria Cross and is now buried in Perth (China Wall) Cemetery. Fred Birks was born in Wales but migrated to Australia as a young man. He enlisted only 10 days after the outbreak of war, served through the Gallipoli campaign and won the Military Medal at Pozières in 1916. He was 23 years old at the time of his death.

During the advance to the second objective, a German machine-gun was firing through the Australian barrage and hitting men in the 10th Battalion. Private Reg Inwood ran through the bursting shells and attacked the post, killing several of the crew and bringing back nine prisoners. That night Inwood crept forward more than 500 metres into no man's land and scouted around the German positions, looking for information and noting the locations of German troops. The next day the advance continued until another machine-gun post brought it to a halt. Inwood advanced with an unidentified soldier from the 7th Battalion and bombed the post, killing all the crew except one man. Inwood returned to the Australian line with his prisoner, whom he had ordered to carry the German machine-gun. For his efforts, Inwood received the Victoria Cross. After the war he returned to South Australia, where he lived with his wife until he died in 1971, aged 81.

The attack had gone without a hitch and the Australians dug in at their objectives. The Germans soon launched the inevitable counterattacks, but the British artillery was well prepared and shattered the German columns as soon as they began to advance. The Battle of Menin Road cost the Australians more than 5000 casualties but was a crushing blow for the Germans. The German Official History recorded that 'the new English method of attack had proved its effectiveness . . . The loss of a sector so terribly fought over as Nonne Bosschen and Glencourse Wood was necessarily also of great moral effect.' The success of the attack gave the British a solid platform to launch the Battle of Polygon Wood five days later.

Directions

Glencourse Wood and Nonne Bosschen have merged into a single wood that is dotted with housing developments and holiday homes. From the southern end of Polygon Wood, follow the road across the motorway. You will reach Glencourse Wood/Nonne Bosschen on the right after about 500 metres. The pillbox captured by Lieutenant Birks was in the vicinity of the crossroads leading into the wood. Private Inwood won his VC just inside the south-western boundary of Polygon Wood.

Anzac House

Anzac House was a formidable German blockhouse that was captured by the 18th Battalion on 20 September, during the Battle of Menin Road. It was a double-storey bunker, mostly used for artillery observation, but also contained two machine-guns when captured. It is often incorrectly assumed that Australian troops were responsible for naming the pillbox; it was in fact named by British troops before the Australians even arrived in Belgium. A nearby pillbox was named 'Helles', after the British sector in Gallipoli, suggesting that this pillbox was named after the 'Anzac' sector in Gallipoli. As was common practice in the Ypres Salient, the names 'Helles' and 'Anzac' referred to both the pillboxes and the farms that formerly stood on the sites.

Directions

Anzac House no longer exists but the site is easily located. From Polygon Wood Cemetery (where you parked your car for the Polygon Wood tour), drive south-west, with the wood on your left, and turn right at the intersection at the far end of the wood. Follow this road for about one kilometre until you reach a crossroads. The farm on the northern side of the crossroads is Anzac Farm, the former site of Anzac House.

Black Watch Corner

This intersection at the southern tip of Polygon Wood was named in honour of the legendary Scottish Black Watch regiment, and was a famous wartime landmark. During the Battle of Menin Road a pillbox at the site was causing casualties among the Australians as they dug in on the objective. A group of Australians advanced on the pillbox and the garrison waved a flag in surrender. Captain Frederick Moore of the 5th Battalion was moving in to accept the surrender when one of the Germans who had already surrendered dropped behind his machine-gun and shot Moore dead. The Australians considered this the worst act of treachery and killed half the garrison before their officers intervened. Captain Moore is buried in Menin Road South Cemetery.

In 2014 a memorial to the almost 9000 members of the Black Watch who were killed during the First World War was unveiled at Black Watch Corner. It depicts a fearsome sergeant of the regiment in full battle kit, including kilt and bonnet. The 1st Battalion of the Black Watch held this ground against a much larger German force in a vital action during the First Battle of Ypres in November 1914.

Directions
Black Watch Corner is the crossroads at the southern end of the main road through Polygon Wood. The 5th Battalion advanced towards it from the far side of the motorway.

CEMETERIES NEAR POLYGON WOOD

Buttes New British Cemetery, Polygon Wood Cemetery: see Polygon Wood tour (page 78).

4

Battle of Broodseinde Ridge, 4 October 1917

The Third Battle of Ypres, the huge Allied effort to drive the Germans from the heights of the Ypres Salient, had begun in July 1917 and had steadily pushed the Germans back. By late September the Germans were in disarray and the Allies, used to the carnage of the Somme battles, felt that they had finally come up with a workable plan for victory on the Western Front. For the Australians, the triumph of their attack on Polygon Wood resulted in unfamiliar feelings of optimism—so much so that the 56th Battalion asked not to be relieved, preferring the activity of the front line to the constant shelling in the support area.

The next objective in the advance was the most important: Broodseinde Ridge, the northern section of the sickle-shaped ridge that overlooked Ypres, and the buttress of the German line since 1915. The Australian 1st, 2nd and 3rd divisions replaced the 4th and 5th in the centre of the British line. On their left the New Zealand Division was brought up, placing four Anzac divisions side by side for the first time on the Western Front. Eight British divisions would attack on the left and right of the Anzac troops.

In the drizzly dawn of 4 October the troops lay crowded in the front line, waiting for the order to attack. German shelling, which had been sporadic during the night, suddenly increased and the Australians found themselves caught in the middle of a furious barrage. They sheltered as best they could but, in the open ground, casualties were heavy. One-seventh of the attacking force was hit. At 6 am the British barrage began and the troops moved forward in the dreary light. On the right, the 1st and 2nd divisions had only advanced 150 metres when they saw a line of troops rising from shell holes in front of them. In spite of a few calls of 'They're your own chaps—don't fire!', most of the Australians recognised them as Germans and opened fire. Some of the Germans ran, others charged with bayonets but were soon killed or captured. By an incredible coincidence, the Germans had planned an attack at exactly the same time as the Australians and the two forces had met in the middle of no man's land.

On the left of the Australian advance, the 3rd Division went forward in stages, charging German defenders in trenches and pillboxes. Private Wally Peeler was a Lewis gunner with the 3rd Pioneer Battalion and was attached to the 37th Battalion for anti-aircraft work. Peeler was recklessly brave and, as the attack developed, he led the fighting at several points. Early in the advance the 37th was held up by a group of Germans sniping at them from a shell hole. Peeler dived among the Germans and killed all nine of them, then shouted for the Australians to come on. On two other occasions he led near suicidal assaults on German positions but came through without a scratch. At one point he was instructed to take his gun forward to suppress a German machine-gun that was holding up the advance. Not content with simply suppressing the gun, Peeler rushed the position, killed the gunner and sent the rest of the crew scurrying into a dugout. Peeler lobbed a bomb into the dugout and opened fire as 10 Germans ran out, killing the lot. During the morning, Peeler single-handedly killed 30 Germans and captured many more. In recognition of this one-man offensive, he was awarded the Victoria Cross.

Later, as the 3rd Division neared its objective on top of the ridge, the Germans opened up a murderous fusillade with machine-guns and rifles and the attack stalled. Sergeant Lewis McGee, a train driver from Tasmania, watched dozens of his comrades in the 40th Battalion get hit by machine-gun fire and several officers killed as they tried to rally the men. Ignoring the hurricane of bullets, McGee ran forward and shot the crew of a pillbox with his revolver. He then led a small group of men in a bombing attack on another pillbox and captured it as well. McGee was killed on 12 October, before learning he had been awarded the Victoria Cross. By these and similar acts of courage the 3rd Division reached their objective and consolidated it against German counterattacks.

On the right of the Anzac advance, the 1st and 2nd divisions surged forward behind their protective artillery barrage. They made such good progress and were so keen to press the retreating Germans that their officers had difficulty holding them back to consolidate their objectives. The ridge in this area had been stripped bare of vegetation and buildings by constant artillery fire and the only landmark was the Becelaere–Passchendaele Road, running along the crest. In the 2nd Brigade's sector, the road curved around a huge crater, presumably made when an ammunition dump was blown up earlier in the war. The Germans dug in along the road and around the crater and began pouring machine-gun and field gun fire into the advancing Australians, forcing them to creep forward from shell hole to shell hole. Finding it impossible to flank the row of defences along the ridge top, the Australians decided the only course of action was a bold rush. The bravest officers and NCOs led small groups of men in charges against the strongest positions. At the crater, Captain Harold Annear of the 6th Battalion coolly walked around its rim shooting down at the Germans with his revolver. He was soon wounded by a German bomb but his example inspired his men, who rushed and captured the crater. Annear died of his wounds the next day.

Eventually the Australians fought their way to the crest of the ridge and stood shooting at Germans who were fleeing down the reverse slope. Over the next few hours they pushed out posts further down the ridge and captured hundreds of Germans from trenches and pillboxes. By the end of the day the Australians had dug in on their final objective. The Germans launched a few weak counterattacks but these were beaten off by artillery fire.

The Battle of Broodseinde Ridge had been a triumph and had wrested the Salient's key defensive position from the Germans. The Germans were completely overwhelmed and they knew it. Their commander, Erich Ludendorff, called it a 'black day'. The history of the 5th Foot Guard Regiment considered 4 October 'the hardest day yet experienced by the regiment in the war'. Combined with the successful attacks at Polygon Wood on 20 and 26 September, it seemed the Allies had finally come up with a successful plan to win the war. All they needed to exploit their success was continued good weather.

If warfare followed a script, the Allies would have continued their advance in glorious sunshine and the Great War would have ended in 1917. Of course, it didn't. The troops hadn't even finished digging in on October 4 when rain began to fall. It continued for the next month, turning the battlefield into a morass and setting the stage for one of the war's greatest tragedies: the Battle of Passchendaele.

BROODSEINDE RIDGE TOUR

The Battle of Broodseinde Ridge was one of the largest Anzac assaults of the war and, consequently, the battlefield is huge. It is not feasible to walk the entire area in one cohesive tour, so I have instead focused on the ground covered by the 3rd Division on the left of the Australian advance. This is an interesting walk which can be completed in about 90 minutes (not including time spent at Tyne Cot Cemetery). It can be driven in about 30 minutes. Note that at the end of the tour you will need to walk back the way you came for about 20 minutes to reach your car. There is a slight gradient for most of the walk but it is not too difficult

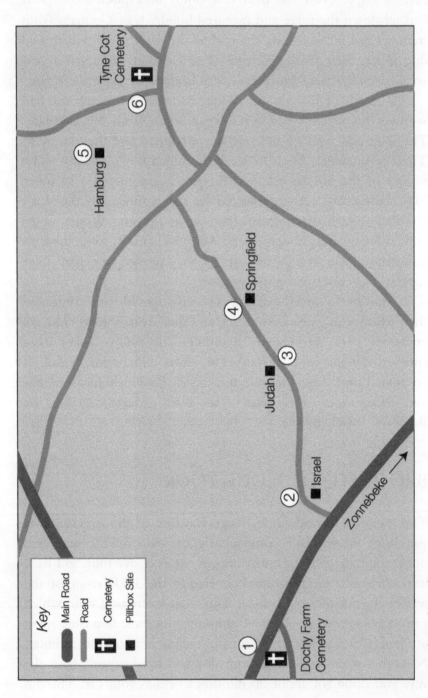

Key

▬	Main Road
▬	Road
✝	Cemetery
■	Pillbox Site

Tyne Cot Cemetery

✝ ⑥

⑤ ■ Hamburg

④ ■ Springfield

③ ■ Judah

② ■ Israel

① ✝ Dochy Farm Cemetery

Zonnebeke →

Broodseinde Ridge

for anyone who is reasonably fit. The tour visits two cemeteries (including Tyne Cot, the world's largest Commonwealth war cemetery) and the sites of two VC actions.

The Broodseinde Ridge battlefield covers an area from Becelaere (Beselare) in the south to Passchendaele (Passendale) in the north. To reach the tour area, leave Ypres (Ieper) and drive to the village of Zonnebeke. In the centre of the village turn left at the large intersection which is signposted to Dochy Farm New British Cemetery. Drive 1.5 kilometres to the cemetery **[1]** and park in front—you will leave your car here for the walking tour. Dochy Farm was a German strongpoint captured by the New Zealanders during the Battle of Broodseinde Ridge. It is one of a handful of large concentration cemeteries built in this area after the Armistice.

The cemetery has 1439 burials from the surrounding battlefields. The ferocious nature of the fighting in this area is illustrated by the fact that only 481 graves could be identified. Australian graves number 305, of which 208 are unidentified. Most of these men were killed during the battles of Broodseinde Ridge (4 October 1917) and Passchendaele (9–12 October 1917). Among them is Private Edward Green of the 10th Battalion (grave VII.C.16), one of the few men from the mysterious Celtic Wood raid whose fate is known (see **Celtic Wood**, pages 98–99). His date of death is incorrectly recorded as 8 October. Also buried here is Lieutenant Robert Glanville MC of the 8th Battalion, who won the Military Cross at Polygon Wood on 26 September 1917. During the fight he lost touch with his men and stumbled into a group of 16 Germans. He brandished his pistol and convinced them to surrender—they were obviously unaware his pistol was empty. He was killed by shellfire during the Battle of Broodseinde Ridge (grave III.B.27).

Stand at the front of the cemetery, facing the road. Ypres is now behind you and you are looking up gently rising ground to Tyne Cot Cemetery on the horizon (slightly to the right). This is Broodseinde Ridge. From this vantage point it is obvious how misleading the term 'ridge' is when applied to this gentle slope. But in the flatness of Belgian Flanders, even a small incline gives an advantage of observation and defence to the side on higher ground. The 3rd Division attacked from near here, with the 2nd and 1st divisions on its right and the New Zealand Division on its left.

Picture the scene: three years of shelling have stripped the landscape bare. The ground is a sea of boggy craters. There are no landmarks except for the occasional skeletal tree or abandoned trench, snaking through the pummelled earth like a scar. The dawn sky flashes like a thunderstorm as distant shells find their mark, and flares—yellow, white, red—arc skyward on the horizon. The Australians lie to your left and right in an extended line along the road, shivering in the cold morning drizzle, anxious for the signal to advance. The dull *crump, crump* of shellfire is constant, and suddenly swells into a roar as the British barrage begins and shells tear the earth on the skyline. As far as you can see in each direction, khaki figures rise, shake off the chill, light cigarettes and trudge forward together. Zero hour has arrived.

Leave Dochy Farm Cemetery and head back towards Zonnebeke. Follow the road for about 450 metres until you reach a smaller sealed road (Maarlestraat). This road conveniently follows the advance of the 10th Brigade during the battle.

It was in this area that Wally Peeler launched the series of assaults that earned him the VC. Peeler had lived and worked in rural Victoria until his enlistment in 1916. He was wounded twice in 1917 and returned to Australia in 1918. Between the wars he served as custodian of Melbourne's Shrine of Remembrance and re-enlisted in the army when the Second World War broke out. Peeler was captured by the Japanese in Java in 1942, while serving in the force commanded by Brigadier Arthur Blackburn, a VC winner from Pozières (see **Battle of Pozières**, page 157). Peeler survived three years of captivity and returned to Melbourne in 1945. His joy at surviving the war was cut short when he learned that his son Donald had been killed in action in the Solomon Islands in 1944. Another son, Alfred, had also served and was killed in an accident soon after the end of the war. Wally Peeler died in Melbourne in 1968, aged 80.

Turn left onto Maarlestraat and follow it until it bends sharply to the right. On the inside of this bend was Israel House [2], a large pillbox that held up the advance and caused a number of casualties. It was overcome when a small party crept behind it and bombed the garrison.

Carry on along the road until you reach a group of red farm buildings on the left. This is the site of a group of German concrete shelters known as Judah House [3], a point that marked the first objective for the attack. The Australians paused here while the New Zealanders on their left navigated through a bog that was holding them up.

A little further on is a red farmhouse on the right side of the road. In 1917 the farmhouse was known as Springfield [4] and had been shattered by shellfire. From the ruins a machine-gun disrupted the 10th Brigade's advance. Captain Frederick Moule moved to attack it but was mortally wounded. Once again, a small group of Australians managed to work around behind the gun position and kill the crew.

Continue along the road until you reach a T-junction, where Maarlestraat meets Schipstraat. Cross the road and stand facing Tyne Cot Cemetery. The two pillboxes that remain in Tyne Cot Cemetery are clearly visible beneath the tall trees—they sit right on the skyline and dominate all approaches. From here it is painfully clear what a formidable obstacle the German pillboxes were. These two alone would present a challenge to attacking troops; in 1917 there were dozens more. The field in front of you was the scene of some of the most ferocious fighting of the battle and was littered with Australian dead by mid-morning. A member of the 40th Battalion described the fighting:

> On the top of the ridge the trench system and line of pill-boxes along it seemed alive with men and machine-guns, and heavy fire was also coming from Bellevue Spur on the front of the New Zealanders. The only possible way to advance was from shell-hole to shell-hole by short rushes. To add to our difficulties, there was a thick belt of wire immediately in front of us, which

had very few gaps in it. On these gaps the enemy had trained machine-guns, and we dribbled through in ones and twos, but dead and wounded remained in each gap. Casualties were very heavy . . .

Diagonally across the field to your left is Hamburg Farm **[5]**, site of the pillbox that was captured by Lewis McGee in his VC-winning action (see page 90). A pillbox still stands in the grounds of the farm but, unfortunately, it is not visible from the road and the farmer does not welcome visitors. Lewis McGee enlisted in 1916. He was assigned to the 40th Battalion and travelled with it to France in late November. He rose quickly through the ranks, receiving his first promotion only 22 days after joining the battalion. He was 29 years old at the time of his death.

Turn right at the T-junction and then left at the next road. This leads to Tyne Cot Cemetery **[6]**, the world's largest Commonwealth military cemetery. (If driving, follow the signs to the parking area behind the cemetery.) Legend suggests that the area now enclosed by the cemetery was dubbed Tyne Cot by British troops who thought the German pillboxes looked like Tyneside cottages. In fact the name Tyne Cot was used long before the Germans built any pillboxes here and was probably given to a group of farm buildings on the site early in the war. Tyne Cot was captured by the 3rd Division immediately following Lewis McGee's assault on Hamburg Farm. Later, one of the pillboxes at the site was used by British troops as an advanced dressing station and men who were killed nearby were buried alongside it. These scattered burials formed the basis for the cemetery, which contained 343 graves at the end of the war. After the Armistice, thousands of graves were concentrated here, so that by 1922 Tyne Cot Cemetery had reached its present size of 11 953 graves. The original graves can be determined by their haphazard arrangement in the centre of the cemetery. At the suggestion of King George V, the Cross of Sacrifice was built over the top of one of the captured German pillboxes (the rough concrete is visible through a panel in the base). Two more pillboxes form the base of the pavilions at the back of the cemetery. The two pillboxes at the front of the cemetery were considered such formidable obstacles they were dubbed 'Irksome' and 'The Barnacle' by British troops. They still stand as brooding sentinels on either side of the entrance.

There are more Australians buried here than in any other cemetery of the First World War: 1368, of which 791 are unidentified. The vast majority of these men were killed in the battles of Broodseinde Ridge (4 October 1917) and Passchendaele (9–12 October 1917) but graves representing Australia's entire period of service in the Ypres Salient can be found. At the rear of the cemetery is the Tyne Cot Memorial to the Missing. During the construction of Menin Gate it was realised that there was not enough space to record the names of all the British missing in the Ypres Salient. This memorial was subsequently built at Tyne Cot to accommodate the overflow. Menin Gate records the names of British servicemen killed up to 15 August 1917 and the Tyne Cot Memorial records the names of those men killed after this date. (Keen to defy British order to the last, Anzac soldiers are the exception. The names of all Australian missing in Belgium, regardless of date of death, are recorded on Menin Gate. The names of the New Zealand missing are recorded at Tyne Cot, Buttes New British Cemetery and Messines Ridge Cemetery.) The Tyne Cot Memorial records the names of 34 827 men who have no known grave.

There are hundreds of notable Australians buried in Tyne Cot Cemetery. An hour spent wandering the rows probably gives a better impression of the extent of Australian service and sacrifice than anywhere else on the Western Front. Certainly one grave worth seeking out is that of Sergeant Lewis McGee VC (grave XX.D.1), who was killed by machine-gun fire near Augustus Wood during the Battle of Passchendaele.

Buried nearby is Captain Clarence Jeffries VC (34th Battalion, died 12/10/1917, grave XL.E.1). Jeffries led his men with distinction during the Battle of Passchendaele and captured several machine-gun posts. He was killed while attacking another machine-gun later in the day (see pages 104–105). Jeffries' body could not be found after the Armistice and his father travelled to Belgium in 1920 to search for it. He was unsuccessful, but later in the year the remains of an Australian captain were found in an isolated grave and identified as Jeffries' by the initials pencilled onto the groundsheet they were wrapped in.

One of the scores of common soldiers with uncommon stories buried at Tyne Cot is Private John Crowley (34th Battalion, died 12/10/1917, grave XIX.D.1). Before the war, John Crowley was the editor of the *Wyalong Star* newspaper in West Wyalong, New South Wales. During an emotional speech before his enlistment he told a crowd of locals he would rather 'sleep the eternal sleep in the cold earth of France' than shirk his responsibilities. He was 52 but lied about his age and joined up, following his brother Matthew and his sons Ossie and John, who had already enlisted. A short time later his youngest son, Reg, who was 16, also lied about his age and joined up. The Crowley family would pay a high price for their commitment to the war effort. As well as John Sr, who was killed at Passchendaele in 1917, Matthew died of wounds at Gallipoli in 1915 and Reg was killed at Villers-Bretonneux in 1918. He had just turned 18. Ossie and John Jr survived the war.

After visiting Tyne Cot, retrace your steps to Dochy Farm Cemetery and your car. For those who are fit and want to make a day of it, the Battle of Passchendaele tour begins and ends at Tyne Cot, and can follow on immediately after the Broodseinde walk.

OTHER SITES OF INTEREST

Celtic Wood

This rather inconspicuous copse would probably be long forgotten had it not been the site of one of the most mysterious tragedies in AIF history.

On 9 October 1917 Lieutenant Frank Scott led 85 men of the 10th Battalion to raid German positions in the wood, south-east of the village of Broodseinde. The raid was intended as a diversion to distract the Germans in that sector from the impending attack on Passchendaele to the north. The Germans were on their guard. Two days earlier parties from the 11th and 12th battalions had raided the wood, causing casualties and taking several Germans prisoner. At dawn on the 9th, Lieutenant Scott led his small group down the slope into the wood—where they disappeared. Only 14 unwounded men returned to the Australian lines. Research by authors Tony Spagnoly and Ted Smith has accounted for 48 of the raiders, but the fate of the other 37 remains a mystery. No graves have ever been found and the Germans produced no records of prisoners. The German regiment facing the Australians also made no mention of the raid in their unit diary. The most likely explanation is that the German defenders took revenge on the Australians for their losses in the earlier raid and killed them all, before burying them in an unmarked grave. Some of the Australian raiders are remembered on Menin Gate and one, Private Edward Green, is buried at Dochy Farm Cemetery, north of Zonnebeke (see page 93). A memorial to the raiders was unveiled in St George's Memorial Church in Ypres in the late 1990s.

Directions

Celtic Wood was destroyed during the war and never grew back, but it's not hard to pinpoint the site of the raid. From Ypres, drive through the village of Zonnebeke and, at the far end of the village, turn right at a roundabout in the direction of Beselare. Follow this road (the N303) for one kilometre and turn left onto Ryselbosstraat. After 250 metres the road turns sharply left at a farmhouse, and a smaller road intersects from the right. Follow the road left and continue for about 100 metres, until you have a good view of the field behind the farmhouse. This is approximately the point where the 10th Battalion's trench crossed the road. From here the raiding party advanced diagonally across the field on your right, down the slope to the German positions in Celtic Wood, which was located about 300 metres away in the middle of the field.

Langemarck German Cemetery

This is the only German cemetery in the battlefield area of the Ypres Salient, although there are four other German cemeteries from the First World War in Belgium. It was started in 1915 and used continuously until this area was lost by the Germans in 1918. During the 1920s and 1930s it was expanded by the concentration of graves from the Salient. By the start of the Second World War more than 14 000 Germans were buried here, including more than 3000 volunteer students. In the 1950s most of the German cemeteries in Flanders were closed and their graves were concentrated in a handful of large cemeteries. Due to a lack of space at Langemarck, more than 24 000 unknown soldiers were buried in a mass grave near the entrance. Since then many have been identified and their names are now recorded on panels surrounding the grave.

Three German pillboxes line one wall of the cemetery, but the most striking feature is the *Mourning Soldiers*, a bronze sculpture of four faceless German soldiers keeping an eternal vigil over the graves of their dead comrades. It was sculpted by Professor Emil Krieger of Munich and stands at the far end of the cemetery. Visitors to Langemarck may be struck by its cold functionality compared to the British cemeteries. The dark mood at Langemarck reflects Germany's isolation at the end of the First World War: it was within Europe but not part of it.

In 1940 Adolf Hitler visited the cemetery while touring the battlefields where he had served during the First World War, and held a commemorative service for the dead from his old unit, the 16th Bavarian Reserve Regiment.

Directions
The village of Langemarck (Langemark) is six kilometres north-west of Zonnebeke and can be reached by following the road opposite the Zonnebeke church. The cemetery is on the road that leads north out of Langemarck, in the direction of Houthulst.

Memorial Museum Passchendaele 1917

Opened on Anzac Day 2004 and renovated in 2013, this museum, housed in the former Zonnebeke Chateau, is one of the best on the Western Front. Zonnebeke Chateau and Lake were well-known landmarks on the Broodseinde/Passchendaele battlefield, even though the chateau had been pounded to dust and the lake pummelled and distorted long before the battles commenced. It was on the banks of the lake that Australian and German troops met in the middle of no man's land in the early hours of 4 October 1917, after coincidentally launching simultaneous attacks (see page 89). Today the chateau has been rebuilt and the lake, described in the *Official History* as 'a bleak waterhole 200 yards long by 100 wide', is a tranquil pond. The museum has a clear narrative describing the fighting all across the Salient, and particularly at Passchendaele, and has some novel features including a re-created dugout and trench system. It makes an excellent introduction to the Western Front and is a good option if time does not allow a visit to the In Flanders Fields Museum in Ypres. The museum is open from 9 am to 5 pm, seven days a week. It is closed in December and January.

Directions
The Memorial Museum Passchendaele 1917 is in the centre of the village of Zonnebeke, on the main road from Ypres.

CEMETERIES NEAR BROODSEINDE RIDGE

Dochy Farm New British Cemetery, Tyne Cot Cemetery: see Broodseinde Ridge tour (page 91).

5

Battle of Passchendaele, 9–12 October 1917

The Battle of Passchendaele was the final chapter in the saga that was the Third Battle of Ypres, a monumental drive to force the Germans from the high ground of the Ypres Salient. Third Ypres was meticulously planned and relied on limited infantry advances well supported by creeping artillery barrages that would, step by step, force the Germans from their strongholds overlooking Ypres. Australian troops had played important roles in earlier advances during Third Ypres, attacking at Menin Road and Polygon Wood in September and Broodseinde Ridge in early October. They had also been instrumental in the advance at Messines Ridge in June, which had swept the Germans from one of their strongest defensive positions and cleared the way for the Third Battle of Ypres to begin.

On 4 October the Australian 1st, 2nd and 3rd divisions had advanced up Broodseinde Ridge and captured key German positions on the slopes below the village of Passchendaele. The attack had been a triumph, catching the Germans completely off guard and forcing them to fall back along a wide front. Now it was time to tackle Passchendaele itself.

The British commander-in-chief, Field Marshal Sir Douglas Haig, knew he was racing against time. The autumn rains were overdue and the ability of the infantry to advance in anything but clear skies was limited. So far, the weather had held and Haig, buoyed by earlier successes and overestimating their effect on German morale, decided on one last gamble: an immediate attack on Passchendaele.

Just as the decision had been made, the weather changed. At noon on 4 October, with the guns still cooling from the attack on Broodseinde Ridge, rain began to fall. The battlefield, pummelled by years of shellfire, turned into a sea of mud. The simple task of marching to the front line became an ordeal. Rain that began as drizzle on 4 October turned to showers on 6 October and to drenching squalls on the 7th. On 8 October the rain became torrential. The chance of success had surely passed.

Haig was not a man to shrink from a challenge. In spite of protests from all fronts, he ordered the advance to proceed. Several trifles, including the complete inability of his artillery to reach the front line in time for the advance, and the exhaustion of his troops after spending a week negotiating a battlefield in thigh-deep mud, didn't bother Haig. In a war characterised by incompetent decision-making, Haig's call to attack Passchendaele was a standout.

The first stage of the advance began at dawn on 9 October. This was mostly a British advance, with the Australian 2nd Division covering the right flank. The 2/8th Lancashire Fusiliers' diary describes their march to the front line in preparation to attack:

> The night was inky, the track led over ground covered with innumerable shell-holes full of mud and water. This march, which would normally take about 1 to 1½ hours to complete, occupied 11½ hours, with the result that the battalion arrived in the front line 20 minutes late.

In spite of these difficulties, the attack started well. German resistance was feeble and the British and Australians made good ground. The Germans regrouped, however, and drove the line back during the night.

This first attack illustrates the great problem with the advance on Passchendaele. The previous attacks during the Third Battle of Ypres relied on fresh troops advancing under the cover of accurate artillery fire. At Passchendaele both advantages were absent. The troops were exhausted from the slog through the mud to reach the front line, and the artillery became bogged and could not reach its proper positions to support the advance. At Broodseinde Ridge the barrage had thrown up a wall of dust, smoke and fire; at Passchendaele it was so thin the troops had trouble even telling where the barrage was.

The second stage of the advance, the attack on Passchendaele itself, was launched on 12 October. Australian troops would play a much larger role in this attack, the 3rd Division tasked with capturing the village and the 4th Division providing support. The New Zealand Division would attack on the Australians' left.

The night before the advance was cold and rainy, and some Australian commanders lobbied for the attack to be cancelled. A little rain was not going to deter Haig, however, and at 5.25 am the troops were ordered to advance. In spite of the dreadful conditions the Australians were keen to attack. One battalion even carried a small Australian flag it intended to raise in Passchendaele once it had captured the village. The troops came under fire from the outset, the limited cover from the weak artillery barrage proving totally ineffective. The advancing troops were struggling in the mud and soon became disoriented and lost touch with the barrage. They were now at the mercy of the German gunners.

On the right, the 9th Brigade was struggling. The 34th Battalion was held up by fire from a pillbox until Captain Clarence Jeffries led a small group to attack it. They captured 25 Germans and two machine-guns and the advance continued. Later another machine-gun was causing heavy casualties and Captain Jeffries again led an assault on the post. He and his men charged towards it but the gunners swung it around and opened fire. Jeffries was killed but his men edged forward and captured the position, allowing the Australians to carry on. For his courage under fire, Jeffries was awarded a posthumous Victoria Cross.

On the left, the 10th Brigade had been badly mauled from the start and was struggling to make ground. Machine-gun fire from Augustus Wood caused heavy casualties, and snipers in a pillbox at Waterfields Farm were taking a toll. Sergeant Lewis McGee, a hero of the 40th Battalion who had won the Victoria Cross a week earlier at Broodseinde Ridge (see page 90), was one of the men killed.

One of the few parties from the 10th Brigade to make any ground was a group of about 20 men from the 38th Battalion who had charged straight for Passchendaele at the start of the advance. Through sheer luck they made it all the way to the village without being hit and stationed themselves by the ruined church. After finding no sign of friend or foe, they lost their nerve and stole back to the Australian line. They were the only Australians to enter the village that day.

Further left, the New Zealanders were also held up by heavy machine-gun fire. Australian lieutenants Allan Grant and Horace Chamberlain crossed a creek on a small bridge and attacked a pillbox that was holding up the advance. They captured it and moved towards two others. Grant was killed but Chamberlain and a handful of men succeeded in capturing the positions, along with 60 prisoners.

The situation was now hopeless. The Australians had only taken a few of their objectives and were being decimated by German fire. German reinforcements were streaming down the ridge and attempting to get behind the Australian positions. In the face of mounting casualties, the Australians withdrew. On the right, the 4th Division had faced similar obstacles and was also forced to pull back with heavy loss. The decision to attack had been ludicrous, the attack itself a disaster. The two Australian divisions had lost more than 4200 men between them.

The Australians were relieved by the Canadian Corps, which spent the next two weeks slogging up the same ridge in the same atrocious conditions. Eventually the Canadians captured

Passchendaele. In taking it, they suffered more than 15 000 casualties and won nine Victoria Crosses, the largest number won by Canadians in a single battle.

Even though it was a 'victory' in the sense that the village was eventually taken, the British troops were so weakened by the attack that they were left dangerously exposed to a German counterattack. The Germans exploited this in March 1918. During their Spring Offensive they swept down the ridge and captured in just a few days all the ground they had lost.

PASSCHENDAELE TOUR

The Battle of Passchendaele was fought in a quagmire; a featureless moonscape of overlapping shell craters where every distinguishing landmark had been blasted from the earth. The entire battlefield was a sea of stinking, cloying mud as thick as paste which clogged rifles and swallowed men.

It has changed since then. The killing fields are now pastures where farmers tend crops and cattle under a warm sun. Today's visitor will struggle to make the leap of imagination required to see the battlefield in its former state. But walking the land gives a good impression of the objectives and outcomes of the battle: why the high ground was so important to both sides, how well-positioned pillboxes held up entire battalions, how gentle valleys and streambeds became choked with the dead. And if the modern visitor gets a sense of the battle, but can't quite visualise the extent of the horror, that is not a bad thing.

This is a fairly long tour (approximately 7 kilometres) with some slight gradients. Allow four hours to do it justice; it can also be driven in a couple of hours. The village of Passchendaele is visited about halfway through the tour and is a good place for a refreshment and rest. The tour takes in one cemetery, several monuments and the site of a Victoria Cross action.

This tour begins at Tyne Cot Cemetery **[1]**, the final stop on the Broodseinde Ridge Tour. For information about the cemetery,

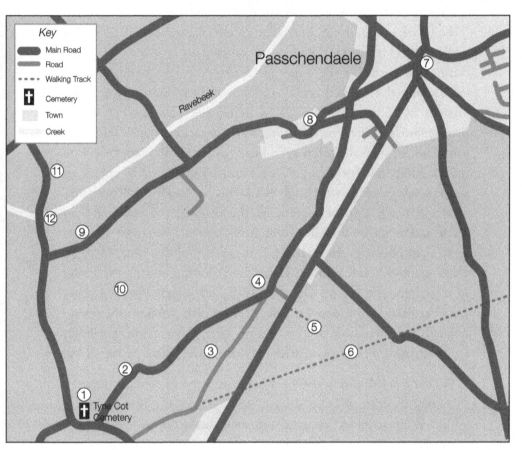

Passschendaele

see pages 96–98. Be sure to visit the grave of Captain Clarence Jeffries VC (grave XL.E.1); the site where he won the Victoria Cross and lost his life will be visited on this tour.

Leave the car park behind Tyne Cot and turn right, then turn left at the next road. Stop by a small grey memorial on the left, inscribed with the Australian rising sun emblem and the words 'Road to Passchendaele Australian Walk, 4 October 1917'. This walking trail follows the ground crossed by Australian troops during the Battles of Broodseinde Ridge and Passchendaele, and leads along the disused Ypres–Roulers railway line between the villages of Zonnebeke and Passchendaele. The railway was a prominent landmark in the otherwise featureless battlefield, and thousands of men sheltered in its banks during both battles. Follow the walking trail for a couple of hundred metres as it enters an old railway cutting, with high banks on both sides. Before long you will reach a short section of the original rail track and an information panel which details how one of the most famous Australian photographs of the war was taken at this spot. Official photographer Frank Hurley was in the front line during the battle of Passchendaele on 12 October 1917 and snapped several shots of exhausted, wounded and dead Australian soldiers sheltering beneath the left bank of the cutting after their attack had been so disastrously repulsed. Hurley described the scene in his diary:

> Under a questionably sheltered bank lay a group of dead men. Sitting by them in little scooped out recesses sat a few living; but so emaciated by fatigue and shell shock that it was hard to differentiate. Still the whole was just another of the many byways to hell one sees out here, and which are so strewn with ghastliness that the only comment is, 'Poor beggar copped it thick', or else nothing at all.

Return to the Tyne Cot car park entry and carry on past it. Just before the road bends to the right, stop. You are now standing on the start line of the Australian attack on 12 October [2]. Turn half right and you are facing in the intended direction of the Australian advance, but because the road traces the top of the ridge, the Australians followed it and advanced along the heights. This caused early confusion and was partly responsible for the advancing troops falling far behind their protective barrage.

Continue along the road. You will soon pass a group of buildings on your right that mark the site of Hillside Farm [3], a German strongpoint that poured heavy fire into the advancing Australians in the early stages of the attack. Machine-gun fire from here and a nearby trench held up the advance for more than an hour until both places were rushed. Thirty-five Germans and four machine-guns were captured. The smashed remains of a large German pillbox can be seen in front of the farm buildings.

Continue along the road until you reach an intersection with a road on the right [4]. It was near here that a pillbox again held up the advance until it was rushed by a party led by Captain Jeffries and Sergeant James Bruce. This was the first act of bravery that led to Jeffries being awarded the VC. For the same actions Bruce received the Distinguished Conduct Medal. He was later promoted to lieutenant and won the Military Cross. He was killed in action on 17 July 1918.

Just past the intersection is a short road leading to the right (Rozestraat). Follow this and, if walking, cross the busy Passendalestraat (Passchendaele Road). If driving, park beside Passendalestraat facing left. Follow a grass path leading to a memorial in the middle of the field. This is the 85th Canadian Infantry Battalion Memorial [5], raised in honour of this Nova Scotia unit on the site of their headquarters during the Passchendaele fighting. It is one of the very few privately erected Canadian memorials in Europe. The original memorial was built by the battalion in 1919, but by 1998 it was in a poor state and repairs were considered unfeasible. A new memorial, made from Nova Scotia granite and identical to the original, was unveiled at the site in 2001. It records the names of 144 members of the 85th Battalion who were killed in the fight for Passchendaele.

Look past the memorial to a tree-covered bank running through the field. This is a continuation of the Ypres–Roulers railway that you visited earlier in the tour. In the field in front of you, between the Passchendaele road and the railway, men of the 34th and 35th battalions came under a hurricane of machine-gun fire during the advance on Passchendaele. Many Australians died within 200 metres of where you are standing. Some of them sank into the mud and still lie there today.

A group of trees and bushes on the old rail line, directly opposite the memorial, is the remains of Decline Copse [6]. It was here that Captain Jeffries was killed attacking a German machine-gun post, the final act that earned him the VC. Jeffries was born in Newcastle and worked as a mining surveyor before joining the AIF in 1916. In June 1917 he was badly wounded by machine-gun fire during the attack at Messines and spent several months recovering in hospital. He was only 22 years old at the time of his death in October.

Return to Passendalestraat and turn right. You now have a walk of about 1.5 kilometres into the village. It's a long and fairly featureless stroll, so reward yourself with a cold drink and some Belgian chocolate when you arrive.

In the centre of Passchendaele village is the church [7], the ruins of which were reached by the group of men from the 38th Battalion in their mad dash for Passchendaele (see page 105). In the square opposite the church is a Bastiaan plaque recording Australia's involvement in the battle.

From this square, follow the street named Canadalaan signposted to the Passchendaele Memorial. This was the road taken by the men from the 38th Battalion. At the end of the street you will reach a memorial set within a picturesque garden. This is the Canadian Memorial [8] and commemorates the capture of Passchendaele by the Canadian Corps on 6 November (see pages 105–106). Although the memorial was raised to honour Canadian troops, the capture of Passchendaele was a joint Dominion effort, with Australian and New Zealand troops also playing vital roles. The gardens surrounding the granite memorial are exceedingly beautiful, with a grove of maple trees encircled by a holly hedge. The tranquillity of the place belies its wartime heritage. This is the site of Crest Farm, a monolithic blockhouse that changed hands several times during the fight for the town and decimated Australian and Canadian forces in the nearby Ravebeek valley.

Walk behind the memorial and look out into the fields. The gentle depression in front of you is the Ravebeek valley, a natural avenue of shelter used by both the Australians and Canadians in their slog for the village. It was well covered by German fire and consequently choked with dead and dying throughout the battle.

From behind the memorial, follow the road to the right down the hill. After about 500 metres, another road (Bornstraat) intersects on the right. Stop here and look across the field to your left. During the assault on the morning of 12 October the 10th Brigade crossed this field from your right to left. They faced murderous fire from the moment they began and suffered heavy casualties as they struggled through the thigh-deep mud. By the time they reached your position their numbers had been shattered and they dug in across this field. This was as close to Passchendaele as they would get. After enduring a day of devastating fire and watching their numbers decline by the hour, they withdrew, leaving 1100 men dead or wounded.

Carry on down the hill until you reach a farm on your left. In the field opposite was Waterfields [9], a pillbox that sheltered German snipers who killed several men on the 10th Brigade's left flank. A group of Australians worked from shell hole to shell hole and captured the pillbox after attacking it with bombs. The undulating ground in this field gives an indication of the churned-up earth that confronted the troops.

Continue along the road until just past the farm. Look across the field to your left. In the middle of the field stood a copse known as Augustus Wood [10]. From here, heavy machine-gun fire caught the 10th Brigade in the open as they advanced and casualties were severe. Sergeant Lewis McGee, the hero of the 40th Battalion who had won the VC on 4 October, was killed by machine-gun fire between the wood and the present day Tyne Cot Cemetery (see **Broodseinde Ridge**, page 88). Lieutenant William Garrard succeeded in leading a small group of men around the wood and charging it from the rear. They captured a pillbox and 20 prisoners, and Garrard received the Military Cross.

Continue along the road and turn right into Tynecotstraat at the crossroads. Cross the small creek and walk to the long red farm building on the right of the road. This is the site of Laamkeek [11], the group of pillboxes that held up the New Zealand advance and was captured by Lieutenants Grant and Chamberlain of the Australian 40th Battalion.

Retrace your steps along the road and pause on the small red-brick bridge across the creek. This was crossed by Grant and Chamberlain as they moved towards the pillboxes at Laamkeek. Look along the creek towards the church spire of Passchendaele. This is the Ravebeek [12], and in 1917 this muddy ditch provided shelter to troops wounded in the attack. By evening on 12 October it was crowded with dead and dying Australians.

Follow the road until you reach Tyne Cot Cemetery, the starting point of your tour.

CEMETERIES NEAR PASSCHENDAELE

Passchendaele New British Cemetery

This is another large concentration cemetery made after the Armistice. The fighting around Passchendaele occurred in dreadful weather conditions and there was not time or opportunity to bury the dead in large, formal cemeteries. Most men killed were buried in isolated graves or in small plots that were later disrupted by shellfire or simply lost in the sea of mud. After the war, the area around Passchendaele was strewn with graves and bodies that could not be identified. These were gathered together in a handful of large concentration cemeteries, the most prominent of which is Tyne Cot. Passchendaele New British is another big one, containing 2101 burials of which the majority are unknown. Australian graves number 292, with 171 unknowns, and mostly contain men killed in the tough slog up

Broodseinde Ridge and towards Passchendaele in October 1917. Interestingly, nine of the Australians buried here were killed in November, after the AIF had been withdrawn from the fighting. These men were unlucky; they were from a handful of units ordered to stay behind to assist Canadian troops who had taken over from the Australians.

The most senior Australian soldier buried here is Captain Elwyn Gould of the 27th Battalion, who had been prominent during the advance on Broodseinde Ridge on 4 October 1917. At one stage he ordered his men to consolidate an old trench they had captured. Their digging uncovered the bodies of British men who had been killed here in 1915, on the same day the Australians had landed at Gallipoli. Gould was killed by shellfire during the disorganised advance near Daisy Wood during the Battle of Passchendaele on 9 October (grave XI.E.16).

Lieutenant Talbert Pitman MC was the signalling officer of the 44th Battalion and had won the Military Cross at Messines in June 1917. At Broodseinde Ridge on 5 October his unit was sheltering in a captured German pillbox and Pitman gave up his place to allow some of his men to sleep inside. He lay down outside and was killed by a shell (grave XIII.C.11).

Directions

From Ypres (Ieper), take the road the Zonnebeke. At the main intersection in Zonnebeke, in front of the church, turn left towards Dochy Farm Cemetery. Pass the cemetery and, after a further kilometre, turn right in Roeselarestraat. Follow this road for four kilometres until you reach Passchendaele New British Cemetery on the left. A memorial to New Zealand troops killed in the Passchendaele fighting is located before the cemetery on the same road.

Part II

French Flanders

French Flanders was the first area of operations for Australian troops on the Western Front. They arrived there in March 1916 after a period of rest and refitting in Egypt and were sent to the sector known as the 'Nursery' to familiarise themselves with trench warfare and learn about weapons and tactics they hadn't used at Gallipoli. The Nursery was a relatively quiet sector and the opposing troops had reached a tacit agreement: we won't attack you if you don't attack us. The Australians set about changing things. Within days of their arrival they began aggressive patrolling, causing mayhem and taking prisoners in the German lines, and sniped at any German head they saw above the parapet.

The next few months saw the Australians increase the intensity of their raiding against the German positions. It was a grubby type of warfare and despised by the men, but as the Australians' skill increased so did the demands placed on them: by the end of June they were raiding the German trenches almost every night.

On 19 July 1916, the 5th Division launched the first major offensive by Australian forces on the Western Front. The Battle of Fromelles was intended as a large-scale diversion that would hold German troops in Flanders and prevent them being sent south as reinforcements to the

Somme. It certainly kept the Germans busy. For a full day and night they were well occupied pouring machine-gun fire into the Australians advancing across no man's land. Poor planning and incompetent leadership contributed to a massacre, and more than 5500 Australians were killed or wounded in one night.

After the debacle at Fromelles the Australians didn't see much of French Flanders until 1918. In March and April of that year the Germans launched a massive offensive along much of the British line and broke through in several places. Australian troops were rushed in to plug the gaps and, in French Flanders, met the Germans in several fierce actions near the Lys River. For most of April the Australians were heavily engaged halting the German advance and recapturing villages that had been lost. They performed magnificently but paid a high price: thousands of Australians now lie in small cemeteries across the area.

French Flanders is an interesting sector of the Western Front and can easily be visited as a stopping off point between Ypres and the Somme. The battlefield at Fromelles is the only essential site, but numerous villages and towns in the area from the 1916 and 1918 fighting also hold interest for Australian visitors.

6

Battle of Fromelles, 19–20 July 1916

Australians best remember 1916 for the heroic capture of the Somme town of Pozières, a magnificent achievement that cost the 1st, 2nd and 4th divisions 23 000 casualties in six weeks of bitter fighting. Less well known, but no less heroic, is the story of the Battle of Fromelles, a brief action by 1916 standards but one of the most costly endeavours for Australian troops in the whole war.

The battle was fought at a time when the murderous Battle of the Somme had been raging for almost three weeks. By this stage British expectations of a stunning breakthrough on the Somme had evaporated, along with the lives of 50 000 men on both sides. Now the British dug in and began a battle of attrition, a torturous five-month slog where success would be measured in inches of ground gained, and more than a million men would be sacrificed to the gods of war.

The attack at Fromelles was ordered to stop the Germans sending troops south to reinforce their battered comrades on the Somme, and was a picture of mismanagement from its conception. General Sir Richard Haking, commander of the British XI Corps and not a man to give up on a plan just because it didn't work, had overseen two disastrous attacks in the Fromelles area in 1915 and another in June 1916. Now he conceived a large-scale 'demonstration' near Fromelles, a diversion that would convince the Germans an attack was imminent and force them to hold troops there to defend their line. The original plan called only for a heavy three-day artillery bombardment, with troops moving around in the rear area as if assembling for an attack. This wasn't a bad plan, but the British generals got greedy. If they were going to spend three days pummelling the German lines, they reasoned, why not send some troops over to capture their trenches as well? It should have been clear that the two goals were incompatible. Doing everything they could to alert the Germans to an impending attack *and then actually launching one* was suicidal.

This logic was apparently lost on the British High Command, and the Australian 5th Division and British 61st Division were selected to attack. The newly formed 5th had men among its ranks who had served at Gallipoli, but as a unit it was inexperienced— so inexperienced, in fact, that only a few weeks before it had been deemed too green to enter the mincing machine on the Somme. About half its troops had not even been issued steel helmets and would wear their slouch hats into battle—the only time the distinctive Australian headgear would be worn in an attack in France. Ironically, Australia's newest division was about to become the first to launch a major attack on the Western Front.

As well as being poorly planned, the Fromelles attack was slapdash in its execution. The attacking troops were rushed into the front line, only to discover that much of their equipment had failed to arrive with them. Trench mortar teams were ordered to set up in hastily built emplacements, only to find that these had been dug too far in the rear and the German trenches were out of range. Exhausted troops were ordered to lug drums of gas into the front line, only to be told that the risk of a mishap from enemy shelling was too great, and they should turn around and lug them back. When a gas attack *was* launched, a breeze sprang up and blew the gas back into the British lines, causing many casualties.

At 6 pm on 19 July, the battle began. The Australians attacked on a front of about two kilometres and had to cross about 200 metres of no man's land to reach the German lines. It had been impossible to dig ordinary trenches in the waterlogged ground of French Flanders, so both sides instead built 'breastworks': walls of sandbags and earth up to three metres thick which effectively formed above-ground trenches. The plan called for the Australians to capture the first German line, consolidate and then push on to capture the German support lines. This was a big ask, but the British 61st Division on their right had an even tougher job. They had to cross more than 400 metres of no man's land and attack head-on the 'Sugarloaf' salient, a huge bulge in the German line that was heavily fortified with wire and machine-guns.

The Australians started well. In spite of their inexperience they successfully rushed the German front line and captured it. But as the troops pushed on, they struggled to find the German support lines they were supposed to capture. Lieutenant Colonel Frederick Toll, commander of the 31st Battalion, went forward with two men more than 400 metres behind the German line, searching in vain for the objective. British aerial photos had shown at least two lines of support trenches behind the main German line, but all the Australians could find were a couple of shallow, half-flooded ditches. Evidently the Germans had found the ground too boggy to dig trenches and had abandoned the construction of their support lines weeks before. Undeterred, the Australians began to dig in, some in the German front line and some in isolated positions in the ditches in front. They filled sandbags with muddy earth and did their best to construct defensible positions against the inevitable German counterattacks. Meanwhile, engineers raced to dig communication trenches across no man's land to enable the safe passage of reinforcements, food and ammunition to the troops in the German lines.

On the right, the British were struggling. The 61st Division had gone forward at the same time as the Australians, but found the going much tougher. The Sugarloaf was proving hard to crack, and the British suffered severe casualties before they even got close to it. The handful of men who managed to reach the German wire were swiftly killed or captured. With the Sugarloaf unsubdued, the Germans could enfilade the Australians on their right with heavy machine-gun fire, and send troops to counterattack along the line.

The 5th Division was now in a desperate situation. With no support from the British on their right, and Germans beginning to counterattack from in front and along the German front line trench, there was a risk of becoming surrounded. As well, German artillery had begun blasting no man's land, making it impossible for reinforcements to reach the troops in the German line. The Australians in the most forward positions held out into the night but were gradually overcome by the advancing Germans. Most were killed, some were captured and a few succeeded in trickling back to the German front line, where they stood back to back with their mates, throwing bombs and fighting hand to hand with any Germans that penetrated the line.

At this point the battle deteriorated into a bloody debacle. On the 61st Division's front, Haking ordered that the Sugarloaf be bombarded and attacked again. The Australian 58th Battalion, a freshly formed Victorian unit that had only been in France for a month, was ordered to send half its force (about 400 men) to support the attack. The young Victorians were keen to prove their worth, particularly to the Gallipoli veterans in their division. At the last minute, Haking cancelled the attack—but the order didn't reach the Australians. Alone and with no artillery support, the 58th Battalion launched, in the words of the *Official History*, 'one of the bravest and most hopeless assaults ever undertaken by the Australian Imperial Force'. The Germans allowed the Australians to get two-thirds of the way across no man's land before opening a hurricane of machine-gun fire from the Sugarloaf. The attacking troops were annihilated, only a handful of them eventually managing to creep back to the Australian line. More than two years later, with the war over, the dead were found lying where they fell in front of the German wire.

The survivors of the 5th Division were still grimly hanging on in the German lines, but their situation was hopeless. Captain Charles Arblaster, a 21-year-old company commander of the 53rd Battalion, organised a desperate defence against fierce counterattacks in the German second line. At one stage he saw German helmets behind him in the frontline trench and, realising he was surrounded, ordered his men to charge. Most of them were hit, including Arblaster, who was later captured. He died from his wounds in a German hospital four days later.

With the situation now lost and Germans swarming into the trenches on all sides, the Australians had no choice but to charge back across no man's land to the Australian front line. With machine-gunners covering the retreat, the Australians began to stream from the German trenches in small groups. German machine-guns opened fire on them from in front, on both sides and the rear and caused terrible loss, but many men reached the Australian trench. Most of the machine-gunners who had stayed behind were killed or captured, but one group of 11 men, under Captain Frank Krinks of the 30th Battalion, decided to run for the Australian lines. Of the original 11, four, including Krinks, survived the dash.

This daring escape had a sad footnote. Two of the men, Privates John Wishart and Tom Watts, went out into no man's land later in the day to search for a wounded comrade. They found him and were bringing him in on a stretcher when they were spotted by a jumpy Australian sentry. Mistaking them for Germans, he fired a single shot which killed both men.

Captain Norman Gibbins of the 55th Battalion, a Gallipoli veteran, had led an inspired defence against the Germans all night and was one of the last men to attempt the dash across no man's land. He reached the Australian lines but was killed before he could climb into the trench.

From no man's land came the haunting cries of the wounded and dying. One young Australian, blinded by his wounds, staggered around in no man's land and cried out for several days. His mates called out to him and vainly tried to direct him back to the Australian lines until the Germans mercifully shot him. Although ordered not to, many Australians crept out to rescue mates. Reverend Spencer Maxted, who had served as a stretcher bearer at Gallipoli and was greatly admired by the Australian troops, ignored an order to stay in the rear and tended to the wounded in the front line throughout the day. He was killed by a shell in the afternoon.

So ended the disastrous Battle of Fromelles. In 27 hours of bitter fighting the 5th Division lost 5533 men and ceased to function as a fighting force. It would be more than a year before the division was sufficiently restored to play a major part in offensive operations again. In the end, even the plan to prevent the Germans from sending troops south was a flop. By the evening of 20 July it was obvious that the attack had been snuffed out and that the Fromelles operation was not a serious attempt to break through the German lines. This was confirmed when the Germans searched the dead and found an order from Haking, directing the troops to advance only as far as the German support line. Safe in the knowledge that the attack was a diversion, the Germans were free to send troops south to the Somme as reinforcements, which they did over the next few days.

FROMELLES TOUR

Fromelles is unique among Australian battlefields. It does not have the victorious aura of Pozières or Hamel, or convey a sense of courage in the face of adversity like the battlefields of Ypres. If any Australian battlefield conforms to the stereotype of the pointless slaughter of the Great War, this is it. It is a sad and lonely place, the dreary plain often rainy and always windy. No visitor to Fromelles will walk away with illusions about the glory of war; instead, they will leave with a hollow sense of loss and deep sadness.

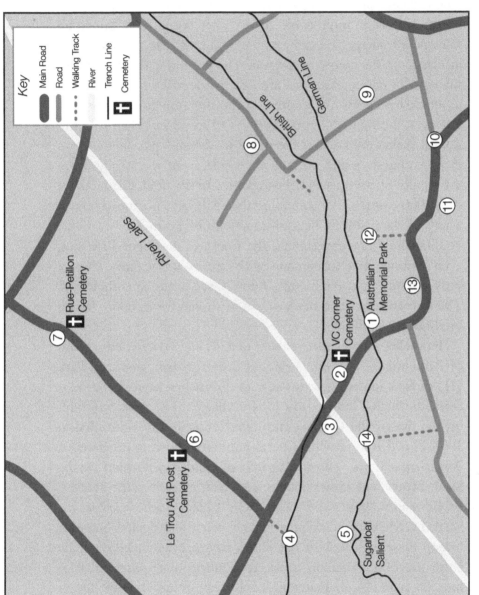

Fromelles

Key

Main Road
Road
Walking Track
River
Trench Line
Cemetery

Rue-Petillon Cemetery

Le Trou Aid Post Cemetery

River Laïes

British Line

German Line

VC Corner Cemetery

Australian Memorial Park

Sugarloaf Salient

As you walk the fields of Fromelles, bear in mind that the whole catastrophic attack was a sideshow. Even if the Australians had pulled off an improbable victory, they would have gained no strategic advantage and the result would have had no discernible influence on the course of the war. The ground in this area was so strategically unimportant that after the battle neither side bothered to attack here again for the rest of the war (the ground was lost, however, during the German Spring Offensive in 1918). And this is what makes the losses at Fromelles so obscene: not only were so many young lives snuffed out, the whole event was a folly. Even the dignity of a proper burial was denied to the dead. Of the more than 2000 Australians killed, more than half have no known grave. Many of them still lie beneath the fields of Fromelles.

Like all of French Flanders, the tour area is millpond flat but, even without hills to contend with, this is still a fairly lengthy walk—about eight kilometres. Allow three hours to complete it. The tour follows good roads so can be driven for its entire length in about 90 minutes.

Fromelles is 20 kilometres west of Lille and 10 kilometres south of Armentières. The tour begins at the Australian Memorial Park [1], three kilometres north-west of Fromelles (follow the signs from the major intersection in the village). The park was built on the site of the German frontline trench and was unveiled in 1998 in order to provide a focal point for growing numbers of Australian visitors. The small patch of field was donated by the local farmer and now contains information panels, the remains of German pillboxes and the emotive *Cobbers* statue. *Cobbers* is a work by Melbourne sculptor Peter Corlett and depicts Sergeant Simon Fraser of the 57th Battalion carrying a wounded comrade from the 60th Battalion to safety. During one of several trips into no man's land, Fraser heard a weak voice call out 'Don't forget me, cobber.' The expression has come to symbolise the bond of mateship that held the Australians together in those terrible days. Later, as a lieutenant in the 58th Battalion, Fraser was Mentioned in Despatches. He was killed during the Second Battle of Bullecourt in May 1917 and is remembered on the

Australian National Memorial at Villers-Bretonneux. The German pillboxes in the park were not there during the battle. They were built by the Germans in 1917 and were damaged by a farmer's attempts to remove them after the war.

Spend some time studying the battle before you begin the tour. The layout of the Fromelles battlefield can be hard to visualise because of curves in the roads and trench lines, and a lack of obvious landmarks, although the information panels at the memorial give a good overview of the orientation of the battlefield.

Leave the park and turn right. You are now walking across no man's land towards the Australian line. On the afternoon of 19 July, men from the 53rd and 54th battalions advanced towards you on either side of this road. Many of them were hit by a German machine-gunner known as Parapet Joe, who fired directly along the road.

After a short distance you will reach VC Corner Cemetery [2]. The name VC Corner is not related to the Battle of Fromelles. The cemetery is named after a nearby intersection that was heavily shelled and was christened VC Corner by British troops earlier in the war, presumably for the courage required to regularly pass through it. This beautiful cemetery is located in the middle of no man's land. Thousands of Australians were killed and wounded in every direction from where you stand. The bodies of most of the dead could not be retrieved until after the war and by then it was impossible to identify them. Not wishing to construct a cemetery where every headstone carried an 'unknown' inscription, the war graves authorities decided to bury 410 Australian casualties in two plots, each marked by a single white cross. A border of rose bushes was planted around each plot, with one plant for each man in the cemetery. This thoughtful and sensitive design makes this cemetery unique. It is the only cemetery in France that is wholly Australian and has no headstones. The only other all-Australian cemetery on the Western Front is Toronto Avenue in Ploegsteert Wood, Belgium (see **Messines**, page 66). Even though the Australians appear to lie in mass graves, these are in fact individual graves, just not marked by headstones. A curved wall behind the Cross of

Sacrifice records the names of Australians who were killed in the battle and have no known grave. Among them are several senior soldiers, including Lieutenant Colonel Ignatius Norris, commander of the 53rd Battalion. He was killed by machine-gun fire while attempting to reach the German support line. His body could not be recovered, but his name appeared on a list of the dead supplied by the Germans in November 1916. In 2010 his body was identified after the exhumation of 250 Australian and British soldiers from a mass grave at nearby Pheasant Wood (see page 140). Also look for the name of Major Arthur Hutchinson, leader of the 58th Battalion's doomed advance against the Sugarloaf.

Other notable officers remembered on the memorial are Majors Thomas Elliott of the 60th Battalion and Victor Sampson of the 53rd Battalion, and Captains Ernest Evans (60th Battalion), Aubrey Liddelow (59th Battalion), Kenneth Mortimer (29th Battalion), Harry Paulin (53rd Battalion) and Thomas Sheridan (29th Battalion). Like Norris, Sampson and Sheridan have now been identified and are buried in Fromelles (Pheasant Wood) Cemetery (see page 140). Private John Wishart, one of the men from the 30th Battalion mistakenly shot by the Australian sentry (see page 123), is also remembered here. As you stand in VC Corner Cemetery, spare a kind thought for all the men who lie here and are commemorated on the memorial. Many of them met dreadful ends, dying from ghastly wounds in no man's land, within sight but out of reach of their comrades in the Australian line. 'Every move they make,' an Australian soldier later wrote, 'the German puts the machine-guns on them. Some are calling for him to do it and end their misery.' As beautiful as it is today, VC Corner is a testament to suffering and despair.

Leave VC Corner Cemetery and turn right. Follow the road to a small bridge over a ditch [3]. This is the 'River' Laies, which crossed the battlefield diagonally and proved a major obstacle to the attacking troops. Finding it too wide to jump and too deep to ford, the Australians struggled through it as best they could. The Germans had set up a machine-gun at the point where the river crossed their line, and enfiladed the Australians and British as they struggled through the slime of the ditch. By nightfall on 19 July this stretch of ditch was crowded with dead and wounded. The Australian front line ran perpendicular to the Laies and crossed the road almost immediately after the bridge.

Carry on to the next intersection and follow the farm track into the field on your left. (If driving, park and walk up the track.) The track ends at about the site of the British front line [4]. From here, British machine-gunners blasted away at the Sugarloaf during the attack. If there are no crops in the field, walk due south. You are now walking in the footsteps of the 58th Battalion in their brave but hopeless assault on the Sugarloaf. As you walk, imagine the men of the 58th advancing alongside you. This is the first action for most of them and their spirits are high. Now imagine a barrage of machine-gun fire erupting from the looming mass of the Sugarloaf, directly in front. Within minutes the 58th is cut to pieces.

After about 350 metres you will reach the site of the Sugarloaf [5]. More than two years after the battle, Charles Bean, the Australian Official Historian, stood in the same place. He wrote:

> We found the old No-Man's Land simply full of our dead. In the narrow sector west of the Laies River and east of the Sugarloaf Salient, the skulls and bones and torn uniforms were lying about everywhere. I found a bit of Australian kit lying fifty yards from the corner of the salient, and the bones of an Australian officer and several men within 100 yards of it.

The sheer volume of machine-gun fire from the Sugarloaf is hard to comprehend. A century later, spent cartridges still litter the ground and German bullets—the actual projectiles—are scattered across the field.

Return along the farm track, cross the road and follow the road opposite. On the left you will reach Le Trou Aid Post Cemetery [6]. Surrounded by a moat and shaded by weeping willows, this intimate cemetery is one of the most beautiful on the Western Front. It is the namesake of an aid post that was established nearby early in the war. The cemetery was first used in October 1914 and contained 123 burials at the time of the Armistice. Most of these were from famous British battles fought before the Australians even arrived in France, including Le Maisnil (21 October 1914), Aubers Ridge (9 May 1915) and Loos (25 September 1915). After the war a further 233 graves were added to the cemetery from smaller burial grounds in the area, giving today's total of 356 graves. Fifty-six Australians who were killed at Fromelles are buried here but only four of them could be identified. They are Lance Corporal John Innes (54th Battalion, died 19/07/1916, grave K.28), Private Percy Matthews (32nd Battalion, died 20/07/1916, grave O.35), 2nd Lieutenant Alexander Paterson (32nd Battalion, died 20/07/1916, grave O.25) and Private Fred Read (54th Battalion, died 19/07/1916, grave O.12).

The houses opposite the cemetery form the hamlet of Le Trou, site of the aid post and the headquarters of Brigadier General Harold 'Pompey' Elliott, commander of the 15th Brigade at Fromelles. Elliott had landed at Gallipoli on the first day of the campaign and was shot in the foot that afternoon. After his brigade had suffered so grievously at Fromelles, Elliott wept as he met the men coming out of the line.

Leave the cemetery and continue along the road until you reach Rue-Pétillon Military Cemetery on your right **[7]**. The cemetery was begun in December 1914 and used until the end of the war, but the vast majority of its graves were added after the Armistice when a number of small cemeteries from a wide area were closed. Rue-Pétillon now contains more than 1500 burials and is a fascinating cemetery for Australian visitors, with burials not just from Fromelles but from other important actions in the near (and not so near) area. The 292 Australian graves in Rue-Pétillon are a snapshot of Australian service in French Flanders throughout the war.

The most senior Australian soldier buried here is also the newest arrival. Major Roy Harrison, second in command of the 54th Battalion, was shot dead in no man's land on the first day at Fromelles, but his body was not found until 1921. It was identified by his monogrammed silver cigarette case (grave I.D.20).

Buried nearby is the heroic Reverend Spencer Maxted, killed while helping the wounded at Fromelles (see page 102, grave I.K.2). And also buried here is Private Tom Watts, the other member of the 30th Battalion killed by the nervy Australian sentry while bringing in a wounded mate (see page 124, grave I.K.59).

Much of Plot I, Row K, is a single long grave containing the remains of 30 men from the 58th Battalion who were killed in a German trench raid on 15 July 1916, four days before the remainder of the battalion was mauled at Fromelles. The most senior officer killed in this raid was Captain Edward Mair (grave I.K.100).

The cemetery also contains 36 victims from a German trench raid on 30 May, mostly from the 11th Battalion. Some of them, including Private Daniel Cocking (grave I.H.23), were Gallipoli veterans.

The earliest Australian casualty in the cemetery is Private Thomas Puddephatt of the 1st Pioneers. He was killed in action on 24 April 1916, less than five weeks after the first Australians arrived in France (grave I.H.66). A late Australian casualty buried here is Lance Corporal Percy Barclay of the 10th Battalion, who was killed during the German defence of Méteren on 24 April 1918 (see page 147). His body was left behind after the Australians withdrew and was later buried by the Germans. It was moved to Rue-Pétillon after the Armistice (grave I.C.23). Lance Corporal Barclay has come a long way since his unfortunate end—Méteren is 25 kilometres away.

Leave the cemetery and continue along the road, and turn right at the next intersection. After a kilometre, turn right onto the Chemin de la Boutillerie. As you walk along this stretch of road you are walking parallel to the British front line, which ran along the left of the road. After about 500 metres you will pass Cordonnerie Farm on your right [8]. This was the site of the German raid on 30 May 1916 that resulted in the 11th Battalion casualties buried in Rue-Pétillon Cemetery. The 11th got their revenge on the night of 2 July, when they launched their own raid against the German trenches opposite the farm. Cordonnerie Farm marked the left flank of the 5th Division's attack during the fighting at Fromelles on 19 July.

Continue along the road for 800 metres until it bends sharply left. Follow the farm track directly ahead until it runs out. (If driving, park and follow the track on foot.) In the field to your left, about 90 metres away, was the British front line, running approximately parallel with the track. No man's land was less than 100 metres wide here and the battalions attacking from this position did much better than their comrades further west. They weren't so lucky during the opening barrage, however. The German trenches were so close that the British artillery had trouble hitting them without also pummelling their own lines.

Return along the track. The clearing on your left just before the intersection with the road is the site of a medieval moated farm that was destroyed during the war. Turn right onto the road, and after about 200 metres you will reach the point where the German front line crossed the road, approximately along the line of the current fence. A major German communication trench, the Kastenweg, joined the front line here and ran along the right-hand side of this road for several hundred metres. In the field to your left are three crumbling German pillboxes, probably constructed in 1917 at the same time as those in the Australian Memorial Park.

Carry on until you reach a small copse on your left. At the far end of the copse follow the grass path to the left. (If driving, park and follow the path on foot.) This leads to a concrete German bunker [9], set deep into the ground and uncovered in 1995. The slanted aperture identifies it as a shelter for a heavy *minenwerfer*, or trench mortar. Shells from this site demolished large sections of the Australian trenches in the lead-up to the battle.

The bunker was located behind the ruined Delangre Farm, a German strongpoint that caused problems for the Australians throughout the battle. It was near here that Captain Krinks and his group of 11 men set up two Lewis guns, which they used to break up German counterattacks and eventually cover the withdrawal of the Australians on 20 July (see page 124). In the fields between here and the Australian Memorial Park, some of the most desperate hand-to-hand fighting of the battle occurred.

Continue along the road and turn right, then carry on until you reach a fork. A stone monument [10] in the centre of the intersection is a tribute to Flight Sergeant Kenneth Bramble, an English Spitfire pilot from 609 Squadron who was shot down near this spot on 21 July 1941. According to locals, Sergeant Bramble managed to bail out of his crippled aircraft but was killed when his parachute failed to open. The memorial was erected by them in 1999.

Continue along the road until you pass a farm dam on the left [11]. This marks the farthest spot reached by Lieutenant Colonel Toll in his search for the German support lines during the opening phase of the battle (see page 121). Looking across the distant fields and realising he was well beyond the objective, and the Australian barrage, he returned to the German line and ordered his men to dig in there, about 350 metres east of the Australian Memorial Park.

Follow the road until it bends sharply to the left and walk along the farm track on the right [12]. German reinforcements poured along this road early on the morning of 20 July and forced their way into their old front line, which crossed the field roughly on the line of the modern electricity poles. From there they launched a bombing attack that eventually forced the Australians out of the trenches. At the end of the track is a scrub-covered German pillbox.

Return to the road and turn right. After a short distance you will reach a crucifix memorial on the right of the road [13]. This commemorates Captain Paul Kennedy of the British Rifle Brigade, who was killed at this spot on 9 May 1915, during an attack on Aubers Ridge. The memorial was erected in 1921 by his mother, who lost two other sons during the war. Captain Kennedy has no known grave and is remembered on the Ploegsteert Memorial to the Missing in Belgium.

Follow the road as it curves to the right and turn left at the next road (Rue Deleval). Just before a small chapel is a farm track leading into the field on your right. If there are no crops in the field, follow the track until it runs out. You are now standing on the German front line, with the Sugarloaf about 200 metres to your left [14]. From this point you have a good view of the battlefield as the Germans saw it. Ahead of you is the River Laies and, about 400 metres beyond it, the farm track that led you to the site of the British front line at point 4, page 125. This is the widest part of no man's land that was crossed during the attack, and the outstanding field of fire afforded the German machine-gunners is obvious. With the Germans forewarned of the attack and the British artillery unable to suppress the enemy machine-guns, the carnage in these fields was inevitable.

Return to the main road and turn left. The Australian Memorial Park, where the tour began, is just ahead on the right.

OTHER SITES OF INTEREST IN FRENCH FLANDERS

Armentières

Armentières was an icon to Allied troops during the war and the humorous ditty 'Mademoiselle from Armentières' made it immortal. As a major British base behind the lines in this sector of the front it was well known to Australian troops, who frequented the restaurants and estaminets around the main square. Unfortunately the Germans destroyed most of Armentières in 1918, so today's sprawling town, much larger than it was during the war, would be unrecognisable to the Diggers. It's one of those places that you should visit because you are in the area, but its extensive industrial areas and maze of arterial roads are unlikely to charm.

Bois-Grenier—Bill Jackson VC

This French village was in the centre of the Nursery sector where the Australians were first sent on their arrival in France, and the fields east of the village were the scene of aggressive Australian patrolling between April and July 1916. During a raid on the night of 25 June, Private Bill Jackson of the 17th Battalion won

Australian troops march past the shattered ruins of the Cloth Hall in Ypres, October 1917. (AWM E04653)

Menin Gate records the names of more than 54 000 Commonwealth soldiers who were killed in the Ypres Salient and have no known grave. The rebuilt Cloth Hall can be seen through the arch.

A horse team races through Hellfire Corner, a notoriously dangerous spot in the Ypres Salient, September 1917. The hessian sheets on the left of the photo were an attempt to screen the intersection from German gunners. (AWM E01889)

A German pillbox toppled by the explosion of a British mine during the Battle of Messines, 7 June 1917. (AWM E01320)

Left: Mud Corner Cemetery is the final resting place of Australians and New Zealanders killed during the Battle of Messines, and is an excellent example of a small battlefield cemetery.

Below: Australian troops passing the cemetery at Polygon Wood, a few days after capturing it in September 1917. The rough mound of the Buttes, a formidable German defensive position, is visible in the background. (AWM E01912)

Polygon Wood today. The Australian 5th Division Memorial stands on the Buttes, overlooking Buttes New British Cemetery.

Throughout the war the Australians were enthusiastic souvenir hunters. Here Private Barney Hines of the 45th Battalion displays booty collected from the Germans in a single morning at Polygon Wood, 27 September 1917. (AWM E00822)

A German prisoner assists a badly wounded Australian during the
Battle of Menin Road, 20 September 1917. (AWM E04635)

Australian soldiers walk along a duckboard track in a sea of mud after the capture of Broodseinde
Ridge, October 1917. The barbed-wire entanglements in the foreground were laid by the Germans
to protect the concrete pillbox visible behind the soldiers. (AWM E01235)

Members of an Australian artillery battery pass through the devastated Chateau Wood soon after the Battle of Passchendaele, October 1917. (AWM E01220)

Tyne Cot Cemetery is the world's largest Commonwealth war cemetery, with almost 12 000 graves. The four trees surround a German concrete pillbox, captured by the Australian 3rd Division during a ferocious fight on 4 October 1917. More Australians lie in Tyne Cot than in any other cemetery of the First World War.

Men of the 53rd Battalion prepare to attack at Fromelles, 19 July 1916. Only three of the men shown here came out of the action alive, and those three were wounded. (AWM A03042)

VC Corner Cemetery, Fromelles, the only wholly Australian cemetery in France.

Members of the 2nd Division man a trench near Bois Grenier, June 1916. The tidy trench, spotless uniforms and theatrical poses suggest that this photo was staged. (AWM EZ0007)

Above: An Australian soldier in the remains of the German OG1 trench after the Battle of Pozières in 1916. The shelling was so heavy during this fight that the trench has been almost completely filled in – the soldier is digging out rifles buried up to their muzzles. The ruins of the windmill, a famous battlefield landmark, can be seen on the horizon on the far right. (AWM E00011)

Right: The Australian 1st Division Memorial at Pozières. Four of the five Australian divisional memorials are of this style – the exception is the 2nd Division Memorial at Mont St Quentin, which depicts an Australian soldier standing defiantly on a stone plinth.

Australia's first Victoria Cross on the Western Front. Jackson was a member of a raiding party that succeeded in crossing no man's land under heavy machine-gun fire and entering the German front line. The German defenders had taken refuge from British shelling in dugouts and offered only token resistance. The raiders captured four prisoners and killed about 30 men during the five minutes they spent in the enemy trench. As they returned across no man's land towards the Australian line the Germans began shelling the area and several men were hit. Private Jackson escorted a prisoner back to the Australian line and then braved the shellfire to rescue a wounded mate. He went out again and was helping to bring in another wounded man when a shell exploded close by, blowing off his arm above the elbow. He refused treatment and led a small group back into no man's land to rescue two more wounded comrades. Jackson's arm, which was still barely attached, was later amputated in the trench.

Jackson was only 18 when he won the Victoria Cross and was Australia's youngest VC winner of the war. He had served with the 17th Battalion at Gallipoli and came with them to France in March 1916. After his actions at Bois-Grenier, Jackson was evacuated to England and spent more than a year in hospital, returning to Australia in September 1917. In the following years he worked in several jobs in New South Wales and was seriously injured in a car crash in 1946. He moved to Melbourne in 1953 and worked at the Melbourne Town Hall until his death in 1959. He was 61.

Directions
Bois-Grenier is five kilometres south of Armentières on the D22. After reaching Bois-Grenier, carry on through the village on the D22 and pass White City Cemetery on your right. After 200 metres the road bends left. Continue for another 100 metres and pull over just past the intersection with a road on your left. This is the point where the British front line crossed the road. The Australian raids (including the one in which Jackson won the VC) took place east of this point, in the fields to your left.

Hitler bunkers

During the First World War Adolf Hitler served as a messenger in the 16th Bavarian Reserve Regiment and spent much of 1915 and 1916 in the Fromelles area. In 1940 he completed a whirlwind tour of his former stamping grounds and visited several bunkers near Fromelles. It is said he sheltered in one or more of them during the Fromelles fighting, but modern researchers are sceptical.

Directions
The bunker most commonly associated with Hitler is on the right of the D141 between Fromelles and Aubers. Film footage of Hitler's 1940 visit shows him inspecting a different bunker, located two kilometres south of the Australian Memorial Park. To find it, leave Fromelles and drive past the Fromelles (Pheasant Wood) Cemetery. After 200 metres, turn left onto the Rue de la Biette. Carry on for 500 metres and park next to a wooden gate on your right, just before a sports field. Walk through the gate and follow a path for 250 metres to a fishing pond. Continue past the pond and cross the field diagonally to your right—another path is signposted in the far corner. Follow this path and you will see the bunker in the field to your left. It was most likely a headquarters bunker constructed behind the German lines in 1916 or 1917. Hitler was a regimental runner during the First World War so it is possible he served here while stationed at Fromelles, but it is more likely that he visited it in 1940 simply because of its arresting and unusual design. The small room on the right is a metal-encased observation post. An information panel provides details about the bunker but, curiously, makes no mention of Hitler's visit.

Hazebrouck

The town of Hazebrouck was a small but important rail junction during the war and became a major support centre for the fighting in French Flanders and the Ypres Salient. Camps and hospitals were established in fields close to the town and tens of thousands of Australians passed through it, particularly during the Flanders fighting from March to July 1916 and the German Spring Offensive in 1918. Hazebrouck was an objective for the Germans during this offensive, but stubborn resistance by the Australian 1st Division saved the town. Hazebrouck is much larger today than it was in 1918 but the main square has not changed dramatically. The town hall is impressive and stands much as the Diggers knew it.

Merris—Phil Davey VC

Merris became prominent during the lull in fighting between the end of the German Spring Offensive in May 1918 and the launch of the Allied Advance to Victory in August. During these months the Australians filled their days by launching limited attacks against soft German targets and by 'peaceful penetration', a system of surprise raids that kept the Germans on their toes. On 28 June the 10th Battalion attacked the town of Merris in support of a British attack further south. The left company of the 10th started well and advanced to the outskirts of the town without suffering a single casualty. While the Australians were digging in, however, the Germans crept forward and opened fire with a machine-gun at point blank range. The Australians were shattered, with several men killed and others either sheltering in a ditch or rushing back to the Australian lines. The attack was verging on disaster when a young corporal, Phil Davey, rushed forward alone and bombed the crew of the machine-gun. After running out of bombs he returned to the Australian line to resupply and then attacked another crew of Germans who had reinforced the gun team. After the smoke cleared, Davey had killed eight Germans and had captured the gun, which he then used to break up a German counterattack. During this attack he was severely wounded in both legs, the back and stomach. For this display of raw courage he was awarded the Victoria Cross.

Phil Davey had joined the 10th Battalion in 1915, just in time for the Gallipoli landing, but was soon evacuated with typhoid.

He was wounded and gassed in 1917 and won the Military Medal in January 1918. After the fight at Merris his wounds were treated in England but he never rejoined his unit, returning to Australia in late 1918. He lived in Adelaide until he died in 1953, aged 57. Brigadier Arthur Blackburn, who had won a VC at Pozières in 1916, attended his funeral and commented, 'I think all agree that no VC was ever better earned than Phil Davey's. He was a terrific soldier.'

Directions
Merris is located 10 kilometres east of Hazebrouck. The 10th Battalion attacked the town from the west and advanced for about 500 metres. Corporal Davey won his VC in the fields immediately west of the village.

Vieux Berquin

Vieux Berquin is remembered in history as the scene of one of the AIF's greatest defensive actions of the war. During the German Spring Offensive in April 1918, the 2nd Brigade was tasked with defending a large sector of the crumbling British line in the area of Vieux Berquin and the Nieppe Forest. On the evening of 12 April the 7th Battalion was stretched out on a front of over six kilometres, a ludicrously long sector for a force of about 500 men. That night the 8th Battalion arrived to reinforce the line. At one stage the two battalions, about 1000 men strong, held 13 kilometres of line, a distance that would normally be allocated to two divisions (about 25 000 men). Between them they stiffly resisted repeated attacks and prevented a strong German force from breaking through. A plaque on the wall of the town hall in Vieux Berquin commemorates this remarkable feat of arms.

Directions
Vieux Berquin is 12 kilometres south–east of Hazebrouck and slightly east of the Nieppe Forest, a landmark that should also be visited (see below). The square opposite the town hall marks the

point where the 7th and 8th battalions linked up in their stoic defence of the town.

Nieppe Forest

This massive wood featured prominently in the Vieux Berquin action just described. Australian support troops sheltered in the wood during the 2nd Brigade's remarkable defence of the British line. At one point during the fight three British officers presented themselves at the post of Lieutenant Leslie McGinn of the 8th Battalion.

'Boy, is this your post?' said the senior officer to McGinn.

'Yes, Sir,' he replied.

'Are you going to make a fight of it?' the British officer asked.

'Yes, Sir.'

'Well, give me your rifle,' replied the officer. 'I am one of your men.' Taking a rifle, he jumped into the post alongside the Australians.

The officer turned out to be the commander of the 1st Lancashire Fusiliers, a regiment that had earlier faced the German onslaught and fallen back with heavy loss. The British officer told McGinn that this was the first time in the regiment's long history that it had retired from a position it had been ordered to hold.

Directions

Nieppe Forest should be seen in conjunction with a visit to Vieux Berquin. During the German offensive, the Australian 2nd Brigade line followed the entire eastern edge of the wood, and beyond. For much of April the road from La Motte au Bois to Vieux Berquin streamed with Australian troops heading to and from the line. La Motte had been abandoned by the villagers in the face of the German advance, but they left behind poultry, pigs and rabbits, which provided a feast for the Australians. Several headquarters were established in the chateau at La Motte. During the Second World War, Nieppe Forest concealed a German V1 'flying bomb' launch site. A large bunker from the complex is on the right side of the road on the way to Vieux Berquin. It is surrounded by craters from Allied bombing raids.

CEMETERIES IN FRENCH FLANDERS

The Australians who died at Fromelles and during the German Spring Offensive now lie in cemeteries scattered across French Flanders. Many cemeteries in the area contain at least a handful of Australian graves. The most interesting for Australian visitors are:

Fromelles (Pheasant Wood) Cemetery

In 2002 Lambis Englezos, a Melbourne school teacher, began investigating the Battle of Fromelles. He believed that the Germans had buried hundreds of Australian and British soldiers killed in the battle in an undiscovered mass grave. After several years of research, a scientific investigation at Pheasant Wood (near the village of Fromelles) indicated that several hundred bodies were buried at the site. Subsequent archaeological work uncovered 250 sets of remains, and a combination of DNA testing and archaeological evidence was used to identify more than 140 of the soldiers who had laid at Pheasant Wood for more than 90 years. In 2010 the 250 soldiers were reinterred at Fromelles (Pheasant Wood) Cemetery, the first new war cemetery built by the Commonwealth War Graves Commission in 50 years. A museum dedicated to the Battle of Fromelles is located next to the cemetery.

Directions
Fromelles (Pheasant Wood) Cemetery is located on the northern outskirts of the village of Fromelles, opposite the church, on the road that leads to the Australian Memorial Park. It is signposted in the village. To reach the site of the mass grave at Pheasant Wood, cross the road from the cemetery, turn right and take the first street on the left after the church (Rue Neuve). At the

end of this street a path leads to the site of the mass grave, in the shadow of Pheasant Wood.

Anzac Cemetery, Sailly-sur-la-Lys

This cemetery was started by Australian field ambulance units in preparation for the Battle of Fromelles in July 1916. It was used by British forces until the area was captured by the Germans in April 1918, and the Germans continued to bury Commonwealth soldiers here while they held the ground. It now contains 320 Commonwealth soldiers from the First World War, six German graves and five British graves from the Second World War. Among them are 111 Australians, including 10 men who could not be identified. Most of these men were killed at Fromelles. This is the only war cemetery in the world with the word 'Anzac' in its title.

One of the heroes of those dark days at Fromelles is buried here: Captain Norman Gibbins of the 55th Battalion, who led his troops back across no man's land to the Australian line only to be shot and killed before he could climb into the Australian trench (see page 123, grave I.A.5).

Pause at the grave of Private James Young of the 55th Battalion. He was wounded in a trench raid on 30 September 1916 and died the next day. He was only 16, one of the youngest Australian casualties of the war. He was apparently well-liked by the men in his company; his sergeant wrote that he was buried with 'the best grave and cross in Sailly' (grave I.G.4).

A late casualty for this sector was Corporal Jack Thomas of the 2nd Australian Tunnelling Company. He was hit by a shell at Cordonnerie Farm on the old Fromelles battlefield on 14 November 1916 and died three days later (grave II.F.3).

Directions

Sailly-sur-la-Lys is eight kilometres north-west of Fromelles. The village can be reached by following the road past the Australian Memorial Park and VC Corner Cemetery. At the crossroads in

Sailly, turn left. Anzac Cemetery is 650 metres along this road on the right. Another 19 Australians lie in the Sailly-sur-la-Lys Canadian Cemetery across the road.

Bailleul Communal Cemetery Extension

Bailleul was first occupied by British troops early in the war and became an important railhead, air depot and hospital centre. The 1st Australian Casualty Clearing Station was based here for a long period and treated wounded men before their evacuation to larger hospitals on the French coast and England. Men who died in the CCS were buried in the local civilian cemetery and, when more space was required, the cemetery extension was created. The extension was used by British hospitals until the Germans captured the town in April 1918, and today contains burials from every year of the war.

Australians number 398 out of 4403 burials, with three unknowns. The cemetery also contains 17 Commonwealth burials from the Second World War and 154 German burials from both wars. A few of the Australians lie in joint graves with another Commonwealth soldier, indicating that the remains could not be individually identified. This is common in the frontline cemeteries where shellfire often mangled bodies but is unusual in a hospital cemetery so far behind the lines. The eternal bond between men who share a grave is symbolised by intertwined unit badges on the headstone.

Buried here is Captain Harry Ground, one of 10 officers in the 60th Battalion to be killed at Fromelles. Ground had enlisted as a private and served at Gallipoli from August 1915 until the evacuation. He was wounded on 19 July and died at the hospital in Bailleul three days later (grave II.F.54).

Buried nearby is Sergeant Arthur Strahan MM of the 57th Battalion (grave II.F.24), who was awarded the Military Medal for bravery at Fromelles. In the face of heavy German fire he moved around the front line encouraging the men and helping to evacuate the wounded. He died of wounds the next day. Three of his brothers also served during the war and survived. His brother-in-law, Private Benjamin Freestone, was not so lucky; he was killed at Flers in November 1916.

Sergeant Tom Fagan MM of the 51st Battalion also lies here. Fagan had tried to enlist on 12 August 1914, eight days after war was declared, but was rejected due to his 'defective teeth'. A manpower shortage in 1916 led to the easing of enlistment requirements and Fagan was accepted into the AIF, bad teeth and all. In April 1917 he was awarded the Military Medal for bringing a Lewis gun into action against German machine-guns at Noreuil, the same attack in which Private Jorgan Jensen won the VC (see pages 284–285). Fagan died of wounds on 9 June 1917, after being hit during the Battle of Messines (grave III.C.124).

Pause at the grave of Sergeant James Batty of the Mechanical Transport Divisional Supply Column. He was sent to France with the very first Australian troops in preparation for the transfer of the AIF from Gallipoli to France. He was accidentally killed on 13 December 1915 while trying to disarm a British shell, making him the first member of the AIF to be killed on the Western Front (grave I.D.127).

Directions
Bailleul is a big town and the cemetery is in a backstreet. From the square in the centre of town, take the D23 towards Ypres (Ieper). After 150 metres turn right into Rue des Soeurs Noires, which is signposted to the cemetery. Take the left branch at a fork and continue for 200 metres until you reach the cemetery entrance. The military cemetery is at the rear.

Brewery Orchard Cemetery, Bois-Grenier

The brewery that originally stood here was ruined fairly early in the war but its deep cellars made a good site for a dressing station. Men who died there were buried in the adjacent orchard and over the course of the war the cemetery slowly grew. It was used until January 1918 and today contains 339 First World War burials plus four Second World War and five German graves. Australian graves number 125, all of which are identified.

All the Australians who lie in Brewery Orchard were killed while serving in the Nursery sector near Bois-Grenier in the first half of 1916. The most notable of them lie in one long grave designated IV.C.25. These 20 men all belonged to the 20th Battalion and were killed in a ferocious bombardment that accompanied a German trench raid on 5 May 1916. The Australians in the front line were taken totally by surprise and had no adequate plan to counter the German attack. Almost 100 men were killed or wounded. Worse still, the German raiders captured two of the new Stokes trench mortars, which the Australians had been given to test. These were the first examples of the weapon to fall into German hands and the AIF was greatly embarrassed by their loss.

Directions
Brewery Orchard Cemetery is on the eastern outskirts of Bois-Grenier, on the D222 road to La Chapelle d'Armentières. The orchard is gone but a modern brewery stands next to the cemetery. There is something reassuringly appropriate about Australian soldiers lying in the shadow of a brewery.

Douai Communal Cemetery

Douai is a large town that was captured by the Germans early in the war and stayed in their hands until October 1918. During this time the Germans used the communal cemetery to bury Allied prisoners of war from both the Western and Eastern fronts. The cemetery was also used during the Second World War when British units launched a push into Belgium in May 1940. Today it contains more than 200 Commonwealth graves from the First World War and almost 50 from the Second World War. Seven Australians lie in Douai Communal Cemetery, all of them men who were wounded at Fromelles and died while prisoners of war.

One of the battle's outstanding leaders is buried here. Captain Charles Arblaster of the 53rd Battalion (see page 123) led a stoic resistance as Germans flooded into the trenches on the night of July 19th (grave D.6).

Another Australian buried here is Private Daniel McKinnon of the 32nd Battalion (grave B.28). McKinnon was badly wounded by a shell blast at Fromelles and was captured, along with some mates from his battalion. As they travelled to the rear, McKinnon wrote a will which he handed to a comrade for safekeeping. He died in Douai on 28 July and was buried at a service organised by French civilians still living in the town. More than 80 French people attended and flowers were laid on his grave. His brother David was killed the following day while serving with the 28th Battalion at Pozières. David has no known grave and is commemorated on the Australian Memorial at Villers-Bretonneux.

Directions

Douai is 40 kilometres south of Lille. From the town centre follow the signs for Denain and Auberchicourt. Cross the bridge over the railway and the cemetery is 45 metres further along on the left. The military burials are at the rear of the cemetery.

Hersin Communal Cemetery Extension

This cemetery is unique: of the 55 Australians buried here, 54 of them are from the 3rd Australian Tunnelling Company. Twenty-one of these men were killed by a single underground explosion on 27 November 1916—it is unclear whether the explosion was caused by a German mine or an Australian mine detonating prematurely.

The tunnellers are often overlooked in military history, but played a vital role. In most cases they came from Australia's gold and coal mines and were tasked with tunnelling under enemy positions and planting huge mines that were used to destroy large sections of German trench. It was dangerous work, with the usual perils of working underground heightened by the dangers of warfare. Apart from the risk of tunnel collapse or asphyxiation, the tunnellers lived in fear of being discovered by the Germans. When they were, the Germans might explode a small mine to destroy the Allied tunnels or, occasionally, break into the tunnels and fight with the miners hand-to-hand. The tunnellers carried out some of the most unenviable work of the war. Hersin Communal Cemetery stands as a tribute to their contribution.

Because of their specialised work, members of the tunnelling company tended to be older than their infantry comrades. The average age of the men buried in Hersin is 35. The most senior soldier buried here is Major Leslie Coulter DSO (grave I.A.2), the commanding officer of the unit. Coulter had won his Distinguished Service Order in the lead-up to the battle of Fromelles in July 1916. To protect the troops as they crossed no man's land, the tunnellers had come up with a clever system: pipes filled with explosives and known as 'push pipes' were buried there. When exploded, they would create a 'trench' that ran from the Australian line and across no man's land towards the German line. In the lead-up to the Fromelles attack a heavy German bombardment uncovered one of the buried push pipes and the plan was in danger of coming unstuck. Coulter braved machine-gun and shell fire to run into no man's land and light the fuse on the exposed push pipe. The pipe exploded and created a trench that was used as shelter by the attacking troops.

Coulter was killed while accompanying the infantry on a trench raid on 28 June 1917. He was from a proud military family. His brother Graham was the commanding officer of the 8th Battalion and won the DSO in 1917. Another brother, Jason, had died of wounds at Gallipoli.

Directions
Hersin is 45 kilometres south-west of Lille. The communal cemetery is in the north-east of the village.

Le Trou Aid Post Cemetery: see Fromelles tour (page 124).

Méteren Military Cemetery

Méteren was prominent in Australian military history during the German Spring Offensive in April 1918 and was an early objective for the Germans in their thrust towards Hazebrouck. They had briefly occupied the town in the early stages of the war, and captured it again on 16 April 1918. The Australian 1st Division attacked the town on 22–24 April but failed to capture it. After repeated attempts, the town was finally secured on 20 July. Méteren Military Cemetery was begun in 1919 and used to bury Commonwealth, French and German bodies. The German and most of the French graves were later removed, leaving 768 Commonwealth burials. This includes 104 Australian graves, most of them belonging to men killed in the fighting in the area in April 1918. Nine of them are unidentified.

Buried here is Lieutenant Percy Reed MC of the 12th Battalion. Reed had originally enlisted in the Royal Australian Navy at the start of the war but when he realised he was unlikely to see action there, he deserted and re-enlisted in the infantry under a false name. His fighting prowess earned him a pardon, and from 1917 he fought under his real name. He was awarded the Military Cross at the Second Battle of Bullecourt in May 1917 for leading a hand-to-hand fight in the German trenches. At Méteren on 24 April 1918 he again led from the front and was killed by machine-gun fire during an assault on the town. His men were forced to fall back and his body was recovered by the Germans (grave I.E.138).

Also buried here is Lieutenant John Sprott MM of the 10th Battalion. As a corporal, Sprott had won the Military Medal at Second Bullecourt for organising Lewis gun teams in the face of heavy German fire. His recommendation describes his 'absolute disregard for danger and great intensity of purpose'. He was killed at Méteren on 24 April 1918, aged 24 (grave IV.B.578).

Directions
Méteren is 14 kilometres east of Hazebrouck. From the centre of the village, take the D18 opposite the *mairie* (town hall). The

cemetery is 200 metres along this road on the left, behind the
civilian cemetery.

Rue-David Military Cemetery, Fleurbaix

'Rue-des-Davids' was a local road that ran through the British rear
area near Fromelles. A cemetery was started here after fighting in
December 1914 and was used continually until the end of 1917.
Some Australians were buried here during that time but hundreds
more were concentrated here after the war. Most of these came from
the killing fields of Fromelles and could not be identified. Today
353 of the 897 graves here are Australian. Unidentified Australians
total 266. There are also 10 German graves near the entrance.

The most senior officer buried here is Captain Hugh Buckley
of the 22nd Battalion. He died of accidental injuries on 27 April
1916 (grave I.D.13).

Buried nearby is Corporal George Dick MM of the 3rd
Battalion, who won the Military Medal for carrying ammunition
to the front line in 1916. He was killed on 25 June.

Directions
Fleurbaix is five kilometres north of Fromelles. To reach Rue-
David Cemetery, drive past the Australian Memorial Park and VC
Corner Cemetery and turn right onto the D175. At the T-junction
at the end, turn left then immediately right. Turn right at the
crossroads. Rue-David Cemetery is 700 metres along this road
(Rue David) on your left.

Rue-Pétillon Military Cemetery: see Fromelles tour
(page 124).

Trois Arbres Cemetery, Steenwerck

This cemetery was started by the 2nd Australian Casualty Clearing
Station in July 1916 and was used to bury men who died of

wounds received in both French and Belgian Flanders. It was used by the CCS until the Germans captured the town in April 1918, and then briefly again when the town was regained by the British in October 1918. It was significantly enlarged after the Armistice by the concentration of graves from the surrounding battlefields. It is now a big cemetery, containing 1704 burials of which 470 are Australian. Because most of these men died of wounds in the CCS, they are all identified.

The most notable Australian buried here is Major General William Holmes CMG, DSO, VD, commander of the 4th Division and the most senior Australian soldier killed on the Western Front. On 2 July 1917 Holmes was escorting William Holman, the Premier of New South Wales, around the newly captured ground at Messines. Holmes usually took the most direct route to the front line, no matter how dangerous it was, but this day chose to drive on a less exposed route and avoid a dangerous corner. The party left the car and was walking along a normally safe track when a salvo of German shells burst nearby. Holmes was the only one hit, but suffered severe chest wounds and died soon after (grave I.X.42).

Also buried here is Major Harold Howden MC & Bar of the 48th Battalion. As a young corporal, Howden had been prominent in the fighting at Quinn's Post at Gallipoli, especially during the Turkish attack in which Major Hugh Quinn, for whom the post was named, was killed. As a captain in the 45th Battalion, Howden won a Military Cross for holding an important part of the line against a German counterattack at Pozières in August 1916. In February 1917 he won another after leading an attack on the village of Gueudecourt. Despite having survived some of the heaviest fighting in Gallipoli and France, his luck ran out on 5 July 1917. He was sitting down to breakfast in his dugout at Hill 63 near Messines when a German shell exploded outside the entrance. Howden was hit by a small fragment in the neck and bled to death as he was being stretchered to the rear (grave I.U.17).

Directions

Steenwerck is seven kilometres west of Armentières. From the centre of the village, follow the D77 in the direction of Nieppe. The cemetery is on your left after two kilometres.

VC Corner Cemetery: see Fromelles tour (page 124).

OTHER CEMETERIES OF INTEREST

Other cemeteries with an Australian connection in French Flanders include:

Aubers Ridge British Cemetery

Australian burials number 104 out of more than 700. Most of these men were killed at Fromelles. Aubers is two kilometres south-west of Fromelles. The cemetery is 500 metres along the D41 in the direction of Herlies.

Cabaret-Rouge British Cemetery, Souchez

Out of 7655 burials, 116 are Australian. The Australian graves date from a range of actions in 1916 and 1917, and include three men killed on 16 March 1916—among the earliest AIF battle casualties on the Western Front. In 2000 an unidentified Canadian soldier was removed from here and reinterred in the Tomb of the Unknown Soldier in Ottawa. Souchez is 45 kilometres south-west of Lille. The cemetery is two kilometres south of the village on the D937.

La Kreule Military Cemetery, Hazebrouck

There are 78 Australian burials here out of 576; mostly men who died of wounds during 'peaceful penetration' operations in this area between May and July 1918. The cemetery is two kilometres north of Hazebrouck on the D916.

Nieppe-Bois (Rue-du-Bois) British Cemetery, Vieux Berquin

Out of 70 burials, 15 are Australian. Most were men from the 8th Battalion killed in the stoic defence of the town in April 1918. There are also 33 British men buried here who were killed during the retreat to Dunkirk in 1940. The cemetery is on the edge of the Nieppe Forest near La Motte au Bois, halfway between Hazebrouck and Merville, about two kilometres along the road to Vieux Berquin.

Ration Farm Military Cemetery, La Chapelle-d'Armentières

Australian burials number 259 out of 1313, mostly casualties of Fromelles. Two brothers are buried here, Private Arthur Matthews and Driver Henry Matthews. They both belonged to the 6th Machine Gun Company and, with another brother, Fred, operated a machine-gun against a German raiding party near Armentières on 4 July 1916. Arthur and Henry were both hit and killed, but Fred continued to operate the gun and beat off the raiding party (graves I.J.8 & 9). Fred was killed later that year at Flers. La Chapelle d'Armentières is a village on the southern outskirts of Armentières. The cemetery is two kilometres south of the village on the road to Fleurbaix.

Rue-du-Bois Military Cemetery, Fleurbaix

The cemetry contains 241 Australian burials out of 844. Most were men killed at Fromelles but some were killed during trench raids at other times in 1916. Fleurbaix is five kilometres north of Fromelles. The cemetery is on the D171, three kilometres south-west of the village.

Y Farm Military Cemetery, Bois-Grenier

There are 163 Australian burials here out of 820; mostly men killed at Fromelles and in fighting in the Nursery sector in 1916. Bois-Grenier is five kilometres south of Armentières on the D22. Leave Bois-Grenier on the D222 towards Fleurbaix and turn left towards the cemetery after a kilometre.

Part III

The Somme

Few placenames in history carry such ominous overtones as the Somme. The fighting in this picturesque corner of France was some of the most ferocious the world has ever seen and the name became synonymous with the horrors of the First World War.

The Somme is both a river and a region. The fighting known as the Battle of the Somme did not occur anywhere near the river, but across the rolling countryside further north. The Somme region, or *département* as it is known in France, saw three great battles during the war, all of which heavily involved Australian troops.

The first big battle in the area is the one best remembered. On 1 July 1916 British (and some French) forces launched the largest attack of the war to date, 27 divisions advancing on a 30-kilometre front. Hopes of a breakthrough were shattered on the first morning when nearly 60 000 British troops were killed or wounded. The losses were shocking and they still are today; 1 July 1916 remains the most disastrous day in the history of the British Army. When it became clear that the German defenders were determined to hang on, the key aim of the battle became 'attrition', that sinister euphemism for persisting with an attack when things have gone wrong and you've run out of ideas. Objectives that were supposed to have been captured in days were not taken for months, and more than a million men on both sides would be killed or wounded before the whole shoddy mess was called off in November.

Australian troops weren't involved in the debacle of the opening days, but soon found themselves thrown into the mincer. On 23 July 1916 the Australian 1st Division was ordered to capture the town of Pozières, located on the highest point of the battlefield and the key to freeing up the Allied advance. Over the next six weeks, Pozières became the scene of the most costly Australian battle of the First World War, drawing in three divisions and leaving more than 23 000 Australians dead or wounded.

The end of the Somme fighting didn't mean the end of the Australian association with the area. In the closing months of 1916 Australian troops carried out a few limited advances, most notably an expensive and ultimately pointless slog through the mud at Flers, and then held sections of the Allied front line during the harshest winter in decades. Few men would ever forget those dark days of 1916.

Attention was diverted from the Somme in 1917. The huge battles at Ypres were doing their own good job of reducing Europe's population, and fighting in the area was limited well into 1918. In March of that year, though, things changed.

By spring 1918 the Germans knew they were running out of time. American troops had been training since 1917 and were due to arrive on the Western Front en masse. The Germans had to act. Bolstered by an influx of 500 000 troops from the Eastern Front, they launched a massive offensive designed to bust through the Allied lines and capture the towns on the Channel coast. On the Somme, things went well at first. The British line buckled under the weight of the German assault and for several days it seemed Germany was about to win the war. But a stiff British rearguard action and the rushing forward of Australian reserve troops halted the German advance. Somme villages that had been support bases during the 1916 fighting now became the front line as the British and Australians desperately resisted the attack. Towns such as Dernancourt, Hébuterne and, particularly, Villers-Bretonneux became legendary in Australian military history after a series of brilliant victories by the AIF.

Once the German Spring Offensive had fizzled out, it was the Allies' turn to attack. Fighting returned to the Somme for the last time as Australian and Canadian forces spearheaded a 100-day advance that pushed the Germans out of France and Belgium and forced them to the Armistice table. As far as the Australians were concerned, this was 'real soldiering', a chance to stretch the legs and advance across open ground that hadn't been turned to wasteland by shelling. The period from August to October 1918 was Australia's most successful of the war, and secured the AIF's reputation as one of the best fighting forces of the First World War.

The Somme battlefields cover a large area and will most likely occupy the largest proportion of your time on the Western Front. The key sites are the battlefield at Pozières (and surrounds), the Australian National Memorial at Villers-Bretonneux, the Australian Memorial Park at Hamel and the battlefield at Mont St Quentin.

7

Battle of Pozières, 23 July– 5 September 1916

No site on the Western Front has a greater association with Australian courage and sacrifice than the French village of Pozières. The fighting here in 1916 cost the lives of nearly as many Australians in six weeks as the entire eight months of the Gallipoli campaign. If the Anzac legend was born at Gallipoli, it grew up at Pozières.

The village sits on a high ridge between the strategically important towns of Albert and Bapaume. As the highest point on the 1916 Somme battlefield, Pozières was a vital objective: whichever side controlled it would have unimpeded views of much of the enemy front. The Allies expected to capture Pozières (and beyond) on 1 July 1916, the disastrous first day of the Battle of the Somme, but three weeks later it was still firmly in German hands.

Australian troops arrived in the area on 14 July and immediately geared up to attack Pozières. The village was the bastion of the German defensive line and was protected by a ring of trenches. 'K' and 'Pozières' trenches ran in front of the village and joined 'OG1' (Old German) and 'OG2' in the fields behind it. Before the war a windmill had stood north-east of the town. It was destroyed early in the fighting but the Germans had turned its foundations into a formidable machine-gun post and, as the highest point on the battlefield, it commanded the surrounding fields.

The Australian 1st Division attacked Pozières in the early hours of 23 July. It was tough going. By this stage of the war the village had been obliterated by shellfire and the Germans defended the ruins tenaciously, often to the last man. In the face of heavy resistance, the Australians moved on through the shattered remnants of the village, overcoming machine-gun posts and wresting trenches and strongpoints from the Germans in savage close-quarter fighting. Over the next 36 hours progress would be measured in inches of ground gained, and thousands of men would die, but the village was captured.

The fighting at Pozières in these first days was characterised by dozens of individual acts of valour. On 23 July, during fighting south-east of the village, the 9th Battalion was locked in a deadly bomb tussle with a German machine-gun post. The Germans had the upper hand until a young private, John Leak, leapt out of the trench and rushed at the German position. After throwing three bombs, he jumped in among the Germans and despatched three unwounded men with his bayonet. His platoon commander arrived in time to find him wiping blood off his bayonet with his slouch hat. For his bravery Leak was awarded the Victoria Cross.

Later that day, in almost the same spot, the Germans had successfully counterattacked and had barricaded the trench. A machine-gun behind the barrier was mauling the Australians and a lieutenant in the 10th Battalion, Arthur Blackburn, was determined to deal with it. He led small groups of men to attack the post four times. After each attempt Blackburn was the only man unwounded. Over the next few hours he reconnoitred the trenches around him and led four more attacks on German machine-gun positions. It was a miracle he survived the day and was deservedly awarded the Victoria Cross.

On 24 July the 8th Battalion attempted to extend its gains from the previous day but came under murderous fire from the moment it began. A Lewis gun team was ordered to a dangerously exposed position to cover the advance and was soon badly knocked around by German fire. Eventually there was only one man left unwounded, Private Thomas Cooke. No one would have blamed Cooke for falling back, but he stuck to his post and poured fire into any German who showed his head. When support troops eventually reached Cooke's position they found him dead beside his gun. For his selfless devotion to duty he was awarded a posthumous Victoria Cross.

On the night of 28 July, the 17th, 18th and 20th battalions were ordered to press towards the German trenches on the far side of the village. The Germans were on edge and fired a volley of flares as they heard the Australians approaching, effectively turning night into day. The Australians were caught in the open and German machine-guns cut them down. The attack was over before it began and more than 140 men had been killed or wounded. Many of the wounded lay in no man's land and faced an agonising death unless help could reach them. Sergeant Claud Castleton of the 5th Australian Machine Gun Company, determined not to see his mates suffer, ran to their aid and brought in a wounded man on his shoulders. Hearing the cries of more men, he went out again and brought in another wounded comrade. He went out into no man's land a third time and was carrying in another wounded man when he was shot in the back and killed. He was posthumously awarded the Victoria Cross.

Over the next week the Germans launched repeated counterattacks in a desperate effort to retake Pozières, but all were repulsed. The Germans then switched tactics: if they couldn't force the Australians out of Pozières, they would destroy them. They launched one of the heaviest artillery barrages of the war and pounded the Australians incessantly. The 1st was Australia's original division, largely made up of men who had been the first to volunteer and who had fought through the Gallipoli campaign, but this unprecedented barrage was more than many of them could bear. The Australian official historian reported seeing Gallipoli veterans sobbing under the strain of the bombardment.

With no attack to prepare for and no counterattack to deflect, all the men could do was crouch as low as they could in the battered trenches and pray for the bombardment to end. The history of the 24th Battalion records that an officer in K Trench came across four men, wide-eyed and skittish, attempting to distract each other from the cascade of shells with a game of cards. Their sergeant had been playing with them until he was killed by a shellburst; his body was dumped on the parapet and another man took over his hand. An hour later the officer returned along the trench and all four men were dead.

After three days the 1st Division had lost more than 5000 men and the rest were exhausted. They were withdrawn and replaced by the 2nd Division. In his excellent account, *Jacka's Mob*, Sergeant Edgar Rule of the 14th Battalion described the condition of the 1st Division as they marched out of the line:

> Although we knew it was stiff fighting, we had our eyes opened when we saw these men march by. Those who saw them will never forget it as long as they live. They looked like men who had been in Hell. Almost without exception each man looked drawn and haggard, and so dazed that they appeared to be walking in a dream . . . Quite a few were silly and these were the only noisy ones in the crowd . . . In all my experience I have never seen men quite so shaken up as these.

The 2nd Division occupied Pozières for 10 days and launched two attacks that pushed the Australian line beyond the village. Fire from the two German trenches east of the village, OG1 and OG2, was devastating and thousands of Australians were hit as they stormed towards them and the nearby windmill. Despite this, the Australians captured the positions.

During a German counterattack on 5 August, Captain Percy Cherry of the 26th Battalion faced a German officer in a neighbouring shell hole. The men were taking pot shots at each other with their rifles and happened to rise and fire simultaneously. Cherry's helmet was knocked off his head from the shot; the German was mortally wounded. Cherry crossed the ground to the fallen man, who passed to him some letters which he asked Cherry to post to his family in Germany. When Cherry promised that he would, the German muttered, 'And so it ends' and died.

On 7 August one of the most dramatic incidents in the history of the AIF occurred in the fields in front of the windmill. Following a heavy artillery bombardment, the Germans launched a strong counterattack in an effort to retake the trenches they had recently lost to the Australians. Captain Albert Jacka of the 14th Battalion, a hero of Gallipoli who had won Australia's first Victoria Cross of the war, was sheltering in a dugout with a small party of his men. The attacking Germans rolled a bomb down the stairs, wounding several men, and placed a sentry at the entrance. Jacka charged up the stairs and shot the sentry with his revolver before rallying his men and leading them to attack the Germans from behind. Jacka was wounded but succeeded in freeing a group of Australians who had been captured in the German advance. Other Australians, seeing Jacka's party taking on the Germans almost single-handedly, joined the fight and in the ensuing melee the German attack was halted with heavy loss. During the fight Jacka was seen diving among parties of Germans sheltering in shell holes, killing and capturing many. He received several severe wounds which nearly killed him, and was awarded the Military Cross. The official historian called Jacka's action 'the most dramatic and effective act of individual audacity in the history of the AIF'. Why Jacka was only awarded the Military Cross and not a second Victoria Cross remains a mystery.

The Germans continued to bombard the 2nd Division and counterattacked relentlessly. By 7 August the division had lost 6848 officers and men. Unable to go on, it was replaced by the 4th Division, which again faced massive German retaliatory barrages and bitter fighting as it extended the line further along the ridge. This cycle continued until 5 September. Each division fought until exhausted and was then replaced. When the replacement division became too battered to fight, the original division was rotated back into the line. Second Lieutenant John Raws, a journalist from Melbourne, served in the 23rd Battalion and described the shelling at Pozières in a letter to his family:

> All is buried, and churned up again, and buried again. The sad part is that one can see no end of this. If we live tonight we have to go through tomorrow night, and next week, and next month. Poor wounded devils you meet on the stretchers are laughing with glee. One cannot blame them—they are getting out of this ... We are lousy, stinking, ragged, unshaven, sleepless ...
> I have one puttee, a dead man's helmet, another dead man's gas protector, a dead man's bayonet. My tunic is rotten with other men's blood, and partly spattered with a comrade's brains.

Raws was killed on 23 August.

The 1st, 2nd and 4th divisions threw themselves against the German strongpoints at Pozières and the neighbouring Mouquet Farm until they were almost destroyed. By early September they could do no more and were relieved by the Canadian Corps just short of Mouquet Farm. More than half the Australians who fought at Pozières had been killed or wounded.

The Battle of Pozières was the toughest task faced by the AIF in the First World War. The remains of thousands of Australians killed in the fighting were never found and still lie beneath the fields in this tiny corner of France. Today Pozières is a shrine to the bravery of the original Anzacs and there are many poignant sites for Australian visitors.

POZIÈRES TOUR

This tour covers the ground where more Australians were killed and wounded than on any other battlefield of the First World War. It is a long walk (about 10 kilometres) with few uphill sections and can be completed in about four hours. It can be driven in about two hours, although parts of the tour follow farm tracks which may provide a bumpy ride for smaller vehicles.

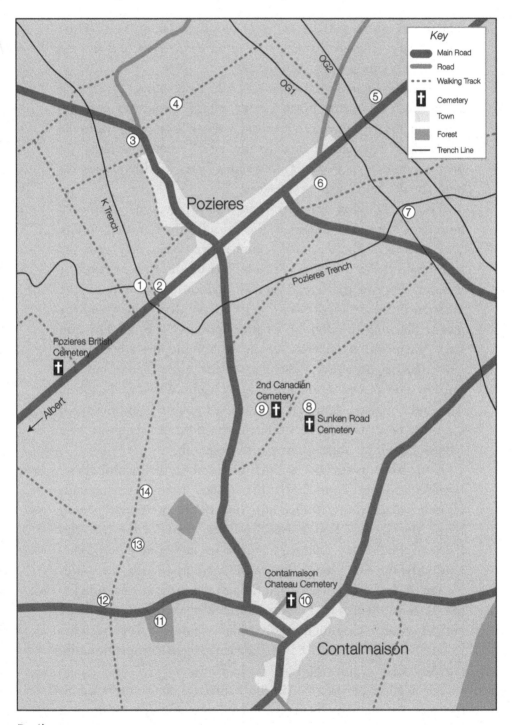

Pozières

This is a walk to get the patriotic blood pumping, visiting the sites of two Australian memorials, three cemeteries and no less than four Victoria Cross actions.

Pozières is located on the razor-straight Roman road (the D929) about seven kilometres north-east of Albert. Leave Albert in the direction of Bapaume, drive through the village of La Boisselle and park in the carpark next to the 1st Division Memorial [1] on the outskirts of Pozières. If walking, you will leave your car here for the remainder of the tour.

The 1st Division chose this site for its divisional memorial because it lost more soldiers in the Pozières fighting than in any other action of the war: 7654 men in six weeks. It placed the memorial on the site of K Trench, one of the first captured at Pozières. Four of the five Australian divisional memorials on the Western Front are of the same style: a large stone obelisk with a plaque detailing the division's battle honours. The 3rd Division has its memorial at Sailly-le-Sec on the Somme, the 4th Division chose the heights above Bellenglise in the Aisne region, and the 5th Division placed its memorial at Polygon Wood in Belgium. The 2nd Division Memorial at Mont St Quentin is distinct from the other four and consists of an oversized bronze sculpture of a Digger in full kit surmounting a stone plinth.

Battle honours for the 1st Division listed on the memorial are: Pozières, Mouquet Farm, Le Barque, Thilloy, Boursies, Demicourt, Hermies, Lagnicourt, Bullecourt, 3rd Battle of Ypres, Menin Road, Broodseinde Ridge, Passchendaele, Battle of the Lys, 2nd Battle of the Somme, Lihons, Chuignolles, and Hindenburg Line. Curiously, the rising sun badge on the memorial carries the words 'Australian Imperial Force'. Even though this is the correct title for the Australian forces in the First World War, their badges actually said 'Australian Commonwealth Military Forces'. On the lawn in front of the memorial is a Bastiaan plaque commemorating the Australian capture of Pozières in 1916.

For a good perspective of the battlefield, cross the road to the wooden viewing platform. From this vantage point it is obvious why the Pozières ridge was such an important objective for both sides. On a clear day the Germans could observe Allied movement all the way to Albert. From near this point German observers watched British preparations for the Battle of the Somme and came up with the defensive plans that helped decimate the attacking troops on the first morning. Panels on the platform point out important landmarks on the Somme battlefield, including Mouquet Farm to your right and the Thiepval Memorial to the Missing, further along the ridge.

Not far from the platform is an excavation site surrounded by a fence. This is the remains of 'Gibraltar' **[2]**, a massive double-storey German blockhouse used as a machine-gun post and for artillery observation. It was captured by 15 men from the Australian 2nd Battalion on 23 July, along with three German officers, 23 men and three machine-guns. The prisoners revealed under interrogation that they knew the troops opposing them were Australian: before the blockhouse was captured, Australian soldiers had been shouting out to the occupants of Gibraltar throughout the night.

Private John Bourke of the 8th Battalion later explored Gibraltar and found in the lower chamber:

> . . . a heap of cake boxes . . . of cardboard and sewn in with calico, just as the parcels come to us from Australia. The addresses were in a child's handwriting as were also one or two letters. In another corner was a coat rolled up. I opened it out, and found it stained with blood, and there, right between the shoulders, was a burnt shrapnel hole . . . The owner of the coat was a German, and, some might say, not entitled to much sympathy. Perhaps he was not, but I couldn't help thinking sadly of the little girl or boy who sent the cakes.

Leave the Gibraltar site and follow the road past the 1st Division Memorial. Turn left onto a farm track and follow it for about 500 metres. (If driving, continue along the road and turn left at the next intersection.) K Trench, a German communication trench, ran parallel to this road in the field on your left. It was captured in a bold rush by the 4th Battalion on 25 July, with the

8th Battalion vigorously chasing Germans out of the village on their right. The two battalions cleared the western side of the village and met at the cemetery **[3]**, which you will soon reach.

The road forks just past the cemetery. The left fork leads to Mouquet Farm, the next obstacle for the Australians after capturing Pozières and the scene of bitter hand-to-hand fighting. Follow the farm track that leads into the fields opposite the cemetery **[4]**. (If driving, park at the cemetery and walk.) This will take you to the site of the German OG1 and OG2 trenches, and into the heart of the ground so bitterly contested east of the village. A track runs parallel to you on the left. This was known as 'Brind's Road' to the Australians, and was named after Major Eric Brind of the 23rd Battalion, who was killed nearby on 29 July. Brind's Road formed the Australian front line north of the village until early August.

As you follow the track you are walking across the ground captured by the Australians with such heavy loss in several attacks between July 25th and 5 August. During those two terrible weeks this field was littered with Australian dead; their bones still come to the surface every year. Imagine crossing this field during one of those attacks, the night sky eerily lit by German flares and the steady chatter of machine-guns blending to a roar as you inch towards the German lines. The windmill—a rough mound on the skyline and a formidable German machine-gun post—looms over you with every step. The thunder of shellfire is constant, the noise deafening, the concussion terrifying. You wonder how anyone could come out of this alive.

Some of the most courageous actions of the Pozières fighting occurred in this small space, including Lieutenant Cherry's rifle duel with a German officer on 5 August and Albert Jacka's audacious counterattack on 7 August.

It is also the site of Private Cooke's heroic fight to the last which earned him a posthumous VC on 25 July. Tom Cooke was a New Zealander who had moved to Melbourne in 1912 with his wife and three children. He enlisted in the AIF in 1915 and served with the 24th Battalion at Gallipoli, achieving the rank of acting corporal. In early 1916 he transferred to the 8th Battalion and, as there was no place for him as a corporal, relinquished his stripes. He was killed in one of the selfless acts of valour that were common during the fighting at Pozières. His body was lost during the fighting and he is remembered on the Australian National Memorial at Villers-Bretonneux, along with more than 10 000 of his comrades.

After about 700 metres the track turns sharply right. Fifty metres before the bend is the point where OG1 crossed the track. OG2 was another 200 metres further on. This section of the German line was attacked in waves by the 25th, 26th and 28th battalions on 29 July. The fourth wave of the 28th reached the German wire to find men who had gone forward with the earlier waves lying down in front of it, apparently preparing to rush the trench. The fourth wave lay down beside them and waited. Several minutes passed before they realised their comrades weren't preparing to attack: they were dead.

Follow the track as it bends to the right and carry on until the intersection with a sealed road. Your next destination is the Windmill Memorial in the field opposite. If there are no crops in the field you can reach it by going cross-country. Otherwise, follow the road to the right then turn left onto the D929 and follow it for 400 metres to the Windmill Memorial **[5]**. (If driving, return to your car and drive to the windmill.)

This rough mound is all that remains of the windmill that stood here for centuries until 1916 and marks the highest point of the entire Somme battlefield. The concrete fortifications of the German machine-gun post can still be seen on the mound. OG1 and OG2 crossed the field in front of the windmill site. After the war the site was acquired by the Australian government. Originally dedicated as a memorial to the 2nd Division, it now unofficially represents all 23 000 Australians who were killed or wounded in the Pozières battle. The inscription reads:

> The ruin of Pozières windmill which lies here was the centre of the struggle in this part of the Somme battlefield in July and August 1916. It was captured on August 4th by Australian troops

who fell more thickly on this ridge than on any other battlefield of the war.

On the other side of the road is the Tank Corps Memorial, dedicated to the men of the British Tank Corps who were killed in action between 1916 and 1918. The first tanks ever used in battle were launched from near here on 15 September 1916 during the battle of Flers-Courcelette. The memorial features four superb miniature tanks, with the surrounding fence made from six-pounder tank gun barrels and tank drive chain. Bullet holes in one of the miniatures are from fighting here during the Second World War.

Return along the D929 towards Pozières. Take the first road on the left, the D73, signposted to Bazentin. Almost immediately you will come to a track leading to the left, which follows the line of a light railway that ran across the battlefield in 1916. Today the track is informally known as Butterworth Lane, after British composer George Butterworth, who was killed near here on 5 August 1916 while serving as a lieutenant in the Durham Light Infantry. By walking 150 metres along this track you will reach the approximate position of the 20th Battalion during their aborted attack on OG1 on 28–29 July.

The field on your left was where Sergeant Castleton rescued several men before he was shot and killed, an action that earned him a posthumous VC [6]. Claud Castleton was born in England and moved to Australia when he was 19. A teacher by profession, he loved nature and geography and spent several years travelling through Tasmania, Victoria, New South Wales, Queensland and Papua. When war broke out he served in several roles before joining the 18th Battalion at Gallipoli. He transferred to the 5th Machine Gun Company in March 1916 and was promoted to sergeant a week later. Witnesses to his heroic rescue efforts at Pozières said it was no surprise that he was killed: while he had strength in his body, he was determined to keep going back out into no man's land to look for wounded. Claud Castleton now lies in the nearby Pozières British Cemetery.

Retrace your steps, turn left at the road and follow it for about 400 metres. This is the point where Pozières Trench crossed the road, joining OG1 about 70 metres into the field on your left. The junction of the two trenches is where Private Leak bombed and bayoneted a German machine-gun crew on 23 July, earning himself the VC [7]. This is also near the site of Lieutenant Blackburn's eight repeated assaults on German machine-gun positions later the same day—at one point he even crossed beneath the road in a German tunnel. He was also awarded the VC.

John Leak was English by birth but moved to Australia as a young man. He worked as a teamster in Queensland and enlisted in 1915, serving with the 9th Battalion at Gallipoli. After his heroics at Pozières, Leak was sent to the rear with the rest of the 1st Division, but rejoined the fight at Mouquet Farm in August, where he was wounded. After recovering, Leak rejoined his unit, only to be gassed in Belgium in March 1918. Leak returned to Australia in 1919 and spent the following years moving around from New South Wales to Queensland and Western Australia. He eventually settled in South Australia, where he died in 1972, aged 80.

Arthur Blackburn was an Anzac legend. He was one of the first to enlist at the outbreak of war, joining the 10th Battalion with the regimental number 31. His first distinguished act came on the morning of the Gallipoli landing, when he and a mate advanced almost two kilometres inland from Anzac Cove. He was commissioned at Gallipoli and promoted to full lieutenant after the evacuation. A month after the fight at Pozières he was evacuated sick and never recovered sufficiently to rejoin his battalion. He was repatriated to Australia in December 1916 and worked as a lawyer for several years before rejoining the army in 1925. At the outbreak of the Second World War he formed and commanded the 2/3rd Machine Gun Battalion and was captured with that unit in Java in 1942. He spent more than three years in a Japanese POW camp and returned to Australia somewhat of a hero. He spent the remainder of his life in various government positions and living happily with his wife and four children. He died in 1960, aged 68.

Continue along the road and turn right at the intersection with a farm track. In 1916 the first half of this track was actually a trench, Sunken Road Trench, which formed the jumping off point for the 3rd Brigade in the attack on 23 July. Continue for one kilometre until you reach two military cemeteries on either side of the track. If driving, continue along the road and turn right at the next intersection. Turn right into Contalmaison and visit point 10 on the tour. Then visit points 8 and 9 from Contalmaison.

The cemetery on the left is Sunken Road Cemetery [8], begun during the Somme fighting and used until November 1916. The Germans buried two of their comrades here in March 1918 but these graves have been removed. Of the 200 Commonwealth soldiers buried here, 61 are Australian. Three of these men could not be found after the war and are remembered on special memorials on the east wall. All the Australians buried here were killed in the fighting at Pozières and Mouquet Farm.

The most senior Australian soldier buried in the cemetery is Captain George Evans (48th Battalion, died 14/08/1916, grave I.A.14). The only other officers are Lieutenant Oswald Law (48th Battalion, died 14/08/1916, grave I.A.12) and 2nd Lieutenant Norbert Tracey (5th Battalion, died 18/08/1916, grave I.A.18). Law was prominent in the fighting led by Albert Jacka on 7 August, holding a section of the front with the remnants of his company against German attacks. Private Arthur McGlashan MM (17th Battalion, died 26/08/1916, grave I.B.9) was a runner who won the Military Medal for bravery during the early Pozières fighting. He was killed in the closing stages of the battle.

The cemetery opposite is the 2nd Canadian Cemetery, Sunken Road [9]. This wholly Canadian cemetery contains the remains of soldiers from the Eastern Ontario Regiment who were killed in fighting around Mouquet Farm in September and October 1916.

Carry on until a T-junction. Turn left, follow the road uphill and at the next T-junction turn left into Contalmaison. Follow the sign left to Contalmaison Chateau Cemetery [10].

The town of Contalmaison was briefly entered by British troops on 1 July 1916 but was not held by them until the 10th. The cemetery was started soon after and, at the Armistice, contained 242 graves. Forty-seven graves were moved here from other parts of the Somme battlefield in the following years. Twenty-one Australians are buried here, mostly killed at Pozières and in actions in the area early in 1917. The area around Contalmaison was home to a number of artillery batteries and there are several gunners buried in this cemetery. Among them are four men from the Australian Heavy Artillery who were killed on 10 November 1916 by a shell that exploded prematurely as it was fired. The most interesting story here is not Australian; it belongs to Private William Short VC (8th Battalion, Royal Yorkshire Regiment, died 07/08/1916, grave II.B.16), who won the Victoria Cross for gallantry in a bomb fight at Pozières. Even after his leg was smashed by a shell he refused to leave the fight and stayed for another five hours, lying in the bottom of a trench and preparing bombs for his mates to throw. He died from his wounds the next day. As you leave the cemetery, note the traces of shell holes in the fields on both sides of the path.

Turn right at the road and leave Contalmaison, then carry on until you reach a small wood on the left. This is Bailiff Wood [11], an objective on the first day of the Battle of the Somme and home to several artillery batteries in later fighting. It is on private land and technically should not be entered without permission, but a brief stroll along the track leading into the wood will reveal deep trench lines and shell holes.

Carry on past Bailiff Wood until you reach a crossroads with a farm track. This is Casualty Corner [12], named after a dressing station that was based here and because the corner was so regularly shelled. It is a famous landmark on the Pozières battlefield—nearly every soldier who served in the sector marched past it on his way to the line. Walk past Casualty Corner for 500 metres until the road bends left. Sausage Valley, the large depression used as shelter by the troops as they marched to the front, is in the field to your left. To your right across the fields is Pozières. Troops marching to the front turned onto the road from Sausage Valley at this point and were greeted by the ominous sight of the rubble piles of Pozières glowing and flickering under the night sky. Flares arced into the darkness and shells flashed as they tore into the remains of the village. The rumble of gunfire and the chatter of machine-guns wafted across the fields, no doubt knotting the stomachs of new troops.

Return to Casualty Corner and turn left into the farm track. (If driving, park here and walk.) The Official History describes the perilous journey past the corner in 1916:

> The road past Casualty Corner to Contalmaison was intermittently swept with shrapnel and high-explosive, and drenched with phosgene gas-shells. At times the corner could only be passed by men running one at a time; those who were hit had to crawl away from the place as best they could, their mates having at that moment one paramount duty—to reach their starting-point for the attack.

Continue along the farm track towards Pozières. This was the main approach route to the village. After 300 metres you will come to a dugout cut into the bank on the right side of the road [13]. This probably served as a battalion headquarters during July and August 1916 and was most likely built by Australians. It is a multi-room dugout with a corrugated iron roof, but it is unstable and partially filled with water. For safety's sake, do not enter it. The Official History mentions a dugout built by Australians in this stretch of road, but I estimate that it was located closer to Pozières, and this is not it.

Continue past the dugout and after 250 metres you will come to an old quarry on the right of the track. This is the Chalk Pit, a well-marked feature on wartime trench maps [14]. Here the Australians established a dump of hand grenades and ammunition, as well as a small medical aid post. The site's historical significance is lost on locals, who today use it as a garbage dump.

Shortly past the Chalk Pit the road becomes sunken as it enters the trees of Pozières. This stretch of road was known as 'Dead

Man's Road' and was where wounded men and troops repulsed in earlier attacks tended to congregate. The British frontline trench, from which the Australians launched their first attack on Pozières, crossed the road about halfway along the sunken section.

Continue along Dead Man's Road and carefully cross the busy D929. Directly opposite is the 1st Division Memorial and your car.

OTHER SITES OF INTEREST

Pozières is in the heart of the Somme battlefields. After visiting the Australian sites in and around the village, follow the road past Mouquet Farm to visit some fascinating sites connected with the British attack on 1 July 1916.

Mouquet Farm

After successfully capturing Pozières, the next objective for the AIF was the heavily fortified Mouquet Farm, located further along the ridge to the north-west. It was large and solid, and the Germans had converted its extensive cellars into a network of tunnels and deep dugouts, providing the defenders with protection and mobility.

The Australians first advanced towards Mouquet Farm on 8 August 1916. Between then and 5 September they threw themselves against the farm seven times, overcoming machine-gun positions, capturing trenches and resisting violent German counterattacks. Throughout this month, artillery fire from both sides was incessant, and the fields around Mouquet Farm were churned into a barren wasteland. The narrowness of the ridge meant that the Australians were advancing on a much smaller front than they had at Pozières, and the effects of German artillery fire were catastrophic in that confined space. Veterans of the Mouquet Farm fighting remembered the smoke and the stench, the bullets and barbed wire but, above all, they remembered the shelling.

Eventually the Australians were within sight of the farm, but the four weeks of constant strain had exhausted them. On 5 September they were relieved by the Canadian Corps, which completed the capture of Mouquet Farm on 26 September.

During an attack on the farm between 9 and 12 August, the Germans responded with a heavy artillery barrage which pummelled the Australian front line and approach routes through Pozières. Carrying parties found it almost impossible to weather the storm of shells, and the troops in the front line were in real danger of being cut off. Private Martin O'Meara, a stretcher bearer in the 16th Battalion, rallied the troops around him and led several excursions through the bombardment to carry water, ammunition and supplies to the front line. Not content to rest on his laurels, he went out into no man's land repeatedly and brought in wounded men. For his selflessness he was awarded the Victoria Cross.

Martin O'Meara was an Irishman who moved to Australia in his youth. He served with the 16th Battalion from its formation, through Gallipoli and until its last battle at Le Verguier in 1918. He was wounded in 1916 and twice more in 1917. He returned to Perth in 1919 but suffered from ill health for many years after the war and spent the rest of his life in a military hospital. He died in 1935, aged 50.

Directions

Mouquet Farm is reached by following the D73 past the civilian cemetery in Pozières—it is signposted in the middle of the village. The farm is still owned by the Vandendriessches, the same family that lived here before the war. It was completely destroyed during the war and has been rebuilt about 150 metres south of the original. Some rough foundations in the trees to the left of the farm are all that remain of the pre-war buildings. In 1993 a Bastiaan plaque was unveiled at Mouquet Farm, recording Australia's involvement in its capture. In the field to the right of the farm is a scrub-covered quarry, the scene of some of the most desperate fighting in the Mouquet Farm attacks. Martin O'Meara won his VC in the fields between the quarry and Pozières.

Thiepval Memorial

Thiepval was one of the principal objectives for British troops on the first day of the Battle of the Somme. On the morning of 1 July 1916, British troops stormed up a steep slope towards the village and were decimated by German machine-gun fire. The town was not captured until the end of September. After the war Thiepval was selected as the site for Britain's main memorial to its missing in France, and a monolithic red brick monument was unveiled on the site of the village chateau in 1932. Today the monument bears the names of more than 73 000 British and South African soldiers who died on the Somme and have no known grave, including seven Victoria Cross winners. The sheer number of missing men is incomprehensible, but it isn't a complete list: memorials in other parts of France, including Arras and Pozières, record the names of thousands more British soldiers missing in other sectors. A combined British/French cemetery behind the Thiepval Memorial symbolises the joint effort of the two great Allies on this part of the Western Front. Even though no members of the AIF are recorded on the Thiepval Memorial, 55 Aussies who were killed while serving with British forces are commemorated there and 10 Diggers are buried in the cemetery.

Directions

Thiepval is reached by following the road from Pozières (the D73) past Mouquet Farm. Turn left in Thiepval and follow the signs to the memorial. An information centre opened next to the memorial in 2004 and provides a moving and informative introduction to the Somme fighting. It is best to visit the information centre before seeing the memorial.

Ulster Tower

This replica of Helen's Tower in Clandeboye, Northern Ireland, was built to commemorate the achievement and sacrifice of the 36th (Ulster) Division during the Battle of the Somme. The Ulster

Division attacked German trenches in this area on the morning of 1 July, charging from the woods across the road to the site of the tower and beyond. By lying out in no man's land before the attack, the men of the Ulster Division had less ground to cover than their comrades and were one of the few units to take their objectives on the first morning of the battle. Without support, however, they could not hold the ground and eventually fell back with heavy loss. The tower was opened in 1921 and has a small information centre and cafe at its base. For many years visitors could climb to a viewing platform high in the tower: during the Second World War a German soldier no doubt enjoyed the view from here before carving a swastika into the stone wall. Unfortunately the platform has been closed due to safety concerns. Visit the copse behind the tower to see shallow trenches and shell holes.

Directions
Ulster Tower is reached by continuing along the D73 from Thiepval. The nearby Mill Road Cemetery is built close to the site of the Schwaben Redoubt, a German strongpoint, and has an unusual layout: many of the headstones are laid flat to counter subsidence caused by German tunnels beneath the cemetery.

Newfoundland Memorial Park, Beaumont-Hamel

This memorial park, with its network of preserved trenches, is one of the most interesting battlefield sites in France. The area now bordered by the park was the scene of one of the most tragic assaults on the first day of the Battle of the Somme. The Newfoundland Regiment attacked here at 8.45 am on 1 July 1916, more than an hour after an attack at the same place had been wiped out by German fire. The communication trenches leading to the British front line were clogged with troops, so the Newfies were forced to cross more than 500 metres of fire-swept ground before they even reached their own front line. Most of the regiment was hit before even entering no man's land. A handful of men managed to advance beyond the British trenches, but were cut down by machine-gun fire well short of the German lines. Of 801 men who marched with the regiment into battle, 733 were killed or wounded.

After the war the scene of this bloody enterprise was purchased by the Newfoundland government (then a self-governing colony, now part of Canada) and dedicated as a memorial to the regiment. Complete British and German trench systems were preserved and a caribou monument, bearing the names of the Newfoundland dead, was constructed overlooking the former battlefield. Today the trenches and shell holes are grassed over, but the park is one of the few places on the Western Front where a complete battlefield—including British and German trenches with no man's land in between—can be seen. A skeletal tree trunk in the middle of no man's land, known ominously as the 'danger tree', marks the furthest point reached by the Newfies on 1 July. The memorial park also contains three cemeteries and an impressive sculpture of a kilted warrior, a memorial to the 51st (Highland) Division, which captured the area in November 1916.

Directions

The Newfoundland Memorial Park is located along the D73, between Hamel and Auchonvillers (this village of Hamel should not be confused with the one captured by Australian troops on 4 July 1918). Entry is free and an information centre in the style of a Canadian log cabin gives an excellent introduction to the battle. Canadian student volunteers are often available to guide visitors around the park. At the rear of the park, behind the German lines, is Y Ravine, a natural feature that was turned into a formidable defensive position by the Germans.

Albert

This large town was the main British base of operations during the Somme fighting. Hundreds of thousands of troops marched through its streets on their way to the front line. Before the war the town had been a pilgrimage site and a magnificent basilica was built in the main square, topped by a gilded statue of the Madonna holding a baby Jesus to the heavens. From early in the war the British had used the basilica as an observation post and the German artillery had taken pot shots at it, badly damaging the building and knocking the statue off its perch. By 1916 the statue was leaning precariously from the tower, and engineers secured it with cable to prevent if from falling. For the next two years the 'Leaning Virgin' was one of the most iconic landmarks on the Western Front and a number of myths sprang up about her perilous state. The British believed that when the statue eventually fell, the war would end. The Germans believed that whichever side toppled the statue would lose the war, a curious interpretation considering how determined they were to blast the basilica from the face of the earth. In any case, neither myth proved correct: British artillery destroyed the church tower in early 1918 after the Germans had captured the town. The statue finally came crashing to earth and disappeared, probably scrapped by the Germans. Soldiers who saw this as an omen were disappointed: the war ground on for another eight months.

Today Albert is a fairly dull town, but it is close to the Somme battlefields and makes a good base for visitors. The basilica has been rebuilt and sports a shiny new Virgin, minus the lean. There is an interesting museum below the basilica which details Albert's involvement in both world wars and has a gift shop selling relics from the battlefield. The town has some nice hotels and a few restaurants, but seems to be deserted by about six every night. If you are looking for nightlife, this isn't your town.

Butte de Warlencourt

The Butte de Warlencourt is an ancient mound that commands the road between Bapaume and Albert. The Germans incorporated the Butte into their Somme defensive line and honeycombed it with trenches, tunnels and dugouts. Machine-gunners on the Butte had commanding fields of fire over the British lines, and used these to deadly effect during the Battle of the Somme. The Butte changed hands more than a dozen times during the fighting but was never genuinely captured by the British: the Germans abandoned it during their withdrawal in February 1917. A British officer, Charles Carrington, described the Butte in his 1929 memoirs, *A Subaltern's War.*

> That ghastly hill, never free from the smoke of bursting shells, became fabulous. It shone white in the night and seemed to leer at you like an ogre in a fairy tale. It loomed up unexpectedly, peering into trenches where you thought you were safe: it haunted your dreams. Twenty-four hours in the trenches before the Butte finished a man off.

Today the Butte is owned by the Western Front Association and is open to visitors. A path leads to the top, where a memorial commemorates all those who fell in the area.

Directions
The Butte de Warlencourt is six kilometres north-east of Pozières, along the D929. It is signposted to the right 500 metres after the village of Le Sars.

Flers

The Battle of the Somme drew to a close in November 1916 as the harshest French winter in decades closed in on the battlefields. Before it was over, however, Australian troops were called on to launch a fairly minor attack by the standards of the Somme fighting, but one that Charles Bean, the official historian, called 'the most difficult in which the AIF was ever engaged'. The objective was the German trench system near the town of Flers. A bulge in the German line stuck out into British territory and the High Command wanted it pinched out.

By 5 November rain had been steadily falling for days and temperatures had plummeted. The battlefield turned to glue and shells failed to explode in the cloying mud. Faced with these atrocious conditions, the Australian 1st and 7th brigades were ordered to attack. The main objective was 'The Maze', a complex of trenches where, at one point, the British and German front lines actually intersected. In a confused attack the Australians managed to capture the German positions but couldn't hold them against counterattacks. At one stage the Germans attacked across the open and offered easy targets to the Australian infantry, but their rifles had clogged with mud and wouldn't fire.

On 14 November the Australians attacked again. This time the 7th Brigade was joined by the 5th and both units managed to break into The Maze. For two days they held on, using German rifles, bombs and ammunition when their own supplies ran out. Just when it seemed the position was safely in their hands, the Germans counterattacked in force on 16 November. The Australians held on as long as they could but were overwhelmed. Many were killed or captured; the rest managed to escape back to the Australian lines.

The attacks at Flers achieved nothing except to demonstrate that men ordered to fight in a quagmire would die by the score. It was a lesson that was sadly forgotten at Passchendaele the following year. More than 900 Australians were killed, wounded or captured in the two attacks at Flers.

After Flers the Australians were forced to endure the hardships of a bitterly cold winter in the mud and slush of the front line. Many could not stand it and left the Australian lines to give themselves up to the Germans, preferring a prison camp to the horrors of the front. At least one Australian shot himself rather than return to the firing line after a rest. The winter of 1916–17 was probably the bleakest period of the war for the AIF.

Directions

Flers is six kilometres east of Pozières. To find the location of The Maze, leave Pozières on the D929 towards Bapaume. In the village of Le Sars, turn right at the crossroads onto the D11 and follow this road for just over a kilometre. Turn left at the T-junction and right at the next crossroads. Follow this road for 700 metres and park near the five-way intersection where the D11 meets two farm tracks. Follow the track heading north-east (to your left) for about 700 metres, until it becomes sunken. This is the point where the German line crossed the track in the area attacked by the Australians.

Fricourt German Cemetery

The village of Fricourt was in the southern sector of the Somme battlefields and was captured on 2 July 1916. Fricourt German Cemetery was started after the war and is a concentration cemetery made up of bodies collected from a wide area. Today it contains more than 17 000 burials, but only 5000 of these are in individual graves. The rest are buried in four *Gemeinschaftsgräber*, or communal graves, where only 5493 bodies are identified. The names of these men are recorded on metal tablets at the rear of the cemetery.

Fricourt Cemetery is the final resting place of men killed in every year of the war but, unsurprisingly, carries a large number of men killed in the 1916 Somme battles. One man who was buried here, however, did not find it his last resting place. Baron Manfred von Richthofen, the 'Red Baron', was buried here after the Armistice. He had originally been buried in Bertangles cemetery after his death on 21 April 1918, but was moved to Fricourt during the great concentration of bodies in the early 1920s. In 1925 he was moved from Fricourt to Berlin. The construction of the Berlin Wall through the middle of the cemetery necessitated the Baron being moved again—hopefully for the last time—to the family plot in Wiesbaden.

Directions
Fricourt is five kilometres east of Albert. The German cemetery is on the right-hand side of the road heading north out of the village, the D147.

Gueudecourt—Harry Murray VC

The story of Harry Murray epitomises everything that has become legendary about the original Anzacs. In three and a half years he rose from the rank of private to lieutenant colonel, commanded a battalion and won more bravery awards than any other soldier in the AIF.

In February 1917 Murray was a company commander in the 13th Battalion and was tasked with leading an assault on the right flank of Stormy Trench, a German position near the town of Gueudecourt. No major action was taking place at this time, but the attack was part of a campaign by the British forces to launch limited assaults on German positions whenever the opportunity arose.

Murray led his company out across the frozen no man's land on the night of 4 February, through a wire entanglement and into the German trench. Finding it practically deserted but confident the Germans would soon counterattack, Murray ordered his men to build a barricade and prepare for action. The simultaneous explosion of 20 hand grenades signalled the start of the German attack and Murray's men at the barricade were soon all wounded. Murray organised a spirited defence and succeeded in holding off the Germans. Later in the night he probed forward and saw another large group of Germans assembling for an attack. Murray called in artillery support and rallied his men to hold off the attackers with bombs. For the rest of the night and the next day they held out in their isolated post, throwing themselves against any Germans who tried to take the position. By the time they were relieved the company had lost 92 of its 140 men. For leading such a spirited defence of a vital position, Murray received the Victoria Cross.

Harry Murray was a born soldier and had enlisted in the AIF in October 1914. He landed at Gallipoli on the first day as a machine-gunner and received his first promotion three weeks later. A week after that, he received the Distinguished Conduct Medal for consistently good work leading his gun teams. By August the high casualty rate among officers led to Murray being promoted by three ranks in one day, from lance corporal to 2nd lieutenant. He was wounded twice at Gallipoli, and travelled with the 13th Battalion to France in March 1916.

During the attack on Mouquet Farm in August, Murray led about 100 men in a fight all the way to the ruins of the farm buildings. They eventually withdrew and the farm was not reached again until it was captured by more than 3000 troops. For this bold charge Murray received the Distinguished Service Order.

Murray's next great achievement was winning the Victoria Cross at Stormy Trench in February 1917. In April of that year the 13th Battalion joined the first attack at Bullecourt. Murray led his men coolly in the face of mounting disaster. With Germans closing in on all sides, Murray gave the order for his men to withdraw through withering fire, passing the order along the line: 'There's only two things now. Either capture—or go into that fire.' Murray and his men dashed back to the Australian lines, among the last men to leave the German trenches. For his stoic leadership in such terrible circumstances, Murray received a bar to his DSO.

Late in 1917 Murray was promoted, temporarily commanding the 13th Battalion before taking permanent command of the 4th Machine Gun Battalion in early 1918. Late in the war he received the French Croix de Guerre. His final tally for his First World War service was the VC, DSO & Bar and DCM, plus numerous Mentions in Despatches and the Croix de Guerre. He was made a Companion of the Order of St Michael and St George (CMG) in 1919.

After the war Murray returned to Australia and took up a large sheep farm in north Queensland. He served as the commanding officer of the 26th Battalion during the Second World War until his retirement in 1944. Murray was injured in a car accident in 1966 and died of heart failure soon after. He was 82.

Directions

Gueudecourt is nine kilometres north-east of Pozières. Harry Murray won the VC in Stormy Trench, east of the village. To find the site, leave Gueudecourt on the D574 towards Beaulencourt, following the signs to a Canadian memorial. Continue for one kilometre until you reach the memorial on your right. The shallow trench that snakes through the park was captured by the Newfoundland Regiment in October 1916, the furthest point reached by British troops during the Battle of the Somme. By early 1917 this sector was occupied by Australian troops, and this trench actually formed part of the start line for the attack on Stormy Trench led by Harry Murray, one of the only remaining trenches on the Western Front that can be definitively linked to Australians. On the night of 4 February, Murray led his company from near this spot to Stormy Trench, which was located in the field behind the memorial.

Lochnagar Mine Crater, La Boisselle

This massive crater, the largest on the Western Front, was created by the explosion of a double-chambered mine beneath German positions on 1 July 1916, the first day of the Battle of the Somme. The results were spectacular: a column of fire, smoke and earth shot more than a kilometre into the air and the German trenches in the area, along with the Germans themselves, were obliterated. It didn't take the Germans long to regroup, however, and men swarmed into the crater, using the shelter of its high lip to pour machine-gun fire into the advancing British troops. The crater was not captured for another two days.

It was purchased in 1978 by Englishman Richard Dunning and is preserved as a memorial to men who fell in the Somme fighting. Commemorative services are held here on 1 July each year. Erosion has reduced its size but it is still enormous—more than 100 metres wide and 30 metres deep. In the interest of preservation, climbing down to its base is no longer allowed.

In 1998 a tourist walking around the rim of the crater noticed a boot heel sticking out of the ground. On closer inspection he realised there was still a foot in the boot. He had discovered the remains of a soldier, killed on 1 July 1916 and lying undiscovered at one of the most frequently visited sites on the Western Front for more than 80 years. A service number carved into the handle of a razor found with the body identified the soldier as Private

George Nugent of the 22nd (Tyneside Scottish) Battalion. Private Nugent now lies in the nearby Ovillers Military Cemetery.

Directions
Lochnagar Crater is near the village of La Boisselle, on the main road between Albert and Pozières. The crater is about 500 metres south of La Boisselle and is signposted in the village—follow the signs to 'La Grande Mine'. A stone bench at the intersection that leads to the crater is a memorial to the Tyneside battalions that captured La Boisselle in the Somme fighting. A field on the right of the road to Lochnagar is a sea of overlapping shell holes and craters. This was an area of intense mining activity known as the 'Glory Hole'.

Sausage and Mash Valleys

These two natural depressions, running roughly parallel on each side of the Albert–Bapaume road, were avenues of shelter for troops moving to the front line during the Somme fighting. Sausage Valley was named after German observation balloons that floated at its head. After this it was probably inevitable that the neighbouring valley was given the complementary name 'Mash'.

Using the parlance they had developed at Gallipoli, Australian soldiers referred almost universally to Sausage Valley as Sausage 'Gully'. It was their main route to the front line during the bitter fighting at Pozières in July and August 1916. During this time the gully was a hive of activity and the bustle of men and vehicles, the batteries of artillery and the dumps of ammunition and equipment reminded many Diggers of the beach at Anzac Cove. Mash Valley was frequently used as a route to the front after Pozières had been captured, particularly during the struggle for Mouquet Farm in August and September 1916.

Directions
The best place to see Sausage Valley is from the rim of Lochnagar Crater. Standing with your back to the crater and facing east

you are looking directly along the valley—it is really only a gentle depression and sweeps past the crater towards Pozières. Gordon Dump Cemetery, named after a British post from early in the Somme fighting and containing 91 Australian graves, is at the valley's head.

Mash Valley is deeper than Sausage Valley and runs along the left side of the Albert–Bapaume road between La Boisselle and Pozières.

Sheffield Memorial Park, Serre

This park is located in the northern sector of the 1 July 1916 battlefield and commemorates the Sheffield 'Pals' Battalion who attacked near here that day. The park is actually on the part of the line held by the Pals from Accrington; the Sheffield Pals attacked from trenches about 100 metres further north. This small piece of land and the four nearby cemeteries neatly reveal the tragedy of the 1 July attack. The park contains grassed-over shell holes and the shallow line of the front line trench from which the Pals attacked. About 200 metres away, up a gradual slope, were the German trenches, well defended by wire and machine-guns. At 7.30 on the morning of the attack, the Pals climbed from the trench and marched, as instructed, in parade-ground formation towards the Germans. They were mown down as they crossed no man's land.

Today three cemeteries—Luke Copse, Queens and Serre Road No. 3—sit in the middle of the old no man's land and contain the bodies of men who were buried where they fell. A fourth cemetery, Railway Hollow, named after a light railway that ran through the area, also contains the remains of many men killed on 1 July.

If the fields are clear of crops, walk from the Sheffield Park frontline trench, past Queens Cemetery and up the slope for another 100 metres. This brings you to the approximate position of the German front line. From here it is clear how the high ground gave the Germans a commanding advantage, and what easy targets the British Pals made as they marched slowly towards the German guns. After the war a German machine-gunner who had served in these trenches that day commented that the British troops were so massed he didn't even need to aim; he just poured fire into the advancing lines.

Directions

Sheffield Memorial Park is near the village of Serre, about eight kilometres north-west of Pozières. From Serre, drive towards Mailly-Maillet on the D919. After about a kilometre you will reach Serre Road No. 1 Cemetery on the right of the road. Park here and then walk 100 metres back along the road towards Serre and turn left onto a farm track. This leads to the memorial park and cemeteries. The track is rough and does not have adequate parking space, so driving to the memorial park is not really an option.

Serre Road No. 2 Cemetery, one of the largest on the Somme battlefields, is further along the D919 towards Mailly-Maillet and also worth a visit (see pages 191–192).

CEMETERIES NEAR POZIÈRES

2nd Canadian Cemetery, Sunken Road: see Pozières tour (page 162).

AIF Burial Ground, Grass Lane, Flers

The village of Flers was captured by British and New Zealand troops during the Battle of Flers-Courcelette on 16 September 1916. The assaulting troops attacked behind tanks, a new weapon that was used for the first time in this battle. Australian military history remembers Flers for the tough fighting that occurred near the village in November 1916, when AIF units attacked in dreadful weather.

The cemetery was started by Australian medical units posted in the nearby chalk caves in November 1916 and was used until the following February. It was greatly enlarged after the Armistice to its present size of 3475 graves. Of these, 417 are Australian, with 142 unknowns. This is the only military cemetery in the world with the acronym AIF in its title.

The most senior Australian officer buried here is Major George Nicholas DSO of the 24th Battalion. Nicholas had won the Distinguished Service Order as a captain at Pozières, when he led an assault on a German machine-gun. He was killed while leading his men to the front line at Flers (grave IV.H.27).

Also buried here is 2nd Lieutenant Fred Matthews of the 6th Machine Gun Company. Matthews first drew attention to himself near Armentières on 4 July 1916. He and his two brothers, Arthur and Henry, were manning a machine-gun when they spotted a German raiding party in no man's land. They opened fire and in the melee that followed both Arthur and Henry were killed. Fred continued to operate the gun and fired more than 1000 rounds at the Germans, breaking up the raiding party (see page 151). At Pozières in August he manned a machine-gun in an advanced position and withstood a heavy German bombardment. When some of his men were buried by a shell he dug them out, and stood by his gun even when the Germans were firing at him from only 25 metres away. For his two great acts of valour he was awarded the Distinguished Conduct Medal. He was killed at Flers on 8 November (grave X.L.2).

Directions
Flers is six kilometres east of Pozières. The cemetery is two kilometres north of the village and can be reached by heading towards Gueudecourt on the D197. Turn right at the crossroads and you will soon come to a sign pointing to the cemetery along a grass track.

Contalmaison Chateau Cemetery: see Pozières tour (page 162).

Côte 80 French National Cemetery, Etinehem

This cemetery is one of only a handful of French cemeteries on the Western Front containing Australian graves. It was started by French field ambulance units during the Battle of the Somme in 1916 and was used until the area was lost to the Germans in March 1918. The Australian 50th Battalion recaptured the ground in August 1918 and the bodies of Australians killed in nearby battles were interred there. Today the cemetery contains 49 Commonwealth graves, of which 29 are Australian. All except one of these are identified. Twelve of the men belonged to the 35th Battalion and were killed in the attack on Bray on 22 August.

Directions
Etinehem is nine kilometres south-east of Albert. The cemetery is one kilometre north of the village on the road to Méaulte. The Australian graves are hidden behind the French graves and consequently the cemetery receives few Australian visitors.

London Cemetery and Extension, Longueval

This large cemetery is located opposite High Wood, scene of some of the bloodiest fighting on the Somme. The wood was eventually secured by British units in September 1916 and the cemetery was begun soon after when 47 British soldiers were buried in a shell hole. By the end of the war the cemetery contained 101 graves but it was enlarged enormously in the following years until it reached its present size of 3872 graves. It is now the third largest Commonwealth cemetery on the Somme. Australian units were not involved in the fighting at High Wood, but their bodies were interred in the cemetery after being collected from isolated grave sites and smaller cemeteries in the surrounding area. London Cemetery now contains 300 Australian graves, mostly men killed in the fighting at Pozières in July and August 1916. Of these, 197 are unidentified. One of the most curious Australian graves belongs to Lance Corporal Frederick Tindall of the 50th Battalion. He was killed by machine-gun fire during the attack at Villers-Bretonneux on Anzac Day, 1918. His body was not found until after the war, and he was reinterred here, more than 35 kilometres from where he was killed (grave 10.E.13).

Directions
Longueval is six kilometres south-east of Pozières. From Pozières, take the D929 towards Bapaume and after two kilometres turn right towards Martinpuich. Carry on through that village and after two kilometres you will reach High Wood (now known as the Bois des Fourcaux). London Cemetery is on the right, directly opposite the wood.

The area around Longueval is a very interesting corner of the Somme battlefield. More than 15 000 Commonwealth soldiers are buried in five cemeteries in the immediate vicinity. An interesting New Zealand memorial is located 1.5 kilometres north of Longueval, and Delville Wood, site of the impressive South African National Memorial, is just east of the village.

Pozières British Cemetery and Memorial

Pozières British Cemetery was begun in 1916, as soon as Pozières had been secured, and was used to bury men killed in and around the village. It was also used during fighting in the area in 1917 and again when the Germans captured the ground in 1918. The cemetery was greatly enlarged after the Armistice, when bodies were brought in from the surrounding fields. Today it contains 2756 graves, 708 of which are Australian. Of these, 251 are unidentified.

At the rear of the cemetery is the Pozières Memorial to the Missing, commemorating 14 652 UK and South African servicemen who were killed on the Somme between 21 March and 7 August 1918 and have no known grave. The major action that took place in this period was the German Spring Offensive, when the British line in the Somme was aggressively driven back across the old 1916 battlefields. The memorial stands as a tribute to all the British soldiers missing from that period of crisis.

The most notable Australian buried in the cemetery is Sergeant Claud Castleton of the Australian Machine Gun Corps (grave IV.L.43), who was awarded a posthumous Victoria Cross for rescuing wounded men during an attack near Pozières on 29 July 1916 (see **Pozières**, pages 159 and 168).

Also buried here is Major Duncan Chapman of the 45th Battalion. As a lieutenant in the 9th Battalion, Chapman was the first Australian to land at Gallipoli on 25 April 1915. He was killed by shellfire at Pozières on the night of 6 August 1916 (grave III.M.22).

Two men who lie in Pozières Cemetery, Sergeants Cecil Heaton and Robert Stone, won the Distinguished Conduct Medal at Gallipoli. Heaton was killed in the 1st Division's initial assault on Pozières on 23 July 1916. Demonstrating how drawn out and confusing the Pozières fighting became, Stone is listed as having been killed sometime between 27 July and 14 August 1916, a window of almost three weeks (graves III.L.14 and I.H.32).

Directions
Pozières British Cemetery is 600 metres south-west of Pozières on the D929 road to Albert.

Serre Road No. 2 Cemetery

The village of Serre was in the northern sector of the Somme battlefield and saw months of sustained carnage between July and November 1916. By early 1917 the area was firmly in British hands but still littered with bodies, so clearance units were brought in to tidy it up and create cemeteries where needed. The battlefield immediately west of Serre became home to several cemeteries, including three on the Serre road. Serre Road No. 2 Cemetery was started in May 1917 and was greatly enlarged after the Armistice when bodies were concentrated here from 16 small cemeteries in the area. It is now the largest Commonwealth cemetery on the Somme, containing 7127 graves. The ferocity of the Somme fighting is reflected in the fact that almost 5000 of these graves are unidentified. Australian burials total 699, of which more than half are unidentified. Most of these men were killed near Pozières in 1916 but some have come from much further afield. Private James Sheldon of the 3rd Battalion was killed during the Australian advance on the Hindenburg Line on 18 September 1918 and was originally buried in the American Cemetery at Bony, more than 50 kilometres from Serre. It is understandable that an Australian grave would be moved from an American cemetery after the war, but why Private Sheldon was not reinterred in one of the scores of Commonwealth cemeteries near Bony is a mystery (grave IX.L.16).

Also buried here is Captain Francis Caless, a well-liked company commander in the 26th Battalion. He was killed during the unit's advance on the German OG trenches east of Pozières on 4 August 1916 (grave XXV.F.11).

Nearby is Sergeant William O'Brien, who features in a famous photograph of B Company, 29th Battalion, taken before the advance on Harbonnières on 8 August 1918. In the photo, O'Brien stands relaxed with 15 of his comrades as they receive orders from their commanding officer. It was to be O'Brien's last photo. He was killed by a shell at Harbonnières the next day (grave XXIV.C.2).

Directions
Serre is 11 kilometres north-west of Pozières. Serre Road No. 2 Cemetery is just over a kilometre south-west of the village on the D919, towards Mailly-Maillet. The Sheffield Memorial Park (see pages 186–187) is nearby.

Sunken Road Cemetery: see Pozières tour (page 162).

Warloy-Baillon Communal Cemetery Extension

Warloy-Baillon is a village close to Albert and was home to British field ambulance units in the lead-up to the Battle of the Somme in 1916. The communal cemetery had been used to bury British soldiers since 1915 but the field ambulances knew the impending battle was going to consume more grave space than was available.

They laid out the cemetery extension and were ready to receive burials by 1 July 1916, the first day of the battle. One can only imagine the thoughts of British infantry who marched by and saw the ambulance units laying out new plots.

The next four months of fighting resulted in over 1000 interments, mostly from the northern sector of the Somme battlefield. Further burials were also made after the German Spring Offensive in 1918. Australian graves number 321, all identified. The majority of these men died of wounds during the Pozières fighting in 1916.

Buried here is Major Terence Garling, commanding officer of the 37th Battery, 10th Field Artillery Brigade. Garling had enlisted two weeks after the outbreak of war and had served through the entire Gallipoli campaign and for two years in France. During the German attack on Dernancourt on 5 April 1918, Garling's battery was stationed in front of Millencourt and provided artillery support to the Australian defenders. During the morning Garling was wounded in the leg by a shell splinter, and he died from blood loss at the Warloy dressing station later in the day. He was only 24 years old. One of his men later wrote: 'I am endorsing the sentiments of everybody who knew him in concluding that all officers and men who ever knew him loved him and mourn for him' (Grave VIII.F.21).

Directions
Warloy-Baillon is seven kilometres west of Albert. The cemetery is on the eastern edge of the village.

Warlencourt British Cemetery

This is another large Commonwealth cemetery, made when bodies were brought in from isolated graves and small cemeteries in the area after the Armistice. Of the 3505 graves, 477 are Australian, including 138 unknowns. Most of these men were killed at Flers in November 1916 and through the bitter winter that followed.

The most senior Australian remembered here is Major Julius Kayser, second in command of the 12th Battalion. He had enlisted three weeks after the outbreak of war and served at Gallipoli. During the campaign he was so badly wounded that he was invalided back to Australia and not expected to return. After an astonishing recovery he returned to Europe and rejoined his battalion in France. He was badly wounded again at Pozières in 1916, but once again recovered and rejoined the battalion. His luck finally ran out at Gueudecourt on 2 February 1917, when he was killed by a German mortar. One of his men later said he was 'almost worshipped by the men of his battalion both as a soldier, and for his sterling qualities as a man'. Kayser was buried at Hexham Road Cemetery but his grave could not be found after the war. He is commemorated on special memorial 6 at Warlencourt British Cemetery.

Four men also buried here won the Distinguished Conduct Medal. They are 2nd Lieutenant William McMullen (25th Battalion, died 05/11/1916, grave III.A.7), Private Frank Murton (19th Battalion, died 14/11/1916, special memorial 11), Lance Sergeant Abel Skinner (25th Battalion, died 05/11/1916, grave II.B.30) and Corporal Leslie Sneyd (27th Battalion, died 05/11/1916, grave II.E.32). All four earned the award within days of each other at Pozières and all four were killed at Flers three months later.

Directions
Warlencourt British Cemetery is on the right side of the D929, seven kilometres north-east of Pozières and one kilometre past Le Sars.

OTHER CEMETERIES OF INTEREST

There are literally hundreds of cemeteries in the Pozières area of interest to Australians. Some others worth visiting include:

Albert Communal Cemetery Extension

39 Australian graves from a total of 822.

Bazentin-le-Petit Military Cemetery

55 Australians out of 182.

Bernafay Wood British Cemetery, Montauban

124 Australians out of 945.

Courcelette British Cemetery

513 Australians out of 1970.

Dartmoor Cemetery, Bécordal-Bécourt

71 Australians out of 768.

Gordon Dump Cemetery, Ovillers–La Boisselle

91 Australians out of 1676.

Guards Cemetery, Lesboeufs

209 Australians out of 3136.

Ovillers Military Cemetery

57 Australians out of 3439.

Puchevillers British Cemetery

417 Australians out of 1763. Look for the grave of Lieutenant
Bert Crowle, 10th Battalion—his private headstone is unique on
the Western Front (grave III.A.11).

Serre Road No. 1 Cemetery

147 Australians out of 2426.

8

Villers-Bretonneux
and Hamel,
April and July 1918

For the AIF, 1918 was a shining year. The tough fights at Gallipoli, Pozières and Bullecourt had demonstrated the Australians were as good as any fighting force in the war; the battles of 1918 made them legendary. Two of the most important Australian actions of the year took place close together between April and July. In April the Australians played a vital role in stopping the attacking Germans at Villers-Bretonneux, an action that was as fine a feat of arms as any of the war. Three months later they captured the village of Hamel in a brilliantly orchestrated assault that would be used as a model for future attacks.

VILLERS-BRETONNEUX, APRIL 1918

The year 1918 had begun with the Germans launching their Spring Offensive in March. It was their last roll of the dice in the war and they knew it. If they could penetrate the Allied lines they stood a good chance of reaching the French coast and opening up supply lines to a Germany debilitated by British naval blockades. If their attack were unsuccessful they would lose the war. America's huge army was finally ready to join the fight and Germany had run out of options.

In the face of this desperate stroke the British line wilted. Led by crack assault troops, the Germans broke through at several points and began pushing the British back. On the Somme the Germans swept across the killing fields of 1916 with breathtaking speed. Battlefields that had cost the lives of hundreds of thousands and had taken months to capture were lost in a matter of days. The German objective was Amiens, the capital of Picardy and the most important rail junction in the region. With Amiens in their hands, the Germans would have a clear run to the coast.

Villers-Bretonneux is a small village 16 kilometres east of Amiens. It had never been famous for much and probably never would have been if the Australians hadn't arrived there in April 1918. On 4 April the Germans attacked Villers-Bretonneux in strength, intending to use it as a stepping stone to Amiens. They were only stopped after a desperate defence by the British 1st Cavalry and the Australian 33rd and 35th battalions. In the afternoon the Australian 36th Battalion launched a counterattack, pushing the German forces out of the village and forcing their line back more than a kilometre.

South of Villers-Bretonneux the Germans still held Hangard Wood, a precarious position that made the British commanders nervous. On 7 April they ordered the 19th and 20th battalions to attack the wood and wrench it from the Germans.

The attack started badly. It seems likely that the battle had been planned on a map that didn't accurately portray the tough lie of the land. The 19th Battalion lost several officers and Lieutenant Percy Storkey took charge of a small group of men. They became separated from the rest of the attacking troops and blundered around in the woods, trying to locate an enemy machine-gun they could hear firing at the Australians. Eventually they stumbled across it and found themselves behind a group of about 100 Germans who were firing from two lines of trenches. An urgent decision was required. If the Germans spotted the small group of Australians they would be cut down. 'Shouting as if the whole battalion was following,' reports the *Official History*, Storkey 'at once led a charge upon the rear of the Germans.' Some immediately surrendered but others tried to swing a machine-gun into action. Storkey shot three with his revolver and his men rolled grenades into the German trenches. When the smoke had cleared, they had killed or wounded 30 men and captured another 53, including three officers, plus the machine-gun. The Australian battalions continued to the objective but found the ground untenable and by nightfall were back where they had started. The two battalions had lost 151 men in the assault. Storkey was awarded the Victoria Cross.

After the war Percy Storkey became a solicitor and eventually a crown prosecutor for the New South Wales Department of Justice. In 1939 he was appointed to the New South Wales District Court Bench, a position he held until his retirement in 1955. He died in England in 1969, aged 78.

The village of Hangard is south of Villers-Bretonneux. Hangard Wood is split into two lobes, and can be reached by following the Rue de l'Eglise north out of Hangard. After two kilometres you will reach the picturesque Hangard Wood Cemetery, which contains the graves of some of the Australians killed in the attack. Continue driving past the cemetery and after 500 metres you will reach the point where the Australian start line crossed the road. Percy Storkey advanced across the field on your right and won the VC just inside the wood on the far side of the field. Numerous trenches and shell holes remain in the wood.

On 17 and 18 April the Germans prepared for a second assault on Villers-Bretonneux by drenching the area with gas. The noxious clouds caused more than 1000 Australian casualties.

By 24 April the Australians had been withdrawn and the protection of Villers-Bretonneux was entrusted to several British battalions. The Germans had yet another trick up their sleeve and attacked the town with their newly developed tanks. Compared to

British models, the German tanks were lumbering and unreliable but they were heavily armed and appeared ferocious as they loomed out of the early morning mist. The British infantry fell back, leaving a few tanks to engage the Germans in the first ever tank-versus-tank battle. The Germans swept into the village and captured the ground the Australians had fought so hard to defend three weeks earlier. (A damaged German tank was later captured by Australian troops near Villers-Bretonneux. It is now on display in the Museum of Queensland in Brisbane, and is the only surviving example of a First World War German tank in the world.)

Orders to recapture the village were immediately issued and the task fell to the Australian 13th, 14th and 15th brigades. North of the village the 59th Battalion, supported by the 57th and 60th battalions, made a bold charge by the light of the moon on the night of 24–25 April, the third anniversary of the original Anzac Day. In an action worthy of that legacy, they drove the Germans out of the village and into the fields to the east.

The fighting during this phase was particularly bloody. The *Official History* referred to it as one of the wildest experiences of Australian infantry during the war, and says that the attacking troops became 'primitive' and 'savage'. One Australian who was in the thick of the action described the brutal half-hour assault:

> With a ferocious roar and the cry of 'Into the bastards, boys,' we were down on them before the Boche realised what had happened. The Boche was at our mercy. They screamed for mercy but there were too many machine guns about to show them any consideration . . . Each man was in his glee and old scores were wiped out two or three times over . . . Here and there a Fritz would hop out of a trench or shell-hole only to fall riddled with bullets and then to be bayoneted by the boys as they came up.

Once the Australians' blood had cooled, however, they faced the consequences of what they had just done. A lieutenant noted that several of his men came up to him with the same remark: 'I can't help thinking of that chap I bayoneted.'

South of the village the 50th and 57th battalions cleared Abbey Wood, while the 51st and 52nd battalions attacked Monument Wood. The two battalions had just begun to advance when flares lit up the night sky and several machine-guns opened fire from a wood on the left. The left platoon was commanded by Lieutenant Cliff Sadlier, a commercial traveller from Perth. He conferred with Sergeant Charles Stokes and determined that the only course of action was a bombing attack against the German machine-guns. Sadlier and Stokes set off with four men and charged towards the German posts. The machine-gunners in the wood were caught totally off guard by the bold rush and, before they could recover from the surprise, the Australians were among the trees and bombing the German posts. At the first post a German put up one hand and called out in surrender but then shot Sadlier in the thigh with a revolver. Sadlier killed him and captured the post, before moving on to the next one. Here he was shot again and was forced to return to the Australian line. Stokes carried on the attack, bombing each position as he found it and leading his small group through the wood. The group of six was now down to three, but Stokes pushed on through a hail of tracer bullets and captured two more machine-gun posts. The attack cleared the way for the battalion to advance. Six machine-guns were later picked up from the posts in the wood.

Both Sadlier and Stokes were recommended for the Victoria Cross. Only Sadlier received it: he was the senior officer involved and the award was probably in recognition of the bravery of the whole group. Stokes, somewhat unfairly, received the lesser Distinguished Conduct Medal.

By this and similar courageous acts, the 13th Brigade completed its sweep south of Villers-Bretonneux and joined the other Australian brigades on the far side of the village. Villers-Bretonneux was back in Australian hands.

Cliff Sadlier had enlisted in the AIF in 1915. He served with the 1st Australian General Hospital in Egypt and transferred to the 51st Battalion in 1916. He rose steadily through the ranks and was promoted to lieutenant only three weeks before the attack at Villers-Bretonneux. The wounds he received in his VC action kept him out of the rest of the war and he returned to Australia late in 1918. After the war he worked in the public service in Perth. He died there in 1964, aged 71.

The wood where Sadlier and Stokes captured the German machine-guns has not changed much since the war. Even though the objective was Monument Wood, the Germans were actually firing from the wood known today as Bois d'Aquennes. To find the spot, leave Villers-Bretonneux heading west on the road to Cachy. Immediately after leaving the village the large Bois d'Aquennes appears on your right. The road soon becomes sunken and curves left. The German machine-guns were spaced out in a line from here across the southern edge of the wood, firing south into the left flank of the advancing Australians. The last gun captured by Stokes was actually in this sunken section of road, at the end closest to Cachy. The Australians advanced from west to east across the fields to your left.

The counterattack on Villers-Bretonneux was one of the most famous Australian actions of the war. Writing in 1936, Brigadier General Grogan, commander of the British 23rd Brigade and one of the senior officers on the scene, called the attack 'perhaps the greatest individual feat of the war'. General Foch, commander-in-chief of all the Allied forces, referred to the Australians' 'altogether astonishing valiance'.

Despite these plaudits (or perhaps because of them), Villers-Bretonneux's place in history remains controversial. In 1918, with the war drawing to a close and the victors jockeying for political advantage, it was lauded by the Australian government as the turning point of the war, the moment when the AIF, all by itself, stopped the German offensive and saved France. Modern military revisionists claim the exact opposite—that the Germans were a spent force by the time they reached Villers-Bretonneux and that it was English troops, rather than the Aussies, who bore the brunt of the assault. The truth is probably somewhere in between. There is little doubt that the action at Villers-Bretonneux was vital in stopping the German Spring Offensive in that sector of the line and that the Australian action, particularly the counterattack on 24 April, was a masterpiece of dash and courage. Did it save France? Probably not. The Germans were at the end of a long advance and realistically didn't stand much chance of reaching the Channel even if they did take Amiens. But the fact remains that the Australians, although significantly outnumbered, managed not only to stop the German advance, but to recapture a large amount of lost territory and inflict heavy casualties on the Germans. The battle at Villers-Bretonneux displayed, probably better than any other action of the war, the characteristics that made the AIF such a great fighting force: resilience, courage, skill and aggression. That is the reason the town is the home of the Australian National Memorial and why strong bonds of affection still unite Villers-Bretonneux and Australia.

HAMEL, 4 JULY 1918

In the summer of 1918, with the German Spring Offensive shut down and the German Army exhausted, the Allies began looking for opportunities to exploit. A major attack was planned but before that took place local commanders were encouraged to make limited advances to keep the Germans on their toes and to secure important pieces of ground.

General John Monash had been appointed commander of the Australian Corps at the end of May and he was keen to demonstrate the skills of his Australian force. The new German line near Villers-Bretonneux bulged in a small salient around the town of Hamel. This was the most obvious place on the Australian front for a limited advance and Monash began drawing up plans.

Monash was a meticulous planner and had some innovative ideas for this battle. He later wrote that 'the role of infantry was not to expend itself upon heroic physical effort, not to wither away under merciless machine-gun fire, not to impale itself on hostile bayonets, but on the contrary, to advance under the maximum possible protection of the maximum possible array of mechanical resources in the form of guns, machine-guns, tanks, mortars and aeroplanes.' At Hamel he put this theory to the test.

Monash's plan called for extremely close cooperation between all the resources at his disposal. Infantry would advance under the cover of tanks and artillery. Aeroplanes, specifically chosen for their noisy engines, would buzz over the German lines, masking the sound of the approaching tanks. And, in probably the greatest innovation of the battle, specially designed carrier tanks would transport supplies and ammunition as the infantry advanced, each one doing the job of 1200 support troops. Aeroplanes would also drop ammunition by parachute at designated drop zones.

As the Australians were gearing up for the battle, several regiments of American soldiers arrived in the sector. The British and Australian generals decided to bolster their own under-strength battalions with about 1000 American troops for the attack on Hamel, even though the Americans were fairly raw. The Australians and the Americans got on well, and the latter were excited to be entering a real fight. As a salute to the Americans, the attack was set for 4 July, American Independence Day.

The troops set off at 3.10 am, covered by a creeping barrage and a strong force of tanks. Monash had ordered that Hamel be bombarded with high explosive and gas shells for days before the attack, in an effort to deny the Germans sleep. It was also hoped that the Germans would be wearing their cumbersome gas masks during the attack.

The Americans set off beside their Australian comrades and were eager to impress but dangerously inexperienced. At several stages of the advance they nearly ran into their own creeping barrage. A young Australian in the 13th Battalion, Corporal Michael Roach, ran forward to pull back some Americans who were too close to the exploding shells and was badly wounded. He died the next day.

The Australian 4th Brigade had been tasked with clearing Vaire and Hamel woods and the 11th Brigade with the attack on the village itself. During the advance the 15th Battalion faced Pear Trench, one of the strongest positions in front of Hamel.

Three tanks had been assigned to deal with it, but when these were late the Australians took matters into their own hands. They rushed the position and, although they suffered heavy casualties from machine-gun fire, managed to break into the trench. It was crammed with Germans and concealed machine-gun and trench mortar emplacements. Some of the Germans tried to surrender but others fought on. The Australians considered this high treachery and killed without mercy. An American observer later counted 40 dead Germans in the trench and adjoining sunken road.

During the attack on Pear Trench a German machine-gun was tearing into the Australians at close range. Private Harry Dalziel rushed towards it armed only with a revolver and killed the entire crew, except for one young German whom Dalziel spared because of his fighting spirit. During the bold rush Dalziel had his trigger finger shot away but he refused to be sent to the rear. He continued with the advance and was later helping to bring some ammunition forward when he was shot in the head. He survived and received the Victoria Cross.

In front of Vaire and Hamel woods a platoon of the 16th Battalion was caught in heavy machine-gun fire and lost many men, including the company commander. Lance Corporal Tom Axford realised that desperate action was required and rushed at the post, throwing bombs as he went. He dived into the German trench, killed 10 men with his rifle and bayonet and took six prisoners. He threw the German machine-guns out of the trench and called to the rest of his platoon to come on. Before the attack Axford had also played an important role in laying out tapes to mark the jumping off line for the attack. For his great work he received the Victoria Cross.

Through these and similar actions the Australians pushed on towards Hamel. Some German posts resisted strongly but were either rushed by the troops or ridden down by the tanks. The 11th Brigade entered Hamel and, escorted by several tanks, cleared the village and pushed into the fields beyond. The 42nd and 44th battalions advanced up a steep slope behind the village and captured a strong German headquarters position known as the Wolfsberg. With this secured, the Australians dug in with all their objectives taken. Monash had intended the battle to take 90 minutes. It took 93.

The Battle of Hamel was one of the turning points of the war. Even though it was a relatively small assault by Western Front standards, it demonstrated how tanks, infantry, artillery and aircraft should work together in an advance. The methods trialled at Hamel would be used in British advances for the rest of the war. The battle had cost the Australians about 1400 men and the Americans 176. But the Germans had lost more than 2000 killed or wounded, plus 1600 taken prisoner. Additionally the Australians captured 179 machine-guns and 32 trench mortars, plus a newly devised anti-tank gun, a .530-inch calibre monster that was basically an oversized rifle that fired from a bipod and required two men to operate it. The rifle is now on display at the Australian War Memorial in Canberra.

VILLERS-BRETONNEUX AND HAMEL TOUR

In 1998 the Australian Office of War Graves published a driving tour of the Villers-Bretonneux and Hamel battlefields, to complement the opening of the Australian Memorial Park at Hamel. The tour kit is no longer available, but the numbered signs marking key sites on the battlefield are still there. I have designed the tour in this book to follow the same route, with a few added extras. Allow four hours to complete it.

The tour begins at the Victoria School in Villers-Bretonneux [1]. The school is in a back street and can be tricky to find, but it is signposted near the *mairie* (town hall) in the centre of the village. The original Villers-Bretonneux school was destroyed during the war and rebuilt in 1927 using funds donated by Victorians, hence the 'Victoria' title. A plaque on the front wall of the school movingly records:

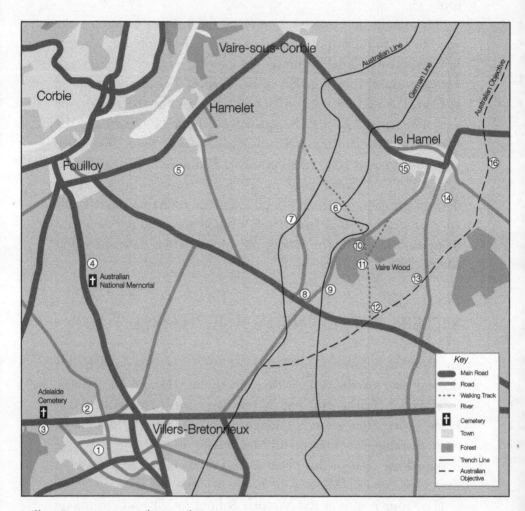

Villers-Bretonneux and Hamel

This school building is the gift of the school children of Victoria, Australia, to the children of Villers-Bretonneux as a proof of their love and good-will towards France. Twelve hundred Australian soldiers, the fathers and brothers of these children, gave their lives in the heroic recapture of this town from the invader on 24th April 1918 and are buried near this spot. May the memory of great sacrifices in a common cause keep France and Australia together forever in bonds of friendship and mutual esteem.

In the school playground a large sign entreats that the school children 'Do Not Forget Australia'. It is written in English, no doubt to stir the hearts of visiting Aussies, but the same words are displayed in French in the town hall. It is a sentiment the people of Villers-Bretonneux do not take lightly—Australian visitors will find themselves welcomed to the town with open arms.

An excellent museum on the upper floor of the school chronicles the fighting in the area in 1918, with a strong focus on Australian achievements. Opening hours vary but are signposted on the door. As is the French custom, the museum is usually closed on Mondays.

Leave the school and turn left on the D1029 towards Amiens. The second stop on the tour was the Red Chateau [2], a landmark well known to the Australian troops during the fighting. After the town was secured the chateau was used by Australian officers planning the great advance on 8 August and by war graves officials after the war. In spite of its significance to Australian visitors for more than 80 years, today's battlefield tourist won't get to see it: it was bulldozed in 2004 to make way for a supermarket.

Continue along the D1029 for a kilometre until you reach Adelaide Cemetery [3] on the right. It was begun in June 1918 and used by the Australian 2nd and 3rd divisions until the Allied advance in August. It contained 90 graves at the end of the war and was enlarged by the concentration of graves from around Villers-Bretonneux until it reached its present size of 955 burials. Of these, 522 are Australian. The most significant grave in the cemetery is located in Plot III, Row M, grave 13. In 1993 the body of an unknown Australian soldier was removed from this grave and reinterred in the Hall of Memory at the Australian War Memorial in Canberra. While the sentiment of the Unknown Soldier is noble, many commentators, myself included, saw the exhumation as a bit callous. This man had laid in peace next to his mates for 75 years before being dug up and shipped back to Australia. A better option would have been to wait for an unknown Australian soldier to be found on the battlefields. Since 1993, dozens of Australian unknown soldiers have been discovered in France.

Lieutenant Ronald Henderson MC (18th Battalion, died 09/04/1918, grave I.F.14) lies in Adelaide Cemetery next to his younger brother Hugh (35th Battalion, died 04/04/1918, grave I.F.15). Ronald Henderson was the intelligence officer for the 5th Brigade and won the Military Cross for courage under fire during the Battle of Menin Road in September 1917. He was killed by a shell during the German advance near Villers-Bretonneux. Hugh Henderson was a private in the 35th Battalion and was only 18 years old when he died of wounds, five days before his brother.

Adelaide Cemetery contains a large number of decorated Australians, including seven men who won the Distinguished Conduct Medal, three who won the Military Cross, one who won the Military Medal twice (MM & Bar), 10 who won the Military Medal, one who won the Croix de Guerre, and one who won both the Military Medal and the Croix de Guerre.

After leaving the cemetery you will need to drive back through Villers-Bretonneux, but the D1029 is a busy road and a U-turn in front of Adelaide Cemetery is not a good idea. Instead, continue in the direction of Amiens and turn around at the first intersection. Drive back through Villers-Bretonneux. Turn left onto the D23, signposted to the Australian National Memorial [4]. The memorial was unveiled in 1938 and is the main monument to Australian forces in France. Stone panels at the base of the tower record the names of 10 772 Australians who were killed in France and have no known grave. This includes men killed in every battle in France except Fromelles. The missing from this disastrous attack are recorded at VC Corner Cemetery (see **Fromelles**, pages 127–128).

The most highly decorated soldier recorded on the memorial is Private Thomas Cooke VC (8th Battalion, died 28/07/1916). Private Cooke won the Victoria Cross for manning a machine-gun under murderous fire at Pozières in 1916. He was killed beside the gun (see **Pozières**, page 159).

Another notable soldier remembered on the memorial is Major Percy Black DSO, DCM (16th Battalion, died 11/04/1917), a hero of the ill-fated First Battle of Bullecourt in April 1917. Black had won the Distinguished Conduct Medal at Gallipoli and the Distinguished Service Order at Pozières in 1916. He was killed trying to hack through the German wire entanglement at Bullecourt after the monumental failure of the supporting tanks (see **Bullecourt**, page 295).

Another hero of Bullecourt recorded here is Captain Gordon Maxfield MC (24th Battalion, died 03/05/1917), who held an advanced post beyond the German lines during the Second Battle. Maxfield's exposed position was overwhelmed by a German counterattack and he was never seen again (see **Bullecourt**, page 298).

A very highly decorated NCO remembered on the memorial is Sergeant James Lihou DCM & Bar, MM (13th Battalion, died 18/09/1918). Lihou was a Lewis gunner and won the DCM at Hamel in July 1918 and the Military Medal in August. During the attack at Le Verguier in September, Lihou and seven other men lost their way in thick fog and smoke and ended up advancing alone in front of the Australian line. They ran headlong into a German machine-gun post which opened fire on them. Lihou rushed forward and bombed the post, killing three men and capturing the rest. He and his small group pushed on and soon reached the objective, well ahead of the rest of the battalion. Several machine-guns opened fire and Lihou charged again, capturing a post and providing covering fire so his mates could reach the safety of a trench. He then led the men in a bombing raid along the trench until they spotted a distant machine-gun about to open fire on the battalion as it approached. Lihou jumped out of the trench and ran straight at the gun, but was caught by its fire and severely wounded. He died that evening and was awarded another DCM. Many men won the Victoria Cross for less.

One of the thousands of 'ordinary' soldiers commemorated here is Private Reg Crowley (34th Battalion, died 04/04/1918), who was killed during the fight for Villers-Bretonneux. According to reports, he was about to bayonet a German officer who threw his hands up and begged for mercy. Crowley hesitated and the German shot him dead with a revolver. Crowley had just turned 18 at the time of his death (he had enlisted at 16). His uncle Matthew had died of wounds at Gallipoli and his father, John, had been killed, aged 52, at Passchendaele in 1917 (see **Broodseinde Ridge**, page 98).

This is only a small selection of the men commemorated on this inspiring memorial. The sheer size of it is overwhelming. It contains the names of 10 times as many Australians as the largest Western Front cemetery. In fact, more than 10 per cent of all Australian soldiers killed in the entire 20th century are recorded here.

In front of the memorial are the 2141 graves that comprise Villers-Bretonneux Military Cemetery. The cemetery was made after the Armistice when graves were brought in from the Villers-Bretonneux battlefield and from small cemeteries in the area. Of these, 779 are Australian, mostly men killed in the fighting in this area in 1918. Forty-eight of them are unknown.

The most senior Australian buried here is Major William Craies of the 52nd Battalion, who died of wounds received at Villers-Bretonneux on Anzac Day, 1918 (grave X.E.9).

Some of the headstones in this cemetery have interesting inscriptions. The family of Sergeant Philip Ball MM (43rd Battalion, died 28/03/1918, grave III.E.1) were apparently still very bitter about the loss of their son in the early 1920s when the headstones were made. They chose the inscription: 'I died in the Great War to end all wars. Have I died in vain?' First World

War headstones almost always carry inscriptions celebrating the life of the lost soldier or the glory of his death. It is unusual to see such a cynical (and unfortunately prophetic) inscription.

Another unusual inscription is on the headstone of Lieutenant Hugh McColl (38th Battalion, died 12/08/1918, grave II.E.8). Unusually lengthy, it reads: 'James H. McColl, father, with wife and daughter visited this grave August 25th, 1923, bringing loving remembrances from family and friends in Australia.' The McColls must have been a prosperous family to afford the long voyage to Europe in 1923.

Bullet damage to some of the headstones in the cemetery, the Cross of Sacrifice and the memorial tower is from fighting here in 1940. French colonial troops had stationed a machine-gun in the tower in expectation of the German advance. When the Germans arrived they dealt with the improvised strongpoint by strafing the tower with a Messerschmitt fighter and driving a tank through the cemetery.

Leave the Australian National Memorial and continue along the D23 towards Fouilloy. On the outskirts of the village turn right towards Hamelet, which is signposted. The fields to your right as you approach Hamelet [5] were the assembly grounds for the 64 tanks that accompanied the Australians and Americans into battle. They set off from here towards Hamel on the night of 3 July, arriving in time to support the troops as they left their jumping-off lines at 3.10 am.

Continue along the D71 to Vaire-sous-Corbie and turn right towards Le Hamel. Take the right fork at the first intersection you reach. After a kilometre you will reach another fork marked by a crucifix in a clump of trees. Park here and walk up the unsealed sunken road (the left fork) for about 800 metres. This will bring you to the site of Pear Trench [6].

It was near here that Private Harry Dalziel won the Victoria Cross. Harry Dalziel had worked as a railway fireman before enlisting in 1915. He served with the 15th Battalion at Gallipoli and France, and came through unscathed until he was wounded in 1917. The head wound he received at Hamel smashed his skull and only skilled medical treatment in England kept him alive. He returned to Australia in 1919 and worked as a farmer and miner. He later served in the Guard of Honour at the Queensland Parliament and became a renowned songwriter. He returned to Hamel in 1956 but couldn't place the site of his VC action. 'The whole place was covered with greenery,' he said. 'It just didn't seem to be the same place.' Harry Dalziel died in 1965, aged 72. His Victoria Cross was the 1000th awarded since the award's inception in 1856.

Return to your car and take the right fork. Follow this sealed road to the top of the hill until you reach a sign indicating stop 7 on the tour. (Note the remains of First World War dugouts in the banks on both sides of the sunken road.) This is where the Australian front line crossed the road [7] and is also near the boundary between the 15th and 16th battalions. The 16th Battalion start line was about 100 metres into the field on your left. They had to cross 350 metres of ground to reach the German trenches. Their objective was Vaire and Hamel woods, now one large wood that you can see to the south-east.

As you drive between points 7 and 8 you are following the Australian front line, which ran parallel to the road about 350 metres away in the field to your right. Follow the road until the intersection with the D122 [8]. The start line for the 13th Battalion crossed the road near this point. The objective for the 13th lay on the far side of Vaire Wood.

Turn left onto the D122 and then immediately left again at the next intersection. The German front line ran along the right side of this road for 200 metres [9] and then crossed it, heading in front of Vaire Wood and past Kidney Trench before joining Pear Trench in the sunken road. The 16th Battalion crossed this section of road as they cleared Vaire and Hamel Woods during the attack.

Continue until you reach the intersection with a road on your left [10]. This is the other end of the sunken road you followed to reach Pear Trench. The sign indicating stop 10 occasionally goes missing and parking can be tight on this narrow road, so be sure to pull as far off the road as you can. Walk back along the sealed road until it bends to the left. Kidney Trench, where Lance Corporal Thomas Axford won the VC, was about 100 metres into the field on your right. This bend in the road was the site of a number of German dugouts, and the 16th Battalion captured scores of men as they advanced through this area. Many of them, as Monash had hoped, were wearing gas masks. 'This, of course,' wrote Colonel Edmund Drake-Brockman of the 16th Battalion, 'made the task of dealing with them very much easier.'

Tom Axford had worked at a brewery in Kalgoorlie until his enlistment in 1915. He joined the 16th Battalion in France and was shell-shocked in the horrific fighting at Pozières in August. He was wounded again in August 1917 and received the Military Medal early in 1918, a few months before his Victoria Cross. He returned to Australia after the war and worked for the Sunshine Harvester Company. He served in the Records Office during the Second World War and died in Perth in 1983, aged 89.

Walk back past your car and follow the track into the wood on your right. After about 200 metres you will reach the point where the long German communication trench known as Hun's Walk crossed the track. Traces of it can still be found in the wood, but it is difficult to locate in the thick undergrowth. Bush bashing on either side of the track will reveal numerous shell holes—a sign of the good work done by Australian artillery during the attack.

Continue through the wood to the far end. The open area to your right as you leave the wood was the site of one of the four resupply dumps used by the carrier tanks [11]. A little further on is an ammunition drop zone used by the Royal Flying Corps and Australian Flying Corps.

Return to your car and continue towards Le Hamel. At the first intersection turn sharply right and drive through the wood, past the drop zones you walked to earlier. Continue on this road until you reach a sign marking stop 12. You are now near the line of the final Australian objective [12], which ran from the T-junction just ahead, north-east past the village of Hamel, through the area that is now the Australian Memorial Park and on across the Somme River.

Continue along this road and turn left at the T-junction. After 500 metres turn left again, towards Le Hamel. After 750 metres you will reach the point where the Australian objective line crossed the road [13], and after a further 250 metres the point where Hun's Walk crossed the road. After another 400 metres you will reach the site of another tank resupply dump and air drop zone in the field on your left. On your right is Accroche Wood. German support trenches ran through here and parallel to the road all the way to the Australian Memorial Park on the hill above the village.

Continue towards Le Hamel and park on the right beside a small chapel [14]. The 43rd Battalion advanced past this point as they cleared the village, with the 42nd attacking on their left and capturing the German command post known as the Wolfsberg. Today the Wolfsberg is the site of the Australian Memorial Park.

Drive into the village, turn left at the French Memorial and park outside the church [15]. A Bastiaan plaque near the church outlines Australia's role in the battle. Hamel had been knocked around by the time the Australians arrived, but some of the buildings were only damaged and were patched up after the war.

Drive back along the street and turn left at the French memorial. After 50 metres, turn right to the Australian Memorial Park [16]. The park was a long time coming, having been built only in 1998 after decades of lobbying from the late Australian historian John Laffin. It was intended as Australia's equivalent of the Newfoundland Memorial Park on the Somme and the Canadian Memorial Park at Vimy Ridge, but the Hamel site has had a rather rockier start than either of those two great memorials.

Delays during construction led to concerns that the park would not be finished in time for its scheduled unveiling on the 80th anniversary of the battle. In the end it was completed in time, but it was beset by problems. The magnificent curved structure did not withstand the elements, and shed some of its granite tiles. Vandalism was also a problem. The memorial was replaced by a more robust version, slightly different to the original, in 2008. It is made from

Above left: Albert Jacka won Australia's first Victoria Cross of the war at Gallipoli, and the Military Cross at both Pozières and Bullecourt. Many considered his one-man offensive at Pozières warranted a second VC. (AWM A02868)

Above right: The Leaning Virgin on the battered Basilica of Albert was a famous landmark for much of the war. British superstition claimed that the day the statue fell, the war would end. (AWM E02068)

Right: The Newfoundland Memorial Park at Beaumont-Hamel is one of the few places on the Western Front where a complete British and German trench system can be explored.

French children tend to graves of Australians killed during the defence of
Villers-Bretonneux in April 1918. (AWM E05925)

Australian soldiers beside a damaged tank the day after their successful assault on Hamel, July
1918. This attack became a template for British assaults for the rest of the war. Note the French flag
fluttering from the roof of the house in the background – it was placed there by an Australian officer
during the thick of the fighting to herald the liberation of the town. (AWM E03843)

Left: General Sir John Monash. When he assumed command of the AIF in May 1918, the five Australian divisions came together under an Australian commander for the first time in the war. (AWM E02350)

Below: King George V arrives at Bertangles Chateau to knight General John Monash, commander of the AIF, 12 August 1918. The guns lining the driveway were trophies captured from the Germans in the decisive Australian advance four days earlier. (AWM E03895)

The Amiens Gun was a rail-mounted German artillery piece that could hurl a 28-cm shell more than 25 kilometres. It was captured by Australian infantry at Harbonnières in August 1918 – the barrel is now on display at the Australian War Memorial in Canberra. (AWM A00006)

A lieutenant of the 29th Battalion addresses his platoon shortly before the assault on Harbonnières on 8 August 1918, the 'black day' of the German Army. Four of the men pictured would not survive the war, including Sergeant William O'Brien (first on the left) who was killed the day after the photo was taken. This photo gives an excellent impression of the Australian soldier in full battle dress. (AWM E02790)

Left: The original Australian 2nd Division Memorial at Mont St Quentin. German troops who occupied the area in the Second World War objected to the imagery and destroyed the statue. A less controversial sculpture of a Digger in full kit replaced it in 1971. (AWM P02205)

Below: Australian troops from the 54th Battalion man a forward post in Péronne, the day after the town was captured by the 5th Division, 2 September 1918. (AWM E03183)

The First World War was a conflict that belonged to the artillery – more than two-thirds of all casualties were caused by shellfire. Here Australian gunners fire an 18-pounder gun in support of the attack on Bullecourt in May 1917. Note the pile of expended shell cases in the background.
(AWM E00600)

The memorial in Bullecourt commemorates the Australian and British divisions who fought there in April and May 1917. The incorporation of an original First World War slouch hat, coated in bronze, makes this memorial unique in the world.

Left: The Digger statue at the Australian Memorial Park at Bullecourt. The memorial was built on the site of two German trenches captured by Australian troops in April and May 1917.

Below: Troops from the 45th Battalion snipe at fleeing Germans during the advance to the Hindenburg Line near Le Verguier, 18 September 1918. (AWM E03260)

Captain Harry Fletcher, Lieutenant Lindley Scales and Captain Austin Mahony of the 24th Battalion. Fletcher and Mahony were mates from rural Victoria who enlisted together in 1915, served at Gallipoli and won the Military Cross. Both were killed during the attack on Montbrehain on 5 October 1918, the AIF's last day of fighting in the First World War. (AWM P03668)

NOUS N'OUBLIONS PAS
L'AUSTRALIE
1918 – 1998
WE DO NOT FORGET
AUSTRALIA

A plaque on the town hall of Bellenglise demonstrates the affection for Australia that still lingers in many villages in northern France. The town was liberated by the 4th Division during its final action of the war.

green granite and features a large Australian rising sun badge, and a quote from French prime minister Georges Clemenceau.

The remains of trenches, originally constructed by the Germans and fortified by the Australians, snake through the park. More trench lines can be found in the scrub behind the memorial, but this is not part of the park.

The views from the Australian Memorial Park are impressive. To the south-west, the tower at the Australian National Memorial at Villers-Bretonneux is obvious. To the east is the ground captured so brilliantly by the Australians in their advance on 8 August, the 'black day' of the German Army. From where you are standing, the Australians launched the Advance to Victory that ended the First World War.

OTHER SITES OF INTEREST

Red Baron Crash Site, Vaux-sur-Somme

On the morning of 21 April 1918 Australian troops were consolidating their positions on a hill near the village of Vaux-sur-Somme when they were greeted by an astonishing sight. A British Sopwith Camel aircraft came screaming over their lines at tree-top height, hotly pursued by the unmistakable bright red Fokker triplane piloted by the most famous fighter ace of the war. Baron Manfred von Richthofen, the 'Red Baron', had already been credited with 80 kills, and this morning was fixated on increasing the tally. In the melee that followed, Australian machine-gunners opened fire from several positions, the British plane jinked and dived and a second British aircraft piloted by Canadian Captain Roy Brown closed on the Red Baron and fired a long burst. The Fokker briefly stuttered, before ploughing into a field beside the Bray-Corbie Road. Australian troops rushed to the plane, where they found the Red Baron fatally wounded. He died almost immediately and nearly as quickly Aussie souvenir hunters had stripped the wreckage of the plane. From the outset the identity of the man who had shot down the Red Baron was shrouded in controversy. Captain Brown was officially credited with the kill, but later research suggests that the shot that killed Richthofen was most likely fired by an Australian gunner. Richthofen was buried by Australian troops with full military honours in the cemetery at Bertangles, near the Australian headquarters (see page 220). After the war, his body was moved to Fricourt German Cemetery (see page 181) and now lies in Germany.

Directions
The Red Baron crash site is marked by an information panel beside the Bray-Corbie Road, north of Vaux-sur-Somme. To find the site, leave Vaux on the C14 heading towards Méricourt. After a kilometre, turn left onto the D1 and continue past a brickworks on your right. Shortly after, the information panel marking the crash site will be seen on the left, on the edge of the field next to a wood. After visiting the site, return along the D1 and visit the Australian 3rd Division Memorial on the heights above Sailly-le-Sec (see below).

3rd Division Memorial, Sailly-le-Sec

After the war the 3rd Division considered several locations for its memorial. The frontrunner was Messines Ridge, where in 1917 the division participated in an attack considered the finest of the war to date, but it eventually settled on the heights above the Somme River near Sailly-le-Sec, an area where the division had been prominent in 1918. In the fields around the memorial the division carried out some of the most successful acts of 'peaceful penetration', a bold new type of raiding. During this time a German prisoner told his captors, 'You bloody Australians, when you are in the line you keep us on pins and needles; we never know when you are coming over.'

The 3rd Division became so good at harassing the Germans that they captured prisoners three nights out of every five, and a good-natured competitiveness built up between the battalions.

On the night of 17 April 1918, Lieutenant Harry Wiles of the 41st Battalion was so intent on catching a German prisoner alive that he chased one down and tackled him, even though his pistol was out of ammunition and the German was fully armed. For his impetuous bravery he received the Distinguished Service Order.

The 3rd Division Memorial is the standard design, a stone obelisk with a plaque recording the division's battle honours. They are listed as: Messines 1917, The Windmill, 3rd Battle of Ypres, Broodseinde, Passchendaele, Morlancourt, Treux, Hamel, 8th August, Proyart, Suzanne, Bray-sur-Somme, Curlu, Cléry-sur-Somme, Bouchavesnes, Roisel and Hindenburg Line.

Some British commentators have wrongly assumed that the 3rd Division Memorial was sited here to commemorate the division's part in the successful attacks of August 1918, and that it is therefore in the wrong place. While it is true that this was a British area of operation in August, the location for the memorial was chosen because of the 3rd Division's work here in April, when this was a wholly Australian sector.

Directions
The 3rd Division Memorial is eight kilometres north-east of Villers-Bretonneux and two kilometres north of Sailly-le-Sec, at the intersection of the D1 and the Sailly–Méricourt road. It stands alone amid rolling fields and does not receive as many Australian visitors as it should.

Allonville

This unassuming village five kilometres north-east of Amiens went from obscurity to infamy in one night. In May 1918, the Germans captured a handful of Australians who revealed under interrogation that a divisional headquarters was based at Allonville. On the night of 30 May the Germans blasted the place with high explosive shells. Two companies of the 14th Battalion were sleeping in two large barns in the centre of town; the third or fourth shell hit one of the barns and brought the roof and part of the walls down on the sleeping men. Thirteen men were killed and 56 wounded, making this the most costly single shellburst in AIF history. Another shell exploded in the neighbouring barn, killing five and wounding 12. The shelling was a disaster for the 14th, but the heroic rescue work that came after was a credit to the battalion. One wounded man, his legs blown off above the knees, refused to be carried out, telling the stretcher bearers, 'I'm all right—get the badly wounded boys out.' Another Aussie who had lost an arm refused to let his mates help him light his cigarette. 'I'll have to learn to do it with one hand,' he said, 'may as well begin now!'

Directions

Allonville is in the heart of the British rear area, 14 kilometres north-west of Villers-Bretonneux. Records don't indicate exactly where in the village the barns were located but the late Australian historian John Laffin placed them 150 metres from the centre of the village at the chateau farm. Ask a local for directions to the farm and the rebuilt barns.

Amiens

Amiens is the largest city in the area and the capital of Picardy. During the war it was a vital rail junction and one of the most important Allied support bases on the Western Front. British troops knew it well as a rest area, hospital base, supply dump and training centre.

The most famous building in the city is the magnificent Gothic cathedral, larger than Notre Dame in Paris. Thousands of Australian soldiers visited the cathedral while on leave and spent their army pay in shops around the cathedral square. The cathedral was reinforced with sandbags in an effort to protect it from shelling but this proved unnecessary—the building came through the war practically unscathed. It is still the prime tourist attraction. A plaque in the nave commemorates the Australian defence of the town.

The Allied advance in August 1918 is sometimes referred to as the Battle of Amiens. While this title roughly defines the sector of the Western Front where the advance took place, the fighting actually occurred eastwards from the British front line at Hamel, and has no direct connection with Amiens.

Modern Amiens is an attractive city, particularly in the centre near the cathedral, though today it would be unrecognisable to the Diggers who spent so much time walking its streets. As the largest centre in this part of the battlefields, it has good transport connections, accommodation and shopping but its size makes it a less convenient base for battlefield visitors than some of the smaller towns to the east, such as Albert and Corbie. Spend an hour in your car negotiating Amiens' somewhat complex traffic system and you will see why the smaller centres are a better option.

Bertangles

This Somme village is notable in Australian military history as the headquarters of the Australian Corps during its highly successful 1918 operations.

Bertangles Chateau, built between 1730 and 1734 as a hunting lodge (the intricate ironwork about the main gate is a veritable catalogue of hunting scenes), was occupied by General Sir William Birdwood and his successor, Lieutenant General John Monash. Monash had taken command of the corps in May 1918—the first time in the war the five Australian divisions were under the command of an Australian officer. (Until the end of 1917 they had simply operated as independent divisions in the British Army and had not always fought alongside each other.)

At Bertangles Chateau Monash planned the outstanding Australian attack on Hamel, as well as the vital Australian role in the Allied Advance to Victory which began in August 1918. On 12 August Monash was knighted by King George V on the front steps of the chateau, an event attended by hundreds of Australian troops, with captured German guns lining the driveway.

After the successes of August the Australian headquarters moved from Bertangles, in order to keep in contact with the front line which was advancing steadily eastwards. An Australian airfield next to the chateau remained in use until the end of the war.

On 21 April 1918, German fighter ace Baron Manfred von Richthofen, the 'Red Baron', was shot down and killed by an Australian machine-gun crew near Vaux (see page 215). His body was brought to Bertangles and was buried with full military honours the next day at the local cemetery. A party from the Australian Flying Corps fired a gun salute as his coffin was laid to rest. Richthofen's body was removed from Bertangles cemetery after the war, but the empty grave can still be seen.

Directions
Bertangles is 10 kilometres north of Amiens, just off the N25. The chateau is north of the village on the D97. The cemetery is north-west of the village on the Rue du Moulin.

Corbie

This picturesque Somme village was well known to the Diggers, particularly during the fighting in this area in March–August 1918. Even though Corbie was well within range of German guns and was badly knocked around by shellfire, it remained an important railhead and rest area for much of 1918.

After the Australians spearheaded the British advance in early August, Corbie was used by the 1st, 4th and 5th divisions as a rest area, and army field hospitals, post offices and storage dumps were set up in the village. Thousands of Australians spent time recuperating on the banks of the Somme where it lazily curled past the town, and after the war many of them remembered Corbie as their favourite French village.

Directions
Corbie is five kilometres north of Villers-Bretonneux. Its most prominent building is the dramatic town hall in the centre of the village. Many other buildings carry scars from German shelling. Since 2003 a handful of good B&Bs have sprung up in and around Corbie, making it a good base for Australian visitors to the Somme.

CEMETERIES NEAR VILLERS-BRETONNEUX AND HAMEL

Adelaide Cemetery, Villers-Bretonneux: see Villers-Bretonneux and Hamel tour (page 205).

Bonnay Communal Cemetery Extension

Bonnay is a village north of Corbie. Its cemetery was started on 1 April 1918 and was mostly used to bury men killed during the defence and recapture of Villers-Bretonneux that month. It was also used briefly during the great Allied advance in August.

The most notable feature of this cemetery is the Cross of Sacrifice, the only one on the Western Front dedicated by an Australian prime minister. In 1921 Billy Hughes, the long-serving politician best remembered for his controversial conscription drives in 1916 and 1917, toured the former battlefields and was asked to dedicate a Great Cross in one of the thousands of newly constructed Commonwealth war cemeteries. Bonnay was a good choice: of 106 burials, 75 are Australian.

The most senior Australian buried here is Captain Albert Halstead MC of the 42nd Battalion. On enlistment, Halstead had been appointed to the 31st Battalion but he fell ill while the battalion was still training in Brisbane and was reassigned to the 42nd Battalion some months later. He won the Military Cross at Broodseinde Ridge in October 1917 for coolly leading his company under fire and for single-handedly capturing seven Germans from a pillbox. He was killed by a shell at Shrapnel Gully near Sailly-le-Sec on 16 April 1918 (grave A.19).

Directions
Bonnay is nine kilometres north of Villers-Bretonneux and can be reached via Corbie. Drive through Bonnay and the cemetery is signposted to the left on the edge of the village.

Daours Communal Cemetery Extension

The village of Daours was the site of several British casualty clearing stations in the lead-up to the Battle of the Somme. The extension to the communal cemetery was started in June 1916 and used until the front line advanced at the end of November. The Germans captured Daours in their Spring Offensive of 1918 and the cemetery was used again when the British pushed the Germans back in August. For much of August it was practically in the front line. It was closed in September 1918. Today 459 of the 1231 graves are Australian, and all but two are identified. Nearly every Australian here was killed in 1918. The handful of 1916 casualties died at Pozières.

A notable officer buried here is Captain Frederick Woods of the 16th Battalion, who was killed at Hamel on 4 July 1918. Woods was the company commander whose death inspired Lance Corporal Tom Axford to single-handedly attack a German machine-gun post, an act that earned Axford the Victoria Cross (grave III.D.37).

Four Australians buried here won the Distinguished Conduct Medal: Lance Corporal Edward Gibson (59th Battalion, died 18/08/1918, grave V.B.3), Corporal Charles Higginbotham (5th Battalion, died 23/08/1918, grave VI.A.34), Private William Irwin (33rd Battalion, died 01/09/1918, grave VIII.B.32) and Company Sergeant Major Henry Todd (9th Battalion, died 11/08/1918, grave IV.A.8). Gibson won his medal at Harbonnières in August 1918 for capturing a post containing 25 men and three machine-guns. Higginbotham won his at Lihons, also in August 1918, for attacking a machine-gun post and killing six Germans. Private Irwin won the DCM at Road Wood in the same advance that earned George Cartwright the VC (see **Bouchavesnes-Bergen**, pages 261–262). Irwin single-handedly captured three machine-gun posts before being wounded. He died of his wounds the next day. Todd was an outstanding NCO who was awarded the DCM for consistently strong leadership during the tough fighting in the Ypres Salient in September and October 1917. He was killed during the opening days of the Advance to Victory.

Directions

Daours is six kilometres north-west of Villers-Bretonneux. From Villers-Bretonneux, drive north on the D23, past the Australian Memorial, to Fouilloy. Turn left at the T-junction in the village onto the D1 and follow it to Daours. The cemetery is north of Daours on the D115, in the direction of Pont-Noyelles.

Heilly Station Cemetery, Méricourt-l'Abbé

Méricourt-l'Abbé is a village near Albert and close to the Somme battlefields of 1916. Heilly Station Cemetery was begun by British units in the lead-up to the Somme fighting in 1916 and was used to bury men who died of wounds at a nearby casualty clearing station. Between March and May 1918 the cemetery was used almost exclusively by the AIF. Today, 401 of the cemetery's 2890 graves are Australian. Eighty-three Germans also lie here.

Even though Heilly Station was a hospital cemetery, it was located close to the front line in 1916 and 1918 and was in the thick of the action for much of those two years. Consequently, many of the burials were hastily made and many men were buried together in single graves. Today these are marked by multiple names on a single headstone. As this leaves no room for regimental badges to be included, 117 badges have been carved onto the cloister wall on the north side of the cemetery.

The most prominent Australian grave in this cemetery belongs to Lance Corporal John O'Neill of the 13th Battalion, who has a private grave marker in addition to his regulation Commonwealth War Graves headstone. The private marker consists of a marble column topped by a cross on a granite base, and it stands out in stark contrast to the uniform military headstones that make up the rest of the cemetery. It was erected by Lance Corporal O'Neill's comrades after he was accidentally killed during grenade training in 1917, and is almost unique on the Western Front. When constructing the cemeteries the CWGC steadfastly refused all requests for the erection of private grave markers. Lance-Corporal O'Neill's mates beat the system by erecting the headstone soon after the Armistice, so that by the time the CWGC came to construct the permanent cemetery in the 1920s, the grave marker was already in place. The decision to leave it there was remarkably compassionate (grave V.F.29).

The most senior Australian soldier killed in France also lies in Heilly Station. He is Brigadier General Duncan Glasfurd, commanding officer of the 12th Brigade. A Scot by birth, Glasfurd had attended Sandhurst Military College in the UK and, before the war, was the commanding officer of the famous Scottish regiment the Argyll and Sutherland Highlanders. On 12 November 1916, Glasfurd was inspecting a forward position near Flers when he was wounded by a shell. His men carried him for 10 hours on a stretcher to get him to medical attention but he could not be saved (grave V.A.17).

Another beloved senior officer buried here is Lieutenant Colonel Owen Howell-Price DSO, MC, the commander of the 3rd Battalion and one of three officer brothers to be killed on the Western Front. His brother Philip is remembered on the Menin Gate in Belgium and his brother Richmond is buried in Vraucourt Copse Cemetery near Vaulx-Vraucourt. Owen was a distinguished officer, a hero of both Gallipoli and Pozières, and led his men bravely during the tough fight at Flers in November 1916. He was wounded by machine gun fire, and his distressed men carried him for hours to the casualty clearing station at Heilly in the hope that he could be saved (grave V.A.14).

Directions
Méricourt-l'Abbé is about 10 kilometres north-east of Villers-Bretonneux. From Villers-Bretonneux, drive through Corbie and head for Méricourt-l'Abbé. The cemetery is on the right of the road after three kilometres.

Laviéville Communal Cemetery

This is one of the smallest cemeteries on the Western Front. There are only eight graves here and six of them are Australian. They were all killed between 23 and 25 April 1918. Three belonged to the 22nd Battalion, one was from the 21st Battalion and the other two were signallers. Why these men were buried here and not in one of the larger cemeteries in the area is a mystery. The two non-Australian burials are a gunner from the Royal Field Artillery killed in 1917 and, interestingly, a British corporal from the Royal Horse Guards killed during the advance through this area in 1944.

The only officer buried here is Lieutenant Arthur Barker of the 22nd Battalion. Barker served at Gallipoli where, during a Turkish attack, he was blown out of a trench by a grenade. He escaped with a cut hand. On 24 April 1918, he was leading a patrol that ran into a group of Germans in no man's land. During a brief fight he was fatally wounded (grave 3).

Lance Corporal Tom Part of the 2nd Division Signal Company was a Gallipoli veteran and one of four brothers to serve during the war. He was killed by a shell near Laviéville on Anzac Day, 1918. Sapper William Newbigging of the Signal Detail was killed in the same blast and lies beside him (graves 6 and 7).

Directions

Laviéville is 16 kilometres north-east of Villers-Bretonneux and west of Albert on the D119. The cemetery is north of the village on the road to Hénencourt.

Querrieu British Cemetery

This cemetery was started by the Australian 3rd Division during the German Spring Offensive in March 1918. It was used by them and British units until the end of August. The cemetery now contains 187 Commonwealth graves, of which 84 are Australian, all identified. Most of these men were killed between March and June 1918.

The most decorated Australian buried here is Sergeant Alexander Wilson DCM, MM & Bar of the 10th Field Ambulance, who also has the distinction of being the most highly decorated member of any Australian ambulance unit. He received his Distinguished

Conduct Medal at Passchendaele in October 1917, for organising the evacuation of wounded from the front line area. Wilson had won both of his Military Medals in 1917 for courageously leading stretcher bearer teams. He was killed along with several other men in a German bombing raid on Australian support positions at Allonville on 20 May 1918 (grave A.22).

Also buried here is Driver John Farrell of the 9th Battery, 3rd Field Artillery, who died of wounds aged 20 on 28 May 1918 (grave A.45). Unusually, Driver Farrell has a private grave marker next to his regulation military headstone, identical to Lance-Corporal John O'Neill's private headstone in Heilly Station Cemetery (see page 223).

The most notable non-Australian grave here belongs to Lieutenant Colonel Christopher Bushell VC, DSO, of the British Royal West Surrey Regiment. Bushell won the Victoria Cross for rallying troops in the face of a ferocious German attack in April 1918. He was killed on the first day of the Advance to Victory, 8 August 1918 (grave E.6).

Directions

Querrieu is 10 kilometres north-west of Villers-Bretonneux. Follow the directions for Daours Communal Cemetery Extension (page 223) and continue on the D115 to Pont-Noyelles. Turn left in that village for Querrieu then in Querrieu turn left towards Bussy-lès-Daours. The cemetery is 500 metres along this road on the left.

Villers-Bretonneux Military Cemetery and Australian National Memorial: see Villers-Bretonneux and Hamel tour (page 205).

9

Village Battles
of 1918

The Somme region had still not recovered from the devastating battles of 1916 when fighting returned in 1918. The Germans swept through the area in their Spring Offensive of March and April, and then were pushed back even more quickly during the Allied advance that followed. Australian troops played a major role during this period and left their mark on villages throughout the area, either defending them or recapturing them. From August to November 1918, the AIF became a fighting machine, arguably the best force in the war. This is ably illustrated by the fact that between March and October 1918 the Australians captured more than a fifth of the total ground taken by British forces and more than a quarter of the prisoners, even though the AIF made up less than 10 per cent of the British forces. The Somme towns captured by the AIF in 1918 were the scenes of some of the greatest achievements in Australian military history.

This is a compact area and a half-day driving tour can take in most of the villages listed, plus the local cemeteries in the area where many Australians lie.

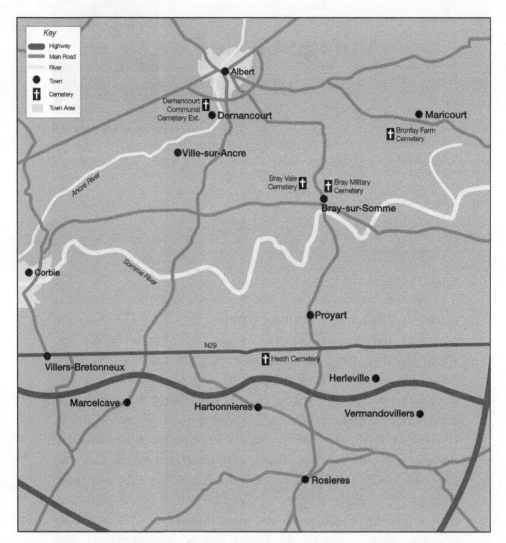

Village battles of 1918

Bray-sur-Somme

The Germans captured Bray during their advance in March 1918 and used it as a forward base. On 5 April Corporal Charles Lane and Private Rinhold Ruschpler of the 24th Machine Gun Company became the first Australians to enter the village since its capture, although they did so as prisoners. They had been manning a machine-gun in the quarry at Dernancourt during a major German attack (see pages 231–232) and were captured without firing a shot. After a harrowing trip to the German rear, which involved dodging shells from both sides, Lane and Ruschpler were locked in a prison cage at Bray. Bray was well within range of British guns and a shell blew a hole in the barbed wire fence. The two Australians seized their opportunity to escape and spent a day dodging German patrols before eventually making a run for it from the German front line, across no man's land and into the Australian trenches.

On 22 August the 33rd, 34th, 35th and 3rd Pioneer battalions were tasked with capturing Bray as part of a larger British advance. The village was in a steep valley shaped like a trident and the battle planners decided it was impossible to adequately cover the troops with artillery fire. The plan therefore called for the troops to pass north of Bray and then swing around and capture it from the rear. The Australians began well but soon became disorganised in the tangles of the valley and were pinned down by heavy fire from Bray. The attempt to capture the village was temporarily abandoned.

The next night the 37th and 40th battalions, again supported by the 3rd Pioneers, took up the fight. Instead of trying to encircle the village they hit it head-on, protected by a creeping barrage. They made good ground and advanced through the town, clearing German machine-gun posts as they went. By the morning of 24 August the town had been captured, along with 186 prisoners and several rail cars loaded with German stores. The attack had cost the Australians 74 casualties, with only three men killed.

Directions
Bray is eight kilometres south-east of Albert on the D329.

Bray Military Cemetery was started during the Somme fighting in 1916 by British field ambulance units. As the front line advanced in 1917 a major dressing station was established in Bray and the cemetery was greatly enlarged. Further graves were added after the war, expanding the cemetery to its current size of 874 burials. Of these, 31 are Australian, including two who could not be identified. Most of these men were killed in and around the town in August 1918.

Pause at the grave of Gunner Albert Derrez. He had immigrated to Australia from France several years before the outbreak of war and was married to an Australian girl. During the war he served in the Australian Field Artillery and was accidentally killed after being run over by an ammunition wagon on 28 August 1918 (grave I.BI.9).

Bray Military Cemetery is reached by following the road to Maricourt. It is on the left of the road shortly after leaving Bray.

Bray Vale Military Cemetery was started in August 1918 and contained just 25 graves at the end of the war. It was enlarged after the Armistice, particularly by the addition of a large number of unidentified bodies from the 1916 fighting near Thiepval and Courcelette, 11 kilometres away. Today it contains 279 graves, the majority of which are unidentified. Seventeen of these are Australian, of which four are unidentified.

Buried here is Captain Harold Dench of the 38th Battalion, who was killed by a sniper on 24 August while helping to organise the British front line on the left of his battalion (grave II.C.10).

Nearby is another decorated officer, Lieutenant Alfred Farleigh MC, who won the Military Cross during a trench raid in March 1918. He was killed by a shell during the 33rd Battalion's advance on 22 August.

Also buried here is Sergeant John Burke MM of the 38th Battalion, who won the Military Medal during the horrific fighting at Passchendaele in October 1917. Burke was killed when a British aeroplane mistakenly bombed an Australian post on 24 August

1918. Several other men killed in the same incident are buried nearby (grave I.B.3).

Bray Vale Military Cemetery is two kilometres from Bray on the right of the road to Méaulte.

Bronfay Farm Military Cemetery was started by the French in 1914 and then used by British troops when they occupied this sector between 1915 and 1917. It was briefly used again during the advance past Bray in 1918, and then enlarged after the Armistice. Today it contains 537 graves, of which 15 are Australian. One of these is unidentified.

An Australian officer buried here died under unusual circumstances. Lieutenant Arthur Bills was leading a platoon of the 50th Battalion during the advance west of Bray in the early hours of 11 August 1918. According to the *Official History*, as the men were digging in a voice called out from the darkness ahead, 'Who are you?' When the men replied that they were Australians, the stranger called back, 'All right, come on Australia' and let fly with a burst from a machine-gun. Thinking that they were being shot at by a confused Englishman or American, the Australians cursed loudly and yelled out to the stranger that they were the 50th Battalion, AIF. Once more the reply came, 'Come on Australia', followed by another burst of machine-gun fire. Realising they were facing a German, the Australians threw a bomb and charged in his direction, but the lone gunner had scarpered, leaving his machine-gun behind. The Australians returned to their positions and found that several men had been hit, including Lieutenant Bills, who was dead (grave II.G.47).

Bronfay Farm still exists and is three kilometres north-east of Bray on the road to Maricourt. The cemetery is opposite the farm.

Dernancourt—Stan McDougall VC

For most of the war this Somme village was only known to the Australians as a stopping point on the railway line to Albert. But during the German Spring Offensive in March and April 1918, that all changed. The Germans had attacked on a wide front and captured Albert. The British defenders had been overwhelmed and were stretched thin. On 28 March the Australian 47th and 48th battalions were attached to the British 35th Division and tasked with defending a 2.5 kilometre line behind the bank of the railway from Dernancourt to the outskirts of Albert. The Australian line was so thin that in many places there were wide gaps that couldn't be defended and were simply watched over by a sentry. Lewis gun crews had been placed in forward positions, at a cutting in the rail line and a railway bridge further south. During the night Sergeant Stan McDougall of the 47th Battalion was keeping watch near the crossing when he heard the sound of bayonet scabbards slapping against the thighs of advancing troops. Peering into the mist he saw Germans advancing along the whole length of line towards the embankment. McDougall gathered some men and began lining them out along the railway embankment when a German bomb exploded next to a Lewis gun team, wounding several men but not damaging the gun. McDougall, who later admitted he had always wanted to get his hands on a Lewis gun, picked up the weapon and ran forward along the bank. He ran headlong into two German machine-gun teams who were crossing the bank, and sprayed fire at them like water from a hose, killing seven before carrying on. McDougall then went on a rampage among the attacking Germans, rushing towards them and hosing them with his Lewis gun, badly blistering his hand on the red hot barrel casing in the process. At the sight of McDougall's heroics, the rest of the Australian defenders stood up and began blasting at the Germans, who were soon killed or captured. McDougall had single-handedly stopped the strongest wave of the German attack and was awarded the VC.

Before the war Stan McDougall was an outstanding horseman and crack shot. Eight days after his VC-winning exploit he won a Military Medal, again at Dernancourt, after skilfully operating a machine-gun during a major German attack. He had enlisted in 1915 and served with the 47th Battalion, before joining the 48th two months after winning the VC. After the war he returned to

Tasmania, working for the Tasmanian Forestry Department and performing several acts of heroism during a number of bushfires. He died in Hobart in 1968, aged 77.

The German attack at Dernancourt on 28 March had consisted of a relatively small force with little chance of success. On 5 April the Germans got serious. They heavily shelled the railway embankment and Australian rear areas, and assembled a large infantry force for an attack. Just before 7 am the Germans moved forward and after a vicious fight managed to penetrate some Australian posts on the railway embankment. The Australian 12th and 13th brigades were holding their own until the Germans brought up field guns and blasted the Australian positions from short range. The Australians fell back, pursued up a steep slope by several waves of German infantry. A group of Australian machine-gunners in a quarry had not even set up their guns when they were overwhelmed by the Germans and captured. The Australians fell back to their support positions and fought tooth and nail to stop the Germans from penetrating the line. The situation was desperate but eventually the Australians succeeded in stopping the German advance.

Later in the day the Australians launched one of their finest counterattacks of the war. Advancing from their support lines, they came under a storm of machine-gun fire but pushed on, wresting their old trench lines from the Germans. On the right they recaptured the railway embankment, but the rest of the line could only advance halfway down the slope. They eventually dug in about 1250 metres from their original line. Against the sheer numbers of Germans facing them, they could do no more.

After the war it was revealed that the two Australian brigades had faced three German divisions: they were outnumbered almost five to one. The German attack at Dernancourt was the largest faced by the AIF during the war and cost them almost 1300 casualties. The Germans lost about the same. Though the Germans had gained some ground, the battle left the Australians feeling supremely confident and the Germans bitterly disappointed. The Australian *Official History* notes that soon after the fight a German correspondent wrote: 'The Australians and Canadians are much the best troops that the English have.'

Directions

Dernancourt is three kilometres south-west of Albert (it is signposted near the centre of town). Drive through the village, follow the road under the railway line and park in the carpark on the left. You are now at the base of the slope up which the Germans attacked on both 28 March and 5 April. Stan McDougall's heroics took place for about a kilometre east along the railway embankment. To your left is Dernancourt Communal Cemetery and Extension, the final resting place of 428 Diggers, many of whom where killed in the Dernancourt fighting. By following the road past the cemetery you are walking in the footsteps of German troops who attacked on 5 April, and you will soon reach the quarry where the Australian machine-gunners were captured. Stand next to the quarry and look back down the slope towards Dernancourt. Imagine the Australians defending against overwhelming odds as the Germans swarmed over the embankment and up this slope towards them.

Harbonnières

The village of Harbonnières was in the southern sector of the great Australian advance on 8 August 1918. On this day Australian and Canadian troops spearheaded the greatest single day's advance by British troops in the war—a day that was dubbed '*der Schwarze Tag*' (the Black Day) of the German Army and led to their capitulation three months later.

The fight at Harbonnières was typical of actions taking place all along the front on 8 August, and involved close cooperation between infantry, artillery, tanks and aircraft. Even the cavalry, accustomed to being shot to pieces in earlier battles, played a limited role on 8 August.

Harbonnières was captured by the 59th and 57th battalions, who were frustrated by German posts in the village and relied on tanks to clear a number of strongpoints. East of the village the

British cavalry and Australian infantry found themselves facing a massive artillery gun mounted on a railway carriage and blasting huge shells at Amiens, more than 25 kilometres away. With the help of a British plane they captured the gun and dozens of prisoners. The barrel of the 'Amiens Gun' is now on display in the forecourt of the Australian War Memorial in Canberra.

Heath Cemetery, Harbonnières was constructed after the Armistice and is one of the most important cemeteries for Australians in the area. It sits in the middle of open country, hence the name, and is a testament to Australian achievement and sacrifice during the pivotal advance in August 1918. All the surrounding countryside was captured by Australians during that advance, and many of the men killed in this great action now lie here.

This large cemetery contains 1860 burials and could well be named 'Heath Australian Cemetery', as 984 of the graves here are Australian. Surprisingly, most of these men are identified, with only 74 unknowns. The skill and bravery of the Australian soldier is well documented in Heath Cemetery by the number of decorated men who lie here. Two won the Victoria Cross, three won the Distinguished Service Order (the highest award for officers after the VC), one officer won the Military Cross twice (MC & Bar) and three won the Military Cross. Heath Cemetery also demonstrates how much of Australia's fighting skill came from the ordinary ranks: two men buried here won both the Distinguished Conduct Medal (the highest award for non-officers after the VC) and the Military Medal, an extraordinary 10 men won the Distinguished Conduct Medal, one man won the Military Medal twice (MM & Bar) and 44 won the Military Medal.

The two most notable Australians buried in Heath Cemetery are Lieutenant Alfred Gaby of the 28th Battalion and Private Robert Beatham of the 8th Battalion, who won the Victoria Cross within a day of each other during the opening phase of the Australian advance in August 1918.

Lieutenant Gaby earned his VC east of Villers-Bretonneux on 8 August by single-handedly attacking a German strongpoint and capturing 50 men and four machine-guns. He was shot through the head by a sniper three days later (grave V.E.14—see page 238).

Private Beatham was awarded the VC at Rosières on 9 August for capturing four German machine-guns and 10 men, and killing another 10. Two days later he attacked another machine-gun post but was caught by its fire and killed (grave VII.J.13—see page 242).

Two senior officers buried in Heath Cemetery were commanders of sister battalions and good mates. Lieutenant Colonel John Milne DSO was the hands-on leader of the 36th Battalion and commanded with great skill during the defence of Villers-Bretonneux in April 1918. He had won the Distinguished Service Order at Messines in 1917 and was killed when a shell struck his headquarters on 12 April 1918 (grave VIII.J.19).

Lieutenant Colonel Ernest Knox-Knight was the commanding officer of the 37th Battalion and according to the Official History, thought that his battalion's objectives for the attack in early August 1918 were so demanding that there would be a 'train load of VCs waiting for us when we get back'. Colonel Knox-Knight didn't win a VC but his reservations about the coming fight were well founded: he was killed by a shell near Proyart on 10 August (grave V.B.15).

Two other notable soldiers buried in Heath Cemetery are Corporal Harry Thorpe MM and Private Bill Rawlings MM. Both were Aboriginal men from country Victoria and were mates. Corporal Thorpe was a natural soldier and served with the 7th Battalion through the storm of fire at Pozières in 1916 and the dogged struggle for Broodseinde Ridge in 1917. While leading his men to mop up pillboxes during this fight he displayed such a disregard for danger that he was recommended for the DCM. He didn't receive it, but was awarded the Military Medal instead. He was wounded in the advance on Lihons on 9 August 1918 and died later that day (grave IV.J.15).

Private Rawlings received his Military Medal for leading a team of bombers along a German trench during the advance near Morlancourt on 28 and 29 July 1918. As the first man in line, Rawlings was responsible for dealing with any Germans the party ran into, and killed several with his bayonet during the advance. His recommendation describes his 'irresistible dash and courage'. During the advance near Vauvillers on 9 August he was killed by machine-gun fire (grave I.A.19). Corporal Thorpe and Private Rawlings well represented the hundreds of Aboriginal men who served during the war, in defiance of rules forbidding their enlistment.

Directions

Harbonnières is 17 kilometres south of Albert and 10 kilometres south-east of Villers-Breonneux.

Heath Cemetery is two kilometres north of Harbonnières on the major D1029 road.

Herleville—William Joynt VC

The village of Herleville was captured by British troops on 23 August 1918 during the Allied advance. North of the village the Australian 1st Division attacked on a wide front, with the 6th Battalion advancing towards Herleville and Plateau Woods. Fire from the woods was merciless and the 6th was badly knocked around before it had reached its objective. The 8th Battalion was in support and was also coming under heavy fire. When a company commander was killed, Lieutenant William Joynt took charge. He scouted forward and found the 6th Battalion taking cover under heavy fire from Plateau Wood. Joynt and another lieutenant from the 8th, Les McGinn, assembled a small group of men and advanced on the wood, capturing a German field hospital and 50 men in the process. As they approached the wood, Joynt and McGinn went forward alone and captured a group of 20 Germans. Joynt then led his men in a rush on the wood and the German defenders broke. The Australians captured the entire wood plus another dozen prisoners.

'They were a very scared crew,' Joynt later wrote in his diary. 'One of them was on the point of howling and looked so miserable—McGinn noticing him and putting his face close to the Hun made a noise . . . "Boo!" The Hun collapsed completely . . .'

Joynt continued to lead the company until wounded by a shell a few days later. He was awarded the Victoria Cross.

William Joynt had had two years of military experience when he joined the 8th Battalion in France in early 1916. He was wounded during a trench raid in September and was Mentioned in Despatches for his good work. The wound he received at the time of winning his VC in 1918 kept him out of the rest of the war and he returned to Australia in 1920. After the war he was a founder of the Legacy organisation and commanded the training centre at Puckapunyal during the Second World War. He was the last surviving Australian VC winner from the First World War, dying in 1986 aged 97.

Directions
Herleville is 17 kilometres south-east of Albert. Herleville and Plateau Woods have now merged into one large wood, the Bois de Rainecourt, located about two kilometres north-west of Herleville. Joynt, McGinn and their small group of men attacked the wood from west to east, just north of the D1029 road from Amiens.

Marcelcave—Alfred Gaby VC

During the advance on 8 August, the village of Marcelcave was a Canadian objective. Further north, the Australian 7th Brigade was tasked with capturing the heavily defended Card Copse and made good ground until held up by machine-guns entrenched behind barbed wire. With casualties mounting it seemed the only option was to charge the position, until Lieutenant Alfred Gaby of the 28th Battalion found a gap in the wire and ran along the German parapet, emptying his revolver into the German garrison. Within minutes he had captured the strongpoint, along with 50 Germans and four machine-guns. Gaby reorganised his men and led them to the objective east of the copse.

Three days later Gaby was in the thick of the action again, leading his platoon in a fresh attack. The Germans began pouring fire into the Australian positions but Gaby stood up and walked undaunted among the Australian posts, encouraging his men to quickly consolidate. Before he could take cover, he was shot and killed by a sniper. Gaby was awarded a posthumous Victoria Cross.

Alfred Gaby was part of a large family from Scottsdale in Tasmania. He was no stranger to military service, having spent three years in the Launceston Regiment before the war and hearing war stories from two of his older brothers who had fought in the Boer War. He enlisted in 1916 and was gassed in Belgium in 1917. He now lies in Heath Cemetery, Harbonnières (see page 212).

Directions

Marcelcave is 18 kilometres south-west of Albert and four kilometres south-east of Villers-Bretonneux. Card Copse no longer exists but was located north-west of Marcelcave on the road to Fouilloy, on the left of the road just before the French Cemetery.

Maricourt—Sid Gordon VC

Maricourt was captured by the British 58th Division on the night of 26–27 August, while several Australian battalions advanced on the Somme Valley further south. During this advance the 41st Battalion was held up by heavy machine-gun fire from Fargny Wood until a Tasmanian lance corporal, Sid Gordon, rushed forward and attacked the post, killing one German and capturing 11. For the rest of the night he continued to single-handedly attack trenches and machine-guns wherever they held up the battalion, ending the advance with the astonishing tally of two officers, 61 men and six machine-guns captured. For his night's work he received the Victoria Cross.

Sid Gordon enlisted in September 1915 and served with the 41st Battalion from its inception. Three weeks before he received the VC he had been awarded the Military Medal at Hamel. He was wounded at Mont St Quentin in September 1918 and returned to Australia the following January. He worked as a dairy farmer in Queensland, where he died in 1963, aged 72. In 2006, Sid Gordon's VC sold at auction for $400 000.

Directions

Maricourt is 10 kilometres south-east of Albert. To reach Fargny Wood, drive east from Maricourt on the D938 and turn right after 2.5 kilometres to Curlu. Drive through the village and turn right at the T-junction. Fargny Wood is 500 metres along this road on the right. Gordon moved from west to east through the wood.

Proyart—Percy Statton VC

The village of Proyart was attacked by the 10th Brigade on the night of 10 August, in an effort to capitalise on the previous two days' advances. The plan called for the brigade to advance along the road south of the village and then swing north as far as the Somme River, encircling Proyart and linking up with other Australian brigades to the north. Six tanks would support the infantry during the advance. The 10th Brigade's commanders had reservations about the plan, and their doubts turned out to be well founded. The tanks were spotted by the Germans as soon as they began to advance and a German plane flew low over the road, destroying a tank with a bomb and sending the infantry to ground. German machine-guns and anti-tank rifles opened a murderous fire on the attacking troops from three directions and the leading battalion was cut to pieces. Lieutenant Colonel Ernest Knox-Knight, commander of the 37th Battalion, was killed when an anti-tank shell exploded beside him (see **Heath Cemetery**, page 236) and most of the tank crews were wounded. In disarray, the tanks turned and began to retreat but an Australian officer, revolver in hand, threatened to shoot the crews if they did not stay put.

Eventually the Australians realised that any chance of success was lost and withdrew. The leading battalions and tank crews had lost a quarter of their men between them.

The following day the 11th Brigade attacked to the north and captured Méricourt, forcing the Germans to abandon Proyart. Patrols from the 10th Brigade occupied the village on 12 August.

During this advance the 37th Battalion was pinned down by machine-gun fire as it moved east of the village. A sergeant of the 40th Battalion, Percy Statton, ordered two Lewis guns to fire on the German position to support the 37th. After watching a dozen men from the 37th cut down as they rushed the German machine-guns Statton took matters into his own hands. With three comrades he crept closer to the German guns, then dashed across 70 metres of open ground and shot the first German crew with his revolver. He then attacked the second crew until his revolver was empty, killing the last German with the man's own bayonet after a hand-to-hand fight. Statton charged towards two other gun positions and the Germans fled, abandoning their machine-guns. While consolidating the position, two of the men who had attacked with Statton were hit by machine-gun fire. One was killed and the other wounded. Statton's final act of gallantry for the day was to brave heavy fire to retrieve the body of his dead comrade and drag the wounded man to safety. Almost single-handedly, Statton had captured a position that was the objective for an entire battalion. Not surprisingly, he was awarded the Victoria Cross. When the award was announced to his battalion, the diarist noted that:

> Although there was much gladness among us all, among the older members of the unit there was an under-current of sadness, when the occasion naturally sent our thoughts back a year to the other gallant Victoria Cross winner, Sgt. Lewis McGee, who never came back out of the sodden waste of mud and shell-holes in front of Passchendaele. [see page 97]

Percy Statton enlisted in the 40th Battalion in 1916 and won the Military Medal at Messines in 1917. He was wounded late that year and gassed at Villers-Bretonneux in 1918, only eight weeks before his VC-winning escapade. Statton returned to Tasmania in 1920 and worked in a timber mill, rescuing several families during a series of bushfires in 1934. He died in Hobart in 1959, aged 69.

Directions

Proyart is 13 kilometres south-east of Albert. The attack on 10 August took place along the D1029 road south of the village, from the intersection with the D41, eastwards to the intersection with the D236. It was near this crossroads (known as Avenue Cross to the troops) that the tanks and leading battalion came under the heaviest fire and Colonel Knox-Knight was killed. Percy Statton won his VC in the fields immediately east of the modern village.

Rosières—Robert Beatham VC

The Australians attacked near Rosières on 9 August, following the astonishing gains they had made the previous day. The main advance was made by Canadian and French forces near Lihons, with Australian units providing the northern flank. The 8th Battalion advanced under heavy fire and suffered severe casualties from German field artillery that blasted away from a hill directly ahead. Older members of the battalion later said the advance across the grassy plain at Rosières reminded them of the battalion's famous attack at Krithia in Gallipoli in May 1915. If this were so, it didn't speak well of the conditions at Rosières: the Krithia attack had been a massacre that wiped out half the battalion.

Fortunately for the 8th, things went more smoothly at Rosières but it was still a tough fight. Much of the success of the day's advance was due to one man, Private Robert Beatham, who ran forward with Corporal William Nottingham and attacked four German machine-gun posts. The two men overcame all four posts, killing 10 men and capturing 10 more, plus the machine-guns. Corporal Nottingham then turned two of the guns on the Germans ahead, enabling the 8th to advance under covering fire.

The fight continued for two more days and eventually the 8th was near its assigned objective. During this final advance the battalion was held up by another machine-gun post and Beatham charged again, even though he had already been wounded. He was caught by the gun's fire and killed instantly. Beatham was awarded a posthumous Victoria Cross. Corporal Nottingham received the Distinguished Conduct Medal.

Robert Beatham had migrated as a teenager from England to Australia. He enlisted in the AIF in 1915 and arrived with the 8th Battalion in France in early 1916. He was wounded at Pozières in August and was hit again in October 1917. He now lies in Heath Cemetery, Harbonnières (see page 235). In 1999 his VC was sold at auction to a private buyer for $178 000.

The advance near Lihons and Rosières eventually succeeded, but the attack had been very poorly planned, especially compared to the outstanding advance made on 8 August, and casualties were alarmingly high. A senior British commander, Major General Archibald Montgomery, described the attack during a lecture in 1929, saying, 'Everyone was so busy congratulating everyone else on their share in the victory that valuable time was lost in preparing for an advance next day.' Charles Bean, always a master of understatement, wrote in the *Official History* that the operations on 9 August 'will probably furnish a classic example of how not to follow up a great attack'.

Directions
Rosières is 21 kilometres south of Albert. To find the area captured by the 8th Battalion, drive to Harbonnières and leave the town on the D337, heading east towards Lihons. After about two kilometres you will reach the intersection with the D329, heading right to Rosières. Do not turn here but continue along the D337. Pass Rosières British Cemetery on your left and turn right at the next crossroads towards Rosières (the Route d'Herleville). Follow this road for 300 metres and then stop. On 9 August 1918, the 8th Battalion was spread out from this point south to the railway line. Over the next two days they advanced from here and helped capture Lihons, to the east. It was near this point that Beatham and Nottingham captured the machine-gun posts that earned them their bravery awards.

Vermandovillers—Lawrence McCarthy VC

During the First World War 66 Australians won the Victoria Cross, but none of them did more to earn it than Lawrence McCarthy. His moment of glory came during the ceaseless Allied advance in August 1918. On the 23rd, British and Australian units were ordered to advance on a wide front from Chuignolles in the north to Herleville in the south. On the right flank the Australian 16th Battalion had a short advance on the outskirts of a copse known as Madame Wood. Their most important task was to provide support to the 16th Lancashire Fusiliers, who would capture a German trench on their left. The Fusiliers' left companies began well and captured their allotted trenches, but the right companies struggled from the outset and could hardly move under a hail of machine-gun fire. A bombing party from the Australian 16th Battalion was supposed to join up with the Fusiliers in the German trench, but when the Australians arrived it was still firmly in the hands of the Germans. The trench was blocked by a solid earth barricade and the Australians and Germans began lobbing grenades at each other across the obstacle. As the company's grenade supplies ran out, the commander, Lieutenant Lawrence McCarthy, decided the only solution was to charge.

Taking one man, Sergeant Fred Robbins, McCarthy scrambled over the barricade, shot a sentry on the other side and attacked a machine-gun post further on. McCarthy shot the crew and pushed on, rounding a bend to find himself standing behind a German officer issuing orders to a group of men. McCarthy shot the officer, and the men around him bolted into a narrow trench. McCarthy and Robbins showered them with bombs until a bloody handkerchief was waved in surrender. Forty Germans emerged as prisoners; 15 more lay dead.

By this stage the rest of McCarthy's company had caught up with him, and the Lancashire Fusiliers could be seen in the trench up ahead. The Australians handed over to them 650 metres of German trench, almost the entire objective set for the battalion. McCarthy had captured 450 metres of this on his own, an act that Charles Bean considered, along with Albert Jacka's actions at Pozières, 'perhaps the most effective feat of individual fighting in the history of the AIF'. McCarthy was more humble. When later asked about the difficulty of capturing so many Germans he replied, 'Oh, it was nothing. I jumped into a trench and got the fright of my life when I found it full of Fritzies. They took my revolver from me then kameraded [surrendered], and all I had to do was to head them back to the Aussie lines.'

Lawrence McCarthy was from Western Australian and enlisted late in 1914. Except for short absences due to illness, he served with the 16th Battalion for the entire war, from Gallipoli to France. He returned to Australia in 1919 and lived in Western Australia and Victoria. He died in Melbourne in 1975, aged 83. His only child, Lawrence Jr, was killed in action in the Solomon Islands in 1945.

Directions

Vermandovillers is 20 kilometres south-east of Albert. To reach Madame Wood, drive to Herleville and leave that village heading south on the Rosières road. After a few hundred metres turn left at the road signposted Vermandovillers. Turn right at the next intersection after 300 metres. Madame Wood (today known as Bois St-Médard) is on your right one kilometre along this road. Courtine Trench, which was captured by McCarthy, ran roughly north–south, 350 metres into the field opposite Madame Wood. A farm track almost opposite the wood leads into the field. Follow it for about 300 metres to reach the site of the trench.

Ville-sur-Ancre—William Ruthven VC

Ville-sur-Ancre is a village lying on the slopes of the Ancre River. The Germans captured it during their Spring Offensive in 1918 and by May of that year had fortified it to protect the higher ground to the south and east.

Fresh from their successful actions in March and April, the Australians began a program of 'nibbling' attacks, designed to capture strategically important patches of ground and frustrate the Germans at every opportunity. Their attentions turned to Ville on 19 May.

The plan called for an attack north and south of the town, with the 22nd Battalion providing the bulk of the attacking force. The 18th Battalion and parts of the 21st and 24th would also provide troops. The main advance would be across the high ground south of the town and the most important objectives were two sunken roads codenamed Big and Little Caterpillar.

The Australians set off in the dark under cover of an artillery barrage and soon came under heavy fire from machine-guns and rifles. The right-hand company of the 22nd Battalion was slowly making ground when the commander, Captain William Hunter, was wounded. The troops were momentarily shaken but Sergeant William Ruthven took control of the situation. With a few sharp orders he organised the men and led them towards Big Caterpillar, the company objective. As they neared the sunken road a machine-gun opened fire from only 30 metres away. Ruthven ran forward and threw a bomb which exploded near the gun. He then dived among the crew, bayoneted one man and captured the gun. German soldiers began to emerge from dugouts in the road bank and Ruthven charged at them, shooting two and forcing the rest to surrender. His men arrived to find him holding six Germans prisoner and two German machine-guns smoking on their mounts.

Ruthven's assault cleared the way for the right of the advance and the Australians were able to secure their objectives. The battle had lasted less than 30 minutes. Ruthven received the Victoria Cross.

'Rusty' Ruthven was working in a timber mill when he enlisted in 1915. He arrived at Gallipoli a month before the evacuation and travelled with the 22nd Battalion to France in early 1916. He was wounded in April 1916 and again on 11 June 1918. He returned to Australia in August 1918 and was discharged in December. After the war he worked as a farmer in rural Victoria before moving to Melbourne and becoming a councillor on the Collingwood Council. He served in various garrison units during the Second World War and was elected to the Victorian Legislative Assembly in 1945. After years of public service he retired in 1961. William Ruthven died in Melbourne in 1970, aged 76.

Directions
Ville-sur-Ancre is five kilometres south-west of Albert. To find the site of William Ruthven's VC action, drive south from the crossroads in the centre of Ville: this road is Big Caterpillar. The 22nd Battalion captured Big Caterpillar on a front stretching from just south of the village to the sharp left-hand bend over a kilometre away. Ruthven's company attacked on the right of the 22nd, slightly north of the bend: this is where Ruthven won the VC. Little Caterpillar, an earlier objective in the advance, is the sunken road immediately west of Big Caterpillar.

Villers-Bretonneux—Wally Brown VC and Albert Borella VC

Villers-Bretonneux is best remembered as the site of the Australian actions in April 1918 that halted the German Spring Offensive in front of Amiens. But the town was also the scene of stiff fighting later in the year, as the Allies moved their line forward in preparation for the big push that began on 8 August.

In July 1918, soon after the successful advance at Hamel, the Australians had the opportunity to refine a tactic that would come to be called 'peaceful penetration'. The term is a misnomer. Peaceful penetration basically involved lightning fast raiding, usually carried out in daylight, which took the Germans completely by surprise and overwhelmed a trench or post before its occupants knew what was happening. The raids were rarely 'peaceful' and usually involved a good number of German casualties, including many prisoners. Many of the Australians were enthusiastic raiders, driven by an innate love of adventure and a desperate desire to collect souvenirs from the German trenches. Peaceful penetration never failed to make the Germans edgy. A captured German battalion order stated:

Forces confronting us consist of Australians who are very warlike, clever and daring. They understand the art of crawling through high crops in order to capture our advanced posts. The enemy is also adept in conceiving and putting into execution important patrolling operations. The enemy infantry has daily proved themselves to be audacious.

The day of 6 July 1918 was a quiet one on the front near Villers-Bretonneux. Both sides were resting in the warmth of the summer sun and recovering from their exertions at Hamel. Sergeant Wally Brown of the 20th Battalion was chatting with a Victorian sergeant who told him that his men had come under intermittent fire from German snipers they couldn't locate. With nothing better to do, Brown decided to 'have a pot at them' himself and walked along a deserted German trench until a shot rang out from a mound about 60 metres away. Guessing that this was the source of the trouble, Brown dropped his rifle, picked up two Mills bombs and ran towards the mound. He threw a bomb to cover his advance and then charged. The mound stood over a small, kidney-shaped trench, with a dugout entrance at the far end and an unmanned machine-gun mounted on the parapet. Brown sprang into the trench and raced towards the dugout entrance, just as a German emerged from it. Brown felled him with a blow to the jaw and then sensed movement behind him. Another dugout opened at the opposite end of the trench and a group of Germans had just appeared from it. Realising that if he threw his last bomb he would be at their mercy, Brown held the bomb high and menaced the group. They promptly surrendered. Brown marched the party back to the Australian lines and handed them over to the intelligence staff. He had captured an officer and 12 men of the 137th Infantry Regiment. News of Brown's one-man raid spread across the entire Australian Corps and he was awarded the Victoria Cross.

Walter Brown was a grocer from Hobart who was working in Sydney at the time of his enlistment in 1915. He was so keen to see action that he joined the Light Horse, then transferred to the Camel Corps. While serving with this unit in Egypt he received permission to travel to Cairo under the pretence that he had lost his false teeth. As soon as he arrived there he asked to be transferred to the infantry and was assigned to the 20th Battalion.

Brown was a born soldier, the type of man 'certain to distinguish himself in this way, if he survived', according to the *Official History*. He won the Distinguished Conduct Medal during the Battle of Passchendaele in 1917 for taking charge of his section after his sergeant had been hit. After the battle he refused the offer of leave in England so that he could search for the body of a mate. He found it and built a wooden cross to place over the grave. Brown was wounded in late 1917 and again a month after his VC action.

After the war Brown lived in country New South Wales until the outbreak of the Second World War. He enlisted in 1940, giving his year of birth as 1900 even though he had been born more than 15 years earlier. He became a gunner with the 2/15th Field Regiment and sailed with the 8th Division for Malaya. On 15 February 1942, the division was surrounded by the Japanese and negotiating terms for surrender. Wally Brown grabbed some grenades, muttered 'No surrender for me' and set off towards the enemy position. He was never seen again.

Ten days after Wally Brown made his famous raid, the 25th and 26th battalions were ordered to straighten the Allied line east of Villers-Bretonneux by advancing near Monument Farm. Lieutenant Albert Borella was leading a platoon of the 26th Battalion south of a railway line when a German machine-gun opened up close ahead. Realising urgent action was needed, Borella rushed forward alone, shot the two German gunners and captured the gun. Once this obstacle had been cleared, Borella led his men forward to the objective, a road that crossed the railway line, but it had been so knocked around by shellfire that he passed over it without recognising it. Before long Borella's group stumbled across Jaffa Trench, a heavily manned section of the German line well beyond the objective. The Germans in the trench were no doubt surprised to find themselves facing a ragged group of Aussies— even more so when they were showered with bombs and Lewis gun fire. They dashed into nearby dugouts but were persuaded to surrender after a few bombs had been rolled down the stairs. Borella sent 30 Germans back as prisoners.

Borella's men consolidated and later helped to break up two German counterattacks. For his courage and leadership over the two days of the advance, Borella was awarded the Victoria Cross.

Albert Borella was born in rural Victoria and had worked as a farmer and fireman before the war. He enlisted in 1915 and served with the 26th Battalion at Gallipoli. He sailed with the battalion to France in 1916 and was wounded there in July. Early in 1917 he was Mentioned in Despatches and awarded the Military Medal for his consistent bravery and devotion to duty. Soon after his VC action in 1918 he was evacuated sick from the front. His health didn't recover before the end of the war and he returned to Australia late in 1918. After the war he worked as a farmer in rural Victoria. During the Second World War he served in a number of garrisons and prisoner-of-war units. Albert Borella died in Albury, New South Wales, in 1968, aged 86.

Directions

The two actions that earned Wally Brown and Albert Borella the VC occurred less than two kilometres apart. Wally Brown's raid took place about two kilometres east of Villers-Bretonneux, along the busy D1029 road. Leave Villers-Bretonneux on the D1029 heading towards Lamotte-Warfusée and drive past the intersection with the road to Marcelcave on your right. Another 350 metres further on, a farm track enters the field on the left. Park wherever it is safe and follow this track into the field. This track roughly follows the line of the trench captured by Brown in his VC-winning raid. The two dugouts were located at the far end of the trench, about 100 metres along the track.

Albert Borella successfully led a platoon of the 26th Battalion on the far side of the railway line, south of the site of Brown's raid. Leave Villers-Bretonneux heading east on the D1029 and drive for 500 metres until you reach a large intersection, signposted 'Le Hamel' to the left. Turn right, ignoring the road that heads back into Villers-Bretonneux, and carry on until the road curves sharply right after 750 metres. Park before the curve and follow a farm track straight ahead into the field. After about 600 metres a bridge crosses a railway line. Cross to the other side of the line. Albert Borella attacked along this side of the railway line heading west to east. This section of track was the battalion's objective that had been so damaged by artillery fire it was unrecognisable. The machine-gun post captured by Borella was slightly west of the track. Follow the track for another 150 metres to reach the point where Jaffa Trench crossed the track. The trench ran north–south through this field and crossed the railway line about 70 metres east of the rail bridge.

10

Battle of Mont St Quentin, 31 August– 2 September 1918

August 1918 was the beginning of the end of the First World War. The Allied Advance to Victory began on 8 August and steamrolled the Germans from the ground they had captured in their Spring Offensive, through the old battlefields of the Somme and out into the open country beyond. Mobility had returned to the fighting for the first time since the opening months of the war and, within 100 days, the Germans were driven from France and Belgium and the war was over. Australian and Canadian troops, long regarded as some of the best fighters in the Allied forces, were given the chance to prove it. They spearheaded the British assault and caused a blow to the German Army that proved fatal.

By the end of August the Australians had pushed the Germans back to the River Somme and their commander, General John Monash, was raising the stakes. Buoyed by his success to date and keen to push his men to the limit, Monash planned a wholly-Australian offensive on the toughest obstacle in the area: Mont St Quentin, a brooding hill 1.5 kilometres north of the town of Péronne. The capture of the mount would render Péronne untenable for the Germans and force them back to their final defensive position, the Hindenburg Line. It's clear Monash was trying to prove to the British High Command that his Australians were unstoppable. It was a big gamble. Thanks to the temerity of the Australian troops, it was a gamble Monash would win, and win well.

The 2nd Division was selected for the assault, with the 17th Battalion tasked with capturing the village on the summit, the 20th Battalion attacking on its left and the 19th providing support on the right. Parts of the 5th Division would launch a noisy attack on Péronne to divert the Germans' attention from the main attack on the mount. By this stage the Australian battalions were desperately short of men. Volunteers from Australia had dried up and two conscription referendums had been defeated, meaning there were simply not enough new men joining the ranks to replace those killed and wounded. At full strength a battalion had more than 1000 men; the ideal number for an attack was at least 800, with 600 considered the bare minimum. For this attack the 20th Battalion had 320 men and the 17th not many more. Facing them were crack troops of the German Second Army who had been ordered to defend Mont St Quentin to the last man. The Australians had quite a task on their hands.

At 5 am on 31 August a furious barrage rained down on Mont St Quentin and the troops set off. They came under fire from the outset. Mont St Quentin was a fortress and the Germans had catacombed its approaches with trenches, protected by wire entanglements and machine-gun nests. In spite of the obstacles the Australians rushed up the slope, 'yelling like bushrangers', according to the unit history. The Germans were completely surprised by the noise and speed of the attack. Many of them surrendered and simply passed through the advancing Australians with their hands raised, walking unescorted back to the Australian line. The Australians reached the summit and, for the time being, the attack was over, the German defenders so completely overwhelmed that the Australians simply walked to their objectives. During a pause, members of the 20th Battalion sat in the open next to a German trench, smoking and chatting, unperturbed by a German machine-gun higher on the mount that sprayed bursts of inaccurate fire over their heads. General Rawlinson, commander of the British Fourth Army, had just got out of bed when he learned the extraordinary news that the Australians had captured Mont St Quentin. It was not quite time to open the champagne, however.

The Australians on the mount soon found they would be hard pressed to hold the ground so easily won. A crash of artillery fire signalled the beginning of the German counterattack and the Australians were soon fighting tooth and nail to hold their ground. Gradually the Germans penetrated the Australian posts and began pushing them back. The Australians finally held the Germans about halfway down the slope and called for reinforcements. These were sent up, with instructions to launch a new attack at dawn the next morning to recapture the mount.

At dawn on 1 September the 21st, 23rd and 24th battalions renewed the attack. The 23rd had been held up as it approached the start line, blocked by a German machine-gun post behind a barbed wire barricade. A young runner, Private Bob Mactier, was sent forward to investigate. He scaled the barrier, bombed the crew and threw the machine-gun out of the trench. The rest of his battalion hurried forward and found that Mactier had pushed on, capturing a group of 20 Germans. Up ahead he encountered another barrier protected by a machine-gun, and killed the crew. Spotting another German machine-gun position, he scrambled out of the trench to attack it but was caught by machine-gun fire and killed. Single-handedly he had cleared the approach for the 23rd Battalion. They arrived at their start position on time and played a vital role in the upcoming attack. Bob Mactier was posthumously awarded the VC, one of the hardest earned of the war.

For several hours the Australians fought their way towards the summit of the mount. Lieutenant Edgar Towner of the 7th Machine Gun Company was wounded when a bullet passed under his helmet and grazed his scalp, but he still succeeded in setting up two of his machine-guns and a captured German gun in a sunken road on the summit. These guns disrupted the Germans and broke up several counterattacks. The Australians were finding the advance tough going and decided the only course of action was to call in an artillery strike on the German positions and attack again in the afternoon.

At 1.30 pm, after the heavy bombardment had pummelled the German defenders, the battalions pushed on under light fire until they passed through a small wood on the summit. On the far side, extremely heavy machine-gun fire erupted from a huge crater and German stick bombs began raining down on the attacking troops. The Australians went to ground and the attack stalled until Sergeant Alby Lowerson of the 21st Battalion rallied a small group of men who charged the crater. Three men were killed and Lowerson was hit in the thigh, but the survivors dived among the German defenders and captured or killed the garrison. Thirty prisoners and 12 machine-guns were taken. For his bravery during this assault and throughout the preceding day, Lowerson was awarded the VC. Lieutenant Towner, who had provided covering fire for this assault and was instrumental in the success of the attack throughout the day, received the same award.

The loss of the crater broke the back of the German resistance and the remaining defenders fled. Mont St Quentin had been captured, an action that General Rawlinson considered the 'finest single feat of the war'. Soon after, following a successful Australian attack on Péronne, the Germans abandoned the town and fell back to the Hindenburg Line, their last line of defence on the Western Front. The attacks on Mont St Quentin and Péronne cost the Australians just over 3000 men, but capped off an astonishingly successful month. Between 8 August and 2 September, the Australians captured more than 14 500 prisoners and 750 guns.

MONT ST QUENTIN TOUR

The attack on Mont St Quentin was considered by many veterans as the greatest Australian action of the First World War. In three days, a handful of desperately under-strength battalions captured one of the most formidable defensive positions on the Western Front and took 2600 prisoners. This tour visits important battlefield sites (including the scene of two Victoria Cross actions) as well as the 2nd Division Memorial, one of the most impressive Australian monuments on the Western Front. The tour is easy to walk, with few uphill sections, and can be completed in about two hours. The tour area is small and includes some farm tracks and woods, so there is no driving option.

Mont St Quentin is close to the major Somme town of Péronne. Leave Péronne by the D1017 in the direction of Bapaume. You will reach the village of Mont St Quentin after about a kilometre's drive. Drive through the village until you reach the 2nd Division Memorial **[1]** on your left. The memorial is set back from the road with houses on either side. It is signposted, but appears unexpectedly if you are driving at speed. Park nearby and visit the memorial—you will leave your car here for the rest of the tour.

The striking 2nd Division Memorial, unveiled on 30 August 1925, the seventh anniversary of the battle, depicts a larger than life Australian soldier in full kit standing astride a stone plinth. The Digger faces north-east, the direction of the Australian advance. Bas-relief panels on four sides of the plinth depict infantry and artillery units during the battle, and contain a dedication to the 2nd Division and the unit's battle honours. The Digger is unique among the Australian divisional memorials—the other four are identical stone obelisks—but it used to be even more distinctive. The original sculpture unveiled in 1925 depicted an Australian soldier bayoneting a German eagle sprawled at his feet. Not surprisingly, German soldiers who occupied the area in the Second World War were affronted by this imagery and removed (and presumably destroyed) the sculpture. The plinth was left intact and in 1971 the current Digger with his imposing stance was added. The extensive battle honours listed on the memorial are: Pozières, Mouquet Farm (misspelled as 'Moquet' Farm), Flers, Malt Trench, Lagnicourt, Bullecourt, Menin Road, Broodseinde,

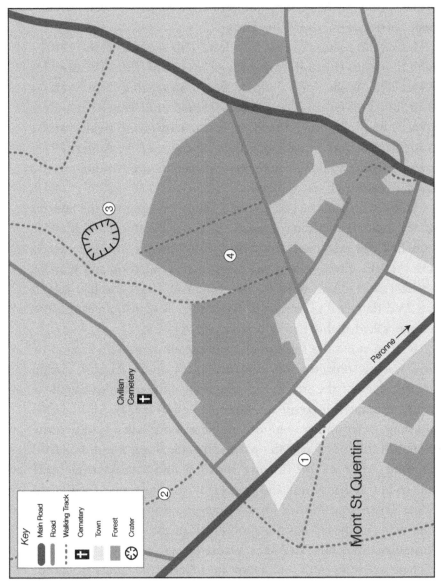

Key

Main Road
Road
Walking Track
Cemetery
Town
Forest
Crater

Civilian
Cemetery

Peronne →

Mont St Quentin

Passchendaele, Ville-sur-Ancre, Morlancourt, Hamel, Villers-
Bretonneux, Herleville, Herbecourt, Biaches, Mont St Quentin,
Beaurevoir Line and Montbrehain. Behind the memorial is a
bronze plaque by Melbourne sculptor Ross Bastiaan which provides
basic information about the battle.

Leave the memorial and turn left. This section of the D1017
which passes through the village is called the Avenue des
Australiens. Walk along the road until you reach a farm track on
your left. Follow this for a short distance until you have a clear
view of the fields down the slope. It was across these fields that the
Australians attacked in the half light of dawn on 31 August 1918,
moving from the distant road, past where you are standing, to the
Digger memorial and beyond.

Directly in front of you, about a kilometre distant at the bottom
of the hill, was Florina Trench. It was here that Bob Mactier
launched the one-man assault that cost him his life and earned
him the VC. Bob Mactier was born in rural Victoria and worked
on his father's farm until his enlistment in 1917. He had joined
the 23rd Battalion in France in November, less than a year before
he was killed in his heroic action. He was 28.

Return along the farm track to the main road. This section of
road was the objective for the Australians on 31 August, during
the first stage of the attack. From here the 17th and 20th battalions
vainly attempted to resist the German counterattacks on the first
morning, before they were driven back about halfway down the
slope behind you. Cross the road and walk along the minor road
opposite. After a short distance turn left into a sunken track [2]
and follow it for about 150 metres. It was here that Lieutenant
Edgar Towner positioned his machine-gun teams on 1 September.
This was an exposed position, about 150 metres ahead of the main
Australian line, but Towner's teams effectively used their two
Vickers machine-guns and a captured German Maxim machine-
gun to devastate Germans amassing for a counterattack in the
woods in front of you. This sunken road was also the starting
point for the left of the attack on the afternoon of 1 September,
which resulted in the capture of the entire mount.

Edgar Towner grew up in the Barcoo district of Queensland and worked on his father's farm until his enlistment in 1915. He served with the 25th Battalion and then the 2nd Machine Gun Battalion in France, and was Mentioned in Despatches twice as well as receiving the Military Cross, in addition to his VC. After the war Towner returned to the land, and during the Second World War served in the 26th Battalion, the same unit commanded by Harry Murray VC (see **Gueudecourt**, pages 182–183). In later years Towner became a well-known historian and geographer. He died in Queensland in 1972, aged 82.

Return to the minor road and turn left. Continue past the civilian cemetery, a prominent landmark mentioned in many accounts of the battle. As you walk along this road the sweeping views to the west and north reveal how tactically important the mount was for both sides. Continue until you reach a farm track heading into the field on your right. Follow the track. As the ground rises the views to the west become even more expansive. The track bends to the right and then to the left. Just before the left bend, look into the field on your left. About 100 metres in is a large depression [3], the remains of the crater that was attacked by Sergeant Lowerson and his courageous group. The Australians advanced from the woods in front of you, towards the German machine-guns in the crater.

Alby Lowerson was working on the goldfields of New South Wales when he enlisted in 1915. He arrived in France with the 21st Battalion in early 1916 and was wounded at Pozières later in the year and again at Bullecourt in 1917. After recovering from the wounds he received at Mont St Quentin, Lowerson returned to the battalion in mid-September 1918 and was wounded for a fourth time at Montbrehain, on Australia's last day of action in the war. He returned to Australia in 1919 and worked as a farmer. During the Second World War he worked in various training units before dying suddenly in 1945. He was 49.

Continue along the path as it leads into the woods. It is well worth leaving the track and exploring the woods on either side [4]: the German trenches captured by the Australians during the attack still snake through the trees. The wood is also a sea of shell craters, evidence of the pounding the area took throughout the war.

Continue along the track through the woods and turn right at the intersection with another track. Turn right at the church and follow this street for about 100 metres. On your right is a battered brick wall that stood here during the war. An undetonated shell from a field gun is still embedded in the wall (about two metres to the right of a small yellow panel). Return along the road and turn right at the first intersection. This will bring you back to the main road through the village. The Australian Memorial and your car are along the road to the right.

OTHER SITES OF INTEREST

Allaines—Lawrence Weathers VC

Following the successful capture of Mont St Quentin on 1 September 1918, the Germans in the area staged a fighting retreat, with Australian and British units hot on their heels. On 2 September the 43rd Battalion, the only unit of the 3rd Division still in the front line, was ordered to join the fight and capture two trenches in front of the town of Allaines, two kilometres north-east of Mont St Quentin.

With Australian and British units closing in, the Germans in Uslar and Fiume trenches decided to stand and fight, opening a murderous machine-gun fire on any Australian who showed his head. The Australians went to ground and there seemed no way out of the stalemate until Corporal Lawrence Weathers took matters into his own hands. Braving the heavy fire, he advanced towards the Germans, throwing bombs as he went, and killed several men, including the garrison's leader. He then returned to the Australian position for more bombs and led three mates in another assault. Weathers stood on the parapet of the trench, lobbing bombs at the Germans until they threw up their hands.

He and his small group captured the trench, along with 180 men and three machine-guns.

Lawrence Weathers was born in New Zealand but came to Adelaide with his family when he was seven. He enlisted in 1916, leaving his job as an undertaker as well as a wife and baby son. He was severely wounded in June 1917 at the Battle of Messines. On 29 September 1918 Weathers was again in the thick of the action during the battalion's advance on the Beaurevoir Line. Early in the attack he was seriously wounded. He died later in the day, before learning he had received the Victoria Cross for his bravery on 2 September. The attack on the Beaurevoir Line was one of Australia's last actions of the war and took place only a week before the AIF was permanently withdrawn from the front line. Corporal Weathers now lies in Unicorn Cemetery, Vendhuile. His brother Tom had been killed at Gallipoli in June 1915.

Directions

From the major crossroads in Mont St Quentin village follow the D43 to Allaines. Drive through Allaines and turn left at Rue de Pont Debray near the far end of the village, signposted 'Centre Equestre'. Follow this road until a T-junction and turn right. This road crosses the Canal du Nord and heads out into farm fields beyond. Drive on for about 300 metres and stop at the intersection with a farm track on the right. The trench captured by Weathers ran parallel to the road about 200 metres into the field on your left. Weathers attacked across the field towards you.

Bouchavesnes-Bergen—George Cartwright VC

During the attack on Mont St Quentin on 31 August 1918, the 3rd Division was tasked with capturing the town of Bouchavesnes, four kilometres to the north. The 33rd Battalion was advancing south of the village towards Road Wood when fire from machine-guns sent the men to ground. In the face of this intense fire, Private George Cartwright stood up and began firing at the nearest machine-gun with his rifle. He advanced on the position and shot the German gunner, plus two more men who took his place. He then threw a bomb to cover his advance and rushed forward, leaping into a trench and capturing nine Germans. At this point, according to the report of the battalion's commander, Lieutenant Colonel Leslie Morshead, 'the whole battalion stood up, vociferously cheered him and renewed the attack with the greatest vigour and determination . . . To have cleaned such a stronghold as Road Wood with so few men seems incredible.' For his inspirational example, George Cartwright was awarded the Victoria Cross.

George Cartwright was English by birth and worked as a labourer after emigrating to Australia. He enlisted at the end of 1915 and was wounded in France in June 1916. He was gassed in April 1918 and wounded again in September, this time seriously enough to be sent to England. He was still there when the war ended. He returned to Australia after the war and served in the 28th Infantry Training Battalion during the Second World War. He died in Sydney in 1978, aged 83.

Directions
Road Wood can be reached by following the D1017 from Mont St Quentin towards Bapaume. After three kilometres, turn left towards Clery-sur-Somme on the D149. After a kilometre you will pass a wood on the right side of the road—this is Road Wood, known today as Madame Wood. The machine-gun captured by Private Cartwright was in the south-west corner of the wood. Park beside the French monument on the side of the road—the 33rd Battalion advanced towards the wood from the fields in front of you.

Péronne—Alexander Buckley VC, Arthur Hall VC and William Currey VC.

In 1918 the major Somme town of Péronne was the recalcitrant cousin of the German bastion at Mont St Quentin. The two places were side by side and you couldn't take one without the other. Between them they formed one of the most formidable obstacles on the Western Front.

Even before the Germans strengthened it with wire and machine-guns, Péronne was a fortress. The town was protected by sturdy ramparts and a moat, constructed in the 17th century by Vauban, the French military architect who had also built the ramparts at Ypres.

On 29 August the Australian 2nd and 5th divisions made half-hearted attempts to cross the Somme and advance on the town but, like their French and British allies before them, found Péronne a tough nut to crack.

A more serious effort was launched on 1 September. It had been hoped that the capture of Mont St Quentin would force the Germans to abandon Péronne but, even with the mount safely in Australian hands, the Germans in Péronne needed a nudge. From their newly gained positions, the 14th Brigade advanced on Péronne from the north-west and began clearing the town street by street, while the 15th Brigade forced its way across the river and wheeled south of the town. Péronne was secured the next day.

During the advance, the 53rd and 54th battalions were tasked with clearing the ground between Mont St Quentin and Péronne. The 54th advanced on the right but was soon blocked by thick wire in front of the first German trench. The Diggers were under heavy fire but, covered by Lewis gunners, they ran forward, wrenched the barbed wire pickets from the ground and crawled under. At the second German trench, machine-guns held up the advance and casualties were heavy. Two corporals, Alexander Buckley and Arthur Hall, ran forward, one on each end of the line, and attacked separate machine-gun posts. Buckley, with the help of one man, shot four Germans and captured his post.

Later in the day the 54th was again held up by extremely heavy fire centred on a footbridge—the only bridge still intact across the moat. Buckley was surveying the bridge and discussing the next move with his comrades when he was killed by machine-gun fire. Inspired by his example up to this point, other Australians rushed across the moat and captured the German positions. This opened the way for the battalion to enter Péronne and help clear the town. Buckley was awarded a posthumous Victoria Cross.

Buckley was a farmer from Coonamble in New South Wales until his enlistment in 1916. He served with the 54th Battalion throughout 1917 and 1918 but went largely unnoticed until his extraordinary acts of courage at Péronne. He now lies in the Péronne Communal Cemetery Extension (see pages 268–269).

While Buckley was dealing with the machine-gun post on the left, Hall, the man who had run forward with him, attacked the one on the right, shooting four Germans and capturing nine, plus two machine-guns. With the position secured the 54th advanced at a half-run, only pausing to take pot shots at the Germans who were fleeing in front of them. As Buckley met his fate while planning an assault across the footbridge, Hall found another bridge across the moat which the Germans had destroyed. He sent a message to headquarters suggesting that the Australians could still cross the moat on planks and debris from the bridge. They crossed under comparatively light fire and by 8.20 am the 54th Battalion was in the centre of town. Throughout the advance Hall had led charges on machine-gun posts and other areas of resistance, ending the day with a tally of 15 Germans and two machine-guns captured. The next day Hall added to his achievements by rescuing a wounded mate under heavy shellfire. Like Buckley, he received the Victoria Cross.

Arthur Hall worked as an overseer on his family farms near Nyngan, New South Wales, before enlisting in 1916. His time spent shooting kangaroos had made him a crack shot and he did well in the infantry. He was wounded in 1917 and was promoted to corporal later that year, and then to sergeant in 1919. He returned to Australia in August and went back to work on the family farm, until the outbreak of the Second World War drew him back into the army as a lieutenant in the 7th Garrison Battalion. After the war he ran his own farm near Coolabah in New South Wales, where he died in 1971, aged 74.

On the 54th Battalion's left, the 53rd were also having a tough fight. Early in their advance they had to pass through Anvil Wood, west of the town, a task made almost impossible by a German field gun that blasted the Australians at point-blank range. Casualties were heavy until a young private, William Currey, sprayed the Germans with fire from his Lewis gun and then charged among them, killing them all and capturing the gun. The 53rd advanced through Anvil Wood, capturing dozens of Germans, several machine-guns and two more field guns. As they emerged from the wood into the open fields near Péronne, the Germans rained fire down on them and the battalion went to ground. Currey used his Lewis gun to subdue a machine-gun post and then single-handedly rushed and captured the position. That night, a small party of Australians under Lieutenant William Waite had advanced ahead of the rest of the battalion and could not be reached with the order to pull back. Currey volunteered to try to find them and crept far out into no man's land. When he had got as close to the Australian post as he could he stood up and yelled at the top of his voice, 'Waitsy, get in!' The Germans launched a volley of fire towards the sound of Currey's voice and even lobbed a few gas shells in his direction. Currey's gas mask was riddled with bullets before he could put it on and he inhaled a good dose of gas, but still managed to crawl back to the Australian line, followed soon after by Waite and his men. Currey recovered from his wounds and was awarded the Victoria Cross.

William Currey was from Newcastle and worked in Sydney until war broke out. He lied about his age and enlisted in 1914, but was found out and discharged. The same thing happened in 1915. In 1916, even though he was now old enough to enlist, he was rejected on medical grounds, but eventually succeeded in joining up late in the year. He served with the 5th Light Trench Mortar Battery before transferring to the 53rd Battalion in 1917. Even after being gassed at Péronne he stayed with the battalion until the end of the war. On his return to Australia he became a keen member of the Labor Party and was elected to the New South

Wales Legislative Assembly in 1941. He was the first VC winner to serve in the New South Wales Parliament and held his seat until his sudden death in 1948. He was 52. As a boy, Currey had attended Dudley Public School in Newcastle. He was one of 93 ex-pupils who served in the AIF. Two of them, Currey and Clarence Jeffries (see **Broonseide Ridge**, pages 97–98), won the Victoria Cross.

Directions

Since 1918 Péronne has expanded north and west, covering much of the ground the Australians captured. To find the site of the trench captured by Buckley and Hall, leave Péronne on the D938 towards Cléry. On the edge of Péronne, turn left at the crossroads towards Halles. Almost immediately a farm track joins this road on the left. Park your car and walk along the track for 300 metres. Johannes Trench ran north–south across these fields and crossed the road where you are standing. This is the area where Buckley and Hall captured the two machine-gun posts.

The footbridge where Buckley was killed was on the southern bank of the lake, the Etang du Cam, south-west of the centre of Péronne. The bridge crossed by Hall was north of the lake and was actually a road bridge on the D938. There is no bridge there now; the moat has been swallowed up by development.

Anvil Wood, where Private Currey captured the German field gun, has been almost overwhelmed by modern buildings. There is only a small patch of greenery left but, fortunately, this is the corner of the wood where Currey won his VC. To find it, follow the directions to Johannes Trench above, but turn right into the Rue du Quinconce just before the crossroads. The remains of Anvil Wood surround the college buildings on the left of this road.

An excellent museum, the Historial de la Grande Guerre (Museum of the Great War), is now housed in the old castle in the centre of Péronne. It is well worth visiting, although it makes scant reference to Australians—strange, considering their role in liberating the town from the Germans.

CEMETERIES NEAR MONT ST QUENTIN

Hem Farm Military Cemetery, Hem-Monacu

Hem Farm Military Cemetery was started by British units in February 1917 and used until the ground was lost to the Germans the following March. In September 1918 the British returned and briefly used the cemetery again. It was greatly enlarged after the Armistice, when graves were brought in from battlefields north and south of the Somme River. Today it contains nearly 600 burials, of which 138 are Australian. Nearly all of these men were killed in the brilliant Australian attacks on Mont St Quentin and Péronne in August and September 1918.

The most notable Australian grave belongs to Private Robert Mactier VC of the 23rd Battalion (see page 254). His lieutenant, who later recommended him for the VC, reported that, after being shot, Mactier 'only lived a few minutes. He tried to speak to me before he died but was unintelligible . . . He was a splendid soldier' (grave II.J.3).

Directions
Hem-Monacu is a village seven kilometres west of Mont St Quentin, just south of the road from Albert to Péronne. From Hem-Monacu, follow the C1 west towards Curlu. The cemetery is signposted south after a kilometre. The farm from which the cemetery takes its name is beside the cemetery.

Herbecourt British Cemetery

The first burials at Herbecourt were made by the French and Germans early in the war, in an extension built next to the civilian cemetery. In 1917 British troops arrived in the area and added a new plot to the cemetery extension. Australian troops then used the British plot almost exclusively in 1918. The French and German plots were removed after the Armistice, leaving the small British plot standing alone in the middle of a field. Today 51 of the 59 graves are Australian, mostly belonging to men killed in the Australian advance in late August and early September 1918.

The most senior officer buried here is Captain Frederick Cotterell MC of the 55th Battalion. Originally from England, Cotterell enlisted in the AIF a month after the outbreak of war and was posted to the 6th Light Horse Regiment. He served at Gallipoli and transferred to the infantry in France. In 1917 he won the Military Cross after bravely leading his men to the objective at Polygon Wood. He was killed on 2 September 1918 while reconnoitring the Australian forward posts near Péronne (grave D.2). His brother Ernest had died while training in Sydney in 1914.

Another decorated officer who lies here is Lieutenant Stanley Colless MC, DCM, also of the 55th Battalion. Colless won the Distinguished Conduct Medal during the disastrous attack at Fromelles in July 1916. He was part of a group of Australians commanded by Captain Norman Gibbins, a hero of the battle, and kept two machine-guns in operation to cover the Australian withdrawal to their own lines (see **Fromelles**, page 123). His Military Cross came in March 1918, after he led a raid on the German trenches, secured several prisoners and personally killed three Germans. Colless was killed by machine-gun fire during the 55th Battalion's advance on Péronne on 1 September 1918 (grave C.1).

Directions
Herbecourt is eight kilometres south-west of Mont St Quentin. The cemetery is west of the village on the D1, the road between Amiens and Péronne.

Péronne Communal Cemetery Extension

The extension to the Péronne Communal Cemetery was begun by British units in March 1917, after the Germans had abandoned the town in their withdrawal to the Hindenburg Line. The Germans also used the cemetery when they took the town back a year later. The Australian 2nd Division became the final unit to use the cemetery after their capture of the town in September 1918. At war's end it only contained 177 graves, but the concentration of isolated graves and the closure of smaller cemeteries in the area has now swelled its size to 1579 graves. Of these, 517 are Australian, nearly all coming from the attack in late August and early September 1918. All except 29 are identified.

A prominent Australian buried here is Corporal Alexander Buckley VC of the 54th Battalion (grave II.C.32), who died while organising an attack across the moat at Péronne (see pages 263–264). Another is Corporal Fred Thurston of the 33rd Battalion. Thurston won the Military Medal three times during the war (MM & two Bars), one of only 18 Australian soldiers to do so. His first award came during the Battle of Messines in 1917, when he acted as company messenger under heavy fire for more than 96 hours straight. The second came in March 1918, after he led a small group to attack a German support trench during a raid near Ypres. His third MM was awarded after he had been promoted to corporal and led his men with cool determination during a counterattack at Marcelcave on 30 March 1918. Thurston's luck ran out during the advance that preceded the attack on Mont St Quentin. He was killed by a shell east of Hem on 30 August 1918 (grave IV.P.6).

An interesting British grave can be found in the Péronne Communal Cemetery, next to the cemetery extension. Corporal Frederick Geard was originally a member of the Royal Engineers but had transferred to the Royal Flying Corps. It is always interesting to find the grave of a member of the RFC, and to ponder the raw courage required to take to the skies in a flimsy wood and fabric machine almost a century ago. What is remarkable about Corporal Geard's grave, however, is that he was killed on 18 August 1914, exactly two weeks after war was declared, making him one of the earliest RFC casualties in France.

Directions

Péronne Communal Cemetery is in the centre of Péronne, near the hospital. From Mont St Quentin, take the D1017 south into Péronne and turn right towards the hospital (hôpital in French) after entering the town. On reaching the hospital, take the small road opposite. The cemetery is at the end of this road.

Part IV

Hindenburg Line

The arrival of 1917 forced both the Allies and Germans to make some tough decisions. The bloody battles of the Somme and Verdun were now behind them and the cruellest winter in decades was finally beginning to wane. The Allies, keen to capitalise on their late successes during the 1916 fighting, planned a series of attacks along the German front. The Germans, battered by the fighting of the past year and losing faith that they could win the war, decided that drastic action had to be taken. Within a few weeks they had changed the course of the war.

For several months German engineers had worked tirelessly to construct a complete trench system, known as the Hindenburg Line, several kilometres *behind* their current front line. In February 1917 the Germans abandoned the positions they had spent so much time and blood defending and withdrew to this line. It was a masterstroke. Not only was the Hindenburg Line straighter and shorter than the original German line, therefore requiring fewer troops to hold it, the Germans had now thrown into disarray the entire Allied plan of attack for 1917. Additionally, because the new line had been constructed in the safety of the rear area, it was built with maximum attention paid to defence and fortification. Multiple lines of trenches had been deeply dug and strongly reinforced. Concrete shelters and machine-gun posts had been built in strategic locations. And the whole thing was protected by the most insidious barbed wire defences ever seen in the war. Thousands of kilometres of wire had been strung out before the front line trenches, extending up to 50 metres into no man's land. The Germans had laid

Hindenburg Line

the entanglement in a zigzag pattern, and sited machine-guns at strategic points. Attacking troops would be drawn into the 'vees' of the zigzag and be mown down by machine-gun fire. For added insurance, the Germans fortified a line of villages in front of the Hindenburg Line and occupied them with a crack force. This outpost line was a tough obstacle that needed to be tackled before the Hindenburg Line itself.

Following the military maxim that a fleeing enemy must be pursued as quickly as possible, Australian troops were thrown in against the outpost villages almost immediately after the German withdrawal. From March to April 1917 they fought in short but fierce encounters with crack German troops in villages whose names would become famous in AIF history. They moved quickly through the area but left many of their mates buried in the local cemeteries.

In April the Australians advanced to the town of Bullecourt and faced the Hindenburg Line itself. In that month and the next they launched two major attacks against the formidable German defences. The first was a disaster and shattered the attacking Australian divisions for no result. The second was better planned and was ultimately successful, but cost the Australians thousands of men. The two great battles at Bullecourt wrecked the Australian divisions involved, and also their confidence in their British commanders.

The Hindenburg Line battlefields are not far east from the Somme. Bullecourt is the essential sight in the area, but the outpost villages are also interesting and can be visited on the drive to Bullecourt.

11

Hindenburg Line Outpost Villages, March–April 1917

Australia played an important role in the taking of the outpost villages in March and April 1917, fanning east from Bapaume and launching repeated attacks. The open, rolling countryside and the lack of significant war damage was something new to the Australians, who had grown accustomed at Pozières and in Flanders to fighting in a quagmire. As they captured each outpost village they stayed only briefly, but the tough fight required at each one left a strong impression on the Australians. Streets and parks across Australia are still named in honour of these villages. Though there are not many wartime sites to see, the villages nevertheless represent an important chapter in Australian military history and should be visited. At most of them, military cemeteries contain the graves of Diggers who paid the ultimate price for liberating the towns. These small, isolated cemeteries are some of the most beautiful and moving in France.

The outpost villages are too spread out to be visited in a walking tour, so driving is the only practical option. All the towns listed in this tour are close to the major D930 road out of Bapaume and can be visited in half a day.

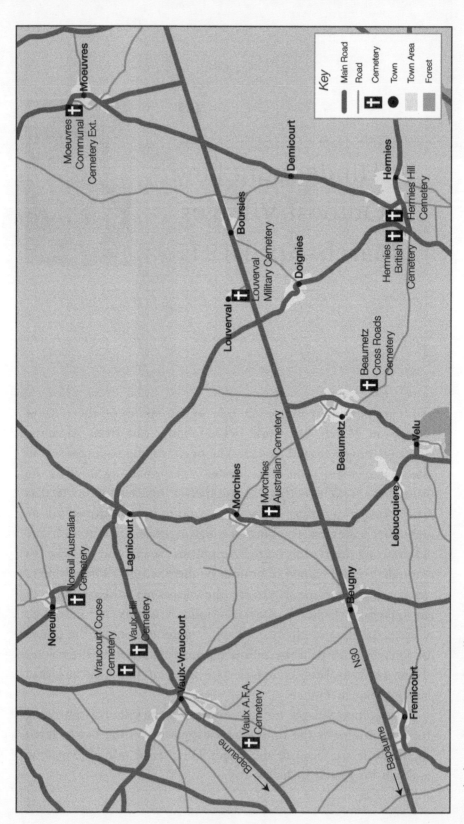

Hindenburg Line Outpost Villages

Vaulx-Vraucourt

This large village was one of the first captured by the Australian troops. It was taken by the 21st Battalion on 18 March without much of a fight. The German occupiers were preparing to abandon the village as the Australians arrived, and fled after a short fight. An Australian field ambulance was stationed here soon after and the town served as a treatment centre for wounded during the outpost village fighting and the later two great battles at Bullecourt. Today there are three cemeteries near the town that have an Australian connection.

Vaulx Australian Field Ambulance Cemetery is located near the site of the field ambulance station and was begun in April 1917. The Germans also used the cemetery when they recaptured this ground in 1918. Today it contains 32 Australians out of a total of 52 Commonwealth burials, and 61 German graves. Decorated Australians buried here include Lieutenant Norman Dougall MC (10th Battalion, died 06/05/1917, grave B.18), Private Jean Gallanty MM (7th Field Ambulance, died 05/05/1917, grave C.13) and Private John Uncle MM (6th Battalion, died 08/05/1917, grave C.15).

The cemetery is located on the right of the road from Beaugnâtre, about one kilometre before Vaulx-Vraucourt, and is set back from the road in a wheatfield.

Vaulx Hill Cemetery was started in September 1918 and contained just 17 burials at the end of the war. After the Armistice several smaller cemeteries in the area were closed and their graves concentrated here. Today it contains 856 graves including 110 Australians, seven of whom are unidentified.

A distinguished senior officer is buried here, Lieutenant Colonel Bertram Watts DSO (4th Artillery Brigade, died 10/04/1917, grave II.B.3). He was killed while commanding his artillery brigade in the lead-up to the First Battle of Bullecourt. Also buried here is Lieutenant Roy Fordham (10th Battalion, died 08/04/1917, grave III.B.). On 25 April 1915 Fordham landed at Gallipoli and was one of a handful of men who penetrated further inland than any other Australian in the campaign. He was killed at Boursies in 1917 (see page 288).

The cemetery is located on the road to Lagnicourt, about one kilometre from Vaulx-Vraucourt.

Vraucourt Copse Cemetery contained 43 graves at the end of the war but was enlarged in 1928. Today it contains the graves of 38 Diggers out of a total of 104. Five of the Australians are unidentified. Buried here is 2nd Lieutenant Richmond Howell-Price MC (1st Battalion, died 04/05/1917, grave II.B.7), one of three officer brothers to die on the Western Front. Lieutenant Colonel Owen Howell-Price DSO, MC, commander of the 3rd Battalion, was killed at Flers on 4 November 1916 and Major Philip Howell-Price DSO, MC was killed at Broodseinde Ridge on 4 October 1917.

To reach the cemetery, leave Vaulx-Vraucourt in the direction of Ecoust-St-Mein and follow the signposted lane to the right.

Morchies

Australia's first contact with Morchies was accidental. On the night of 19 March Lieutenant Mervyn Knight of the 60th Battalion was inspecting his posts when he became disoriented. He entered a village, expecting it to be the Australian-held village of Beugny. To his shock, he heard German voices and realised he had stumbled into Morchies, which was still firmly in German hands. He managed to avoid capture for several harrowing hours and eventually slipped past the German sentries and back to the Australian line. This dramatic incident aside, Morchies didn't prove much of an obstacle for the Australians. The 59th Battalion captured it almost without loss on 20 March.

Morchies Australian Cemetery was started by Australian troops soon after the capture of the town in March 1917 and used until the end of April. It was used briefly by the Germans in March 1918 and again by the British in September. The cemetery contains

61 Commonwealth burials, of which 20 are Australian. Two German soldiers also lie here. As is the case with many cemeteries in this area, nearly all the Australians buried here were killed in the terrible fighting at Bullecourt in April and May 1917.

Morchies Australian Cemetery is reached by following the D18 south out of Morchies. The cemetery is on the left after a short distance.

Beaumetz

This village was attacked by the 60th Battalion in the same action that captured Morchies on 20 March. The fight was tougher at Beaumetz: the 60th faced heavy machine-gun fire and slogged forward all afternoon, eventually digging in just short of the village. They had done good work, however, and the Germans evacuated the village during the night. The 29th Battalion relieved the exhausted 60th the next day and found Beaumetz deserted.

The Germans launched a strong counterattack against Beaumetz on 23 March and captured the village within a couple of hours. But the 29th and 30th Battalions were about to demonstrate the outstanding fighting skills that Australian troops had displayed since Gallipoli. Without the help of supporting troops, the Australians reorganised and rushed the village, retaking the ground they had just lost. During the Australian charge, 2nd Lieutenant Henry Harrison of the 29th Battalion led a dozen light horsemen (who had joined his battalion only the previous night) to attack a German strongpoint. After a short bayonet fight the Germans fled. For his bravery Harrison was awarded the Military Cross.

By 6.30 am the Germans had been entirely overcome and the town was back in Australian hands. The Australians had gotten off relatively lightly, with 12 men killed and 38 wounded. The Germans, on the other hand, had been completely routed and left more than 50 men dead in the streets of Beaumetz, with another 11 taken prisoner.

After the line had been stabilised, Brigadier General 'Pompey' Elliot, commander of the 15th Brigade and a man renowned for his feisty temperament, was outraged by the audacity of the German attack. He impulsively ordered the Australians to attack the German line in retaliation, a move that would likely have wiped out most of his brigade, but was overruled by his superiors before things got out of hand.

The next day the Germans demonstrated how badly they wanted Beaumetz back by attacking again. This time they didn't penetrate far into the village and were driven out by the Australians. Scattered Germans held out in isolated houses, including two snipers who hit eight Australians during the course of the day. They were eventually dealt with by Lieutenant Harold Trevan, who shot one with his last bullet and then used the dead man's rifle to shoot the other one.

During their attack on 24 March, German troops sheltered in the sunken road that runs north from Beaumetz and joins the D930. Many of them were killed or wounded here by Australian fire from the village.

Beaumetz Cross Roads Cemetery was begun after the town's capture in March 1917 and used until the following February. It was used again as British units advanced through the area in September and October 1918. Other graves were concentrated here after the Armistice, enlarging the cemetery to its current 250. Fifty-nine of these are Australian, one of which is unidentified. Buried here is Captain Eric Booth of the 29th Battalion, who bravely led a company in the recapture of the village from the Germans on 23 March. Later in the day he was killed by shellfire (grave B.43).

The cemetery is on a minor road and is best found by following the signs from the centre of Beaumetz.

Lagnicourt—Percy Cherry VC, James Newland VC and Jack Whittle VC.

On 26 March the 26th and 27th battalions were tasked with capturing Lagnicourt, known to be strongly occupied by the

Germans. Under cover of a thin artillery barrage the Australians advanced from house to house through the village, clearing machine-gun posts and taking prisoners in the shell-damaged buildings. At one stage a team of Lewis gunners under the command of Captain Percy Cherry of the 26th Battalion, a popular officer who had excelled during the fighting at Pozières in 1916, edged along the main street of the village, firing their guns from the hip. After clearing several houses the barrels of the guns were too hot to touch. In the centre of the village they faced heavy fire from German machine-gunners sheltering in a massive mine crater and the advance stopped. Cherry called for trench mortars to be brought up to shell the Germans but soon grew impatient at the delay and took matters into his own hands. Under the cover of Lewis gun fire he organised a party to rush the crater, overcoming several machine-guns and killing the garrison. During this action Cherry's commanding officer received three messages from him:

1. 'Held up by strong point. Have you any Stokes [trench mortars]?'
2. (Half an hour later) 'Can't wait for Stokes; having a go at it; will report result later.'
3. 'Got them with Lewis guns and rifle bombs from the flanks. The lot killed. Damned good.'

The Australians continued to advance through the village and set up defensive posts on the far side, ready to meet any German counterattack. They didn't have to wait long: the Germans attacked strongly in the afternoon, capturing several of the posts and threatening the entire Australian line. Cherry decided that the only solution was to launch a counterattack of his own, but in the face of Australian machine-gun fire the Germans called off their assault and retreated. Later in the day Cherry was conferring with fellow officers in a sunken road east of the village when he was killed by a shell. He was posthumously awarded the VC.

Percy Cherry worked as a fruit picker in Tasmania until his enlistment in 1915. He was wounded at Gallipoli and distinguished himself at Pozières in 1916 (see **Pozières**, page 160–161). He was awarded the Military Cross for attacking machine-gun posts at Warlencourt—the announcement made the same day he was killed. He now lies in Quéant Road Cemetery, Buissy (see pages 312–313).

The capture of Lagnicourt cost the Australians 377 casualties but brought them within sight of the Hindenburg Line.

The crater captured by Cherry was located in the centre of modern-day Lagnicourt, in front of the church and town hall.

The Battle of Lagnicourt

On 15 April Lagnicourt was again the scene of bitter fighting when the Germans launched a strong counterattack in an attempt to regain several of the outpost villages. The Australians were involved in a desperate defence of a long line from Lagnicourt to Hermies and fought stoically at isolated posts along the line. Captain James Newland, assisted by Sergeant Jack Whittle, both of the 12th Battalion, resisted wave after wave of German assaults and held vital posts around Lagnicourt. For this and for bravery in assaults earlier in the month they were both awarded the VC. An Australian counterattack late in the day stabilised the line and took back ground lost to the Germans. The day's action cost the Australians 1010 casualties, including more than 300 men taken prisoner.

James Newland was a Boer War veteran who enlisted in 1914, only two weeks after the war began. He landed at Gallipoli on the first day and was wounded in May. At Pozières in 1916 he was Mentioned in Despatches for his leadership and organisation. He was wounded for a second time in early 1917 but rejoined his unit in time for the actions that led to his VC. He was wounded again at Bullecourt in May. He returned to Australia in 1918 and served as an officer in the Permanent Forces, a role he held until his retirement in 1941. He died suddenly in Melbourne in 1948, aged 66. Newland was 35 years old at the time of winning the VC: the oldest Australian VC winner of the war.

Jack Whittle was also a Boer War veteran who served in the navy before the Great War. He enlisted in the AIF in 1915 but was too late to serve at Gallipoli. He was wounded in one of the

12th Battalion's first actions in 1916 and received the Distinguished Conduct Medal at Le Barque in 1917, shortly before winning the VC. Whittle was wounded twice more in 1918 and returned to Australia late in the year. He worked as an insurance salesman and, in 1934, rescued and resuscitated a three-year-old boy who had fallen into a lake. Jack Whittle died in Sydney in 1946, aged 62. His son Ivan was killed while serving at Port Moresby in 1943.

Moeuvres—Charles Pope VC

The ground between Moeuvres and Louverval was in the heart of the German attack during the Battle of Lagnicourt on 15 April. The Australians were spread out on a long front and, without enough men to hold a continuous trench line, occupied the ground in a series of posts, separated by several hundred metres. As the Germans advanced on 15 April, a large group moved between two Australian posts without being observed and occupied a trench in rear of the Australians. Lieutenant Charles Pope of the 11th Battalion was the commander of one post and realised he was surrounded when several men were hit by fire coming from behind them. Pope sent back a runner to call for reinforcements and ammunition. After a harrowing journey through the German positions, the runner reached the Australian headquarters, but no Australians could get back through the German line to reach their isolated comrades. Without reinforcements and running low on ammunition, Pope could not have been faulted for surrendering to the Germans. Instead, he ordered his men to hang on until their last shot had been fired and then to charge the Germans with their bayonets. Pope's entire party was killed in the charge. For holding his vital post to the last man, Pope was awarded a posthumous Victoria Cross.

Charles Pope was English by birth and had served on the London Metropolitan Police Force before emigrating to Perth in 1910. He enlisted in 1915 and served with the 11th Battalion until his death. He had married an Australian girl before the war and had left her and two children living in Perth. He now lies in Moeuvres Communal Cemetery Extension. His brother John was also killed during the war.

Pope's post was west of Moeuvres, about 2.5 kilometres from Louverval on the road to Inchy-en-Artois.

Moeuvres Communal Cemetery Extension was begun by German units in 1917 and used by British troops who captured the village in September 1918. It was greatly enlarged after the Armistice and now contains 565 Commonwealth burials and a German mass grave. Only eight Australians are buried here, all of them killed during the outpost village fighting. The most notable is Lieutenant Charles Pope VC of the 11th Battalion (grave V.D.22).

The cemetery is on the northern edge of the village on the road to Inchy-en-Artois.

Noreuil—Jorgan Jensen VC

After the capture of Lagnicourt, the Australians swung north and, on 2 April, advanced towards the village of Noreuil. They had attacked the village three weeks earlier across open fields from the west and failed miserably, so the new plan called for the 50th Battalion to approach stealthily along the sunken roads from Lagnicourt, while the 51st Battalion attacked further north. The 52nd Battalion would provide support.

It was a good plan, but the Germans saw it coming and blocked the sunken roads with barricades and machine-guns. The 50th Battalion, encountering two of these barricades, was badly mauled by machine-gun fire. After a barrage of trench mortar shells failed to suppress the Germans, a party of six bombers was sent forward to deal with the obstacles. Private Jorgan Jensen, a Dane who spoke German, rushed forward alone, dived over the barricade and pulled the pin from one of his grenades with his teeth. Menacing the 45 German defenders with his grenade, he bluffed them into thinking they were surrounded and convinced them to surrender. He then sent one of the Germans to the other post with instructions that they should surrender as well, which they did without a whimper. As Jensen sent his prisoners to the rear, a distant group of Australians, unaware of the situation, opened fire on the Germans. Jensen jumped onto the bank of the sunken road and into the line of fire, waving his helmet until the Australians stopped shooting. Single-handedly he had cleared the way for the 50th Battalion and was awarded the Victoria Cross.

With these obstacles out of the way, the two battalions cleared Norueil and overcame isolated German posts on the far side of the village. The attack cost the Australians more than 600 men, the 50th Battalion alone losing 360. Twenty of these men had been killed by Australian fire after being captured and mistaken for Germans as they were marched to the rear.

Jorgan Jensen had migrated to Australia from Denmark as a young man and was naturalised in 1914. He enlisted in 1915 and arrived at Gallipoli a few months before the evacuation. He was wounded in France in 1916 and again during a patrol at Villers–Bretonneux in May 1918. He spent several months in hospital and returned to Adelaide at the end of the year. He died in 1922, aged only 31.

The barricade captured by Jensen was located about 250 metres out of Noreuil on the sunken road to Lagnicourt, at the point where the road rises and bends to the left.

Noreuil Australian Cemetery was begun soon after the village was captured and used until the following September. The cemetery contains 244 burials, of which 182 are Australian. A row of special memorials along one wall commemorates 82 men who were buried here but whose graves were destroyed by shellfire. Nearly all these men were from the 50th Battalion and were killed during the attack that earned Jensen his VC. Private Edward Clayton (age 29) is buried beside his brother, Private William Clayton (age 42). Both served in the 52nd Battalion and were killed during the First Battle of Bullecourt on 12 April 1917 (graves E.5 and E.6).

The cemetery is reached by turning off the road to Ecoust-St-Mein. Look for the sign in the centre of Noreuil.

Doignies

On 2 April, the same day as the attack on Noreuil, the 55th Battalion was tasked with capturing Doignies, south of the Bapaume–Cambrai road. In the same attack, its sister battalion, the 56th, would capture Louverval, just north of the road. The plan was clever and called for the advancing battalions to bypass both villages to the north and then wheel south, encircling the villages and attacking the Germans from the rear. In spite of miscommunication between the battalions and poor navigation by some of the attacking troops, the attack on Doignies went smoothly. The German defenders fired a few scattered shots but soon fled to avoid becoming surrounded.

The Germans were taken totally by surprise and had left warm breakfasts uneaten on tables. They had mined the village and intended to destroy it before evacuating, but had not had a chance to detonate the explosives. This good fortune was slightly negated by the first Australian troops who arrived in the village. On finding detonator wires stretched across the streets, they pulled them, setting off the charges and injuring several men. In one case a private hurrying across a bridge tripped over a wire and exploded a charge in the river. Fortunately the bridge—and the private—were not damaged.

Later in the day the Germans counterattacked but were driven off with sharp loss by the battalion's supporting artillery.

Louverval

The attack on Louverval was made by the 56th Battalion on the morning of 2 April, in conjunction with the 55th Battalion's attack on Doignies. This attack did not quite go according to plan. Next to the village was a chateau and large wood, which proved a tough obstacle. The Germans had cut down most of the trees and the Australians found the trunks were either too close to the ground to scurry under or too high to climb over for men burdened with heavy packs. In spite of these obstacles and mounting casualties, the Australians eventually trickled through the wood and adjacent village. A group of 20 Germans was cut off and attempted to surrender, but the Australians' blood was high and most of this group was shot.

On losing the wood and village, the Germans began shelling the Australians in their new positions and attempted to counterattack the wood. Australian Lewis gunners broke up the attack but the shelling caused many casualties.

The attacks on Doignies and Louverval cost the two battalions 484 casualties between them. War is never glorious but this day's fighting, particularly at Louverval, had been grubby and the Australians resented their casualties. This is evident in the number of Germans taken prisoner: between the two battalions, only 12 Germans were captured alive.

Louverval Military Cemetery was used between April and December 1917. After the Armistice it was enlarged by the addition of graves from the nearby Louverval Chateau Cemetery, and now contains 124 burials. Four of these are Australian. Corporal Edward Davidson had enlisted within a month of the outbreak of war and served throughout Gallipoli with the 12th Battalion. He was probably killed during the attack on Boursies on 9 April 1917 but, because this is uncertain, his date of death is recorded as 6/10 April 1917 (grave B.22). Private Charles Kirkness was a stretcher bearer, a group rarely given enough credit for their courage and commitment to duty. He was killed on 17 April 1917 while carrying a wounded man to an aid post after the German attack at Lagnicourt (grave C.19).

On a high terrace overlooking the cemetery is the impressive Cambrai Memorial, which commemorates more than 7000 soldiers from the UK and South Africa who were killed in the Battle of Cambrai (November and December 1917) and have no known grave.

Boursies

By 3 April there were only three outpost villages standing between the Australians and the Hindenburg Line: Boursies, Demicourt and Hermies. It was decided that the best way to capture them was to strike Boursies and Hermies simultaneously on 9 April. If all went according to plan and these villages were captured, the Germans would evacuate Demicourt, which sat between them. Once again, the plan called for the attacking troops to encircle the villages rather than attack them head-on. This had worked well at Doignies; surely it would work here too.

Unfortunately, there are no certainties in battle. The tactic that had taken the Germans by surprise at Doignies and routed them in a couple of hours turned into a gruelling 26-hour ordeal at Boursies. The attacking battalions, the 10th and 12th, came under heavy fire the moment they left their line, and casualties were severe and disruptive. Several officers in both battalions were killed early in the advance, including Lieutenant Roy Fordham, one of a handful of men who had advanced the furthest inland on the day of the landing at Gallipoli (see **Vaulx Hill Cemetery**, pages 277–278). That the 12th Battalion made any ground at all was mostly due to the work of Captain James Newland, who led an attack on a German strongpoint at an old mill and then held it against German counterattacks. For his work here and at the Battle of Lagnicourt a week later, Newland was awarded the VC (see page 282).

Eventually the Australians clawed their way through the village and pushed the Germans into the fields beyond. The attack had cost the 10th and 12th battalions 341 men. The Germans had lost less than 100. For the day's fighting to be considered a success, the attack on Hermies would have to be something special.

Hermies—Bede Kenny VC

The plan to capture Hermies called for the Australians to attack it unexpectedly from the north-west, skirting behind the German wire barricade and clearing the village. The 2nd Battalion was given the job, supported by two companies from the 3rd Battalion who would attack from the south-west. One company of the 2nd

Battalion was tasked with setting up a line of posts east of the village to cut off any Germans trying to escape.

The early stages of the attack were tougher than expected. Before the 2nd Battalion had even set off, a German flare ignited a haystack and lit up the field where the Australians were assembling. Heavy fire broke out and several men were hit, so the 2nd Battalion set off early. They quickly overcame the isolated German posts north of the village but were held up by extremely heavy fire from an abandoned brickworks. The attack was in real danger of falling apart: dawn was fast approaching and the Australians would be sitting ducks once the sun rose. Just when it seemed the only option was a near-suicidal charge at the brickworks, the German fire suddenly ceased. A company from the 2nd Battalion who had advanced further east had heard the commotion and outflanked the Germans, killing several and taking more than 70 prisoners. The brickworks had been the key defensive position near the village and its capture cleared the way for the Australians. They pushed through Hermies, capturing Germans in most of the buildings and cellars they passed. The Germans were caught totally off guard. In spite of the noise of fighting that had been going on for the last hour, some of them were asleep and others were making breakfast.

The only other delay occurred when the left company of the 2nd Battalion was trying to establish its line of posts east of the village. One platoon came under heavy machine-gun fire from a sunken road. Eight bombers crept forward and saw a German post in a sandpit next to the road. A lanky corporal, Bede Kenny, asked two mates to cover him and then rushed the position, throwing bombs as he went. A German charged forward and Kenny shot him dead. He then dived among the others and found all of them wounded by his bombs, except for one officer, who Kenny killed after a close fight. The rest of the platoon arrived at the sandpit to find Kenny in total control of the position, guarding a group of wounded prisoners and their machine-gun. Kenny's swift action had overcome a dangerous obstacle and enabled the company to form its line of posts. He was awarded the Victoria Cross.

With Australians closing in on all sides, nearly every German in Hermies was either killed or captured. The action had been a complete success. The two battalions lost 253 men but captured more than 200 Germans. The tough nature of the fight is revealed in the fact that more than a third of all the Australian casualties had been killed.

With both Boursies and Hermies lost, the Germans began to evacuate Demicourt. The 1st Battalion moved towards the village soon after Hermies was taken and secured it by midday. The capture of Hermies was the first time the Australians had been involved in an attack that had gone, from start to finish, almost exactly to plan.

The Australians advanced on Hermies in the fields on the eastern side of the Doignies road, the D34. The sunken road where Bede Kenny won his VC is still there, although the sandpit has disappeared. From the centre of Hermies, take the D5 east in the direction of Havrincourt. Before leaving Hermies, turn left at a crossroads. Follow this road until it heads north-east out of the village and becomes sunken. Kenny attacked along this stretch of road from near the edge of the village. After 250 metres the road bends left. The sandpit captured by Kenny was in the field on the inside of this bend.

Bede Kenny had worked at a chemist in Bondi before enlisting in 1915. He joined the 2nd Battalion early in 1916 and served with the unit throughout the war. After his VC-winning action he was wounded at Méteren in 1918 and returned to Sydney. After the war he worked as a salesman for a wine company but suffered from ill health later in life. He died in Sydney in 1953, aged 56.

Hermies British Cemetery was started by the Australians soon after they had captured Hermies and was used by British units until December 1917. Today 27 of the 109 burials are Australian, nearly all men of the 2nd Battalion killed in the advance on the village. Buried here is 2nd Lieutenant Malcolm Paterson of the 2nd Battalion, who was killed trying to find a way to overcome the strong German position at the brickworks (grave A.7).

Hermies British Cemetery is on the west side of the village and is signposted at the three-way intersection of the D34, D5 and D19 roads.

Hermies Hill British Cemetery was started in November 1917 and used on and off for the rest of the war. After the Armistice it was greatly enlarged when graves were brought in from the surrounding fields and several small cemeteries. There are now over 1000 graves in the cemetery, of which 43 are Australian. Four of these are unidentified. Twenty-one Australians who lie here were originally buried in Hermies Australian Cemetery north-west of the village. It was closed after the Armistice and the graves relocated here. Buried here is Lieutenant Victor Robins, who led a company of the 2nd Battalion in the attack on Hermies. Demonstrating how depleted the Australian ranks had become, Robins was the senior officer in the attack, despite being only 22 years old. He was killed early in the advance (grave III.D.11). Also buried here is 2nd Lieutenant Alfred Cassidy of the 1st Battalion, the only officer killed in the capture of Demicourt on the morning of 9 April (grave I.H.35).

Hermies Hill British Cemetery is directly opposite Hermies British Cemetery.

With Hermies and Demicourt taken, the Australian advance on the outpost villages ended. General Hubert Gough, commander of the British Fifth Army, said in a telegraph to the 1st Division: 'Throughout the advance since the end of February the enterprise, tactical skill, and gallantry of the whole Anzac Corps has been remarkable and is deserving of the highest commendation.' The Australians now dug in facing the Hindenburg Line, the capture of which would prove one of the bloodiest chapters in the history of the AIF.

12

Battles of Bullecourt, April and May 1917

Bullecourt is one of the most important placenames in AIF history. The two great battles fought here in 1917 were among the most ferocious ever endured by Australian troops and cost the four Australian divisions involved more than 10 000 men.

Bullecourt was one of the villages incorporated into the complex defences of the Hindenburg Line. The Hindenburg Line consisted of two deep trench lines, 'OG1' and 'OG2', protected by massive belts of barbed wire. The Germans had laid out the wire entanglement in a zigzag pattern, so that attacking troops would become separated and be drawn into the 'vees' of the zigzag, where they would be bunched up in the sights of well-placed machine-guns. Deep dugouts and concrete emplacements provided extra protection to the defenders.

The 'mastermind' behind the First Battle of Bullecourt was General Hubert Gough, a Boer War veteran and cavalryman who commanded the British Fifth Army. Gough was impulsive and prone to underestimating the Germans. In spite of strong evidence to the contrary, he convinced himself that the Hindenburg Line at Bullecourt was weakly held and ripe to be captured. His excitement peaked when General Douglas Haig, the British commander, gave Gough 12 tanks to help break down the German wire and clear a path for the infantry.

The tanks were still relatively untested. They had been tentatively used during the Battle of the Somme six months earlier but the jury was still out as to their effectiveness in battle. Their officers couldn't even agree on *how* they should be used: should they be spaced out across a wide front and follow the infantry in an attack, or bunched up to attack in front of the infantry? The only thing certain was that the early tanks were mechanically unreliable, vulnerable to artillery fire and operated by inexperienced crews. Gough's enthusiasm could not be contained, however. In spite of protests from General William Birdwood, commander of the Australian troops, the tanks were ordered to support the troops in place of an artillery barrage and given the vital responsibility of breaking down the German wire.

The attack was set for 10 April and was intended to support a large British attack on nearby Arras. Two brigades of the Australian 4th Division, the 4th and 12th, were tasked with the assault. The British 62nd Division would attack the village of Bullecourt itself, on the left of the Australians. At this stage of the war the 4th Division was probably the toughest in the AIF, but its task was monumental.

Captain Albert Jacka, intelligence officer of the 14th Battalion, scouted in front of the Australian lines and found a sunken road in no man's land that would be a good jumping off point for the attack. The night before the advance he was patrolling no man's land when he ran headlong into a German officer and a companion. He captured them both, preventing the Germans from discovering the jumping off tape and providing valuable intelligence about the opposing units. Jacka, who had already received the Victoria Cross at Gallipoli and the Military Cross at Pozières, was awarded another MC.

At 4 am on 10 April the troops lay out in fresh snow, waiting for the tanks to arrive and the attack to begin. An hour later the scheduled time of the attack had come and gone and there was no sign of the tanks. Apparently they had lost their way during the drive to the front line. Worried that the troops would be spotted in the dawn light, the 4th Division commanders called off the attack and the troops streamed back to the Australian line 'like a crowd from a football match'.

If the fiasco of the tanks was not portent enough that this battle was in trouble, a serious breakdown in communication should have been. The 4th Division failed to inform the British 62nd Division that the attack had been called off. The 62nd attacked Bullecourt, as instructed, at 4.30 am and was mauled by machine-gun fire.

The 4th Division's troops had just returned to their rest areas when their commanders received an order that the attack had been rescheduled for the next day. Despite strong protests from the Anzac leaders, General Haig had ordered that the attack should go ahead on the 11th.

The troops who lay out in the snow in the early hours of 11 April must have felt a strong sense of deja vu. Once again, they were preparing to attack without adequate artillery support. Once again, they were relying on the support of tanks that, so far, had not shown up. After making the return trip from the rear to the front line twice in two days, the troops were exhausted. Private Wilfred Gallwey of the 47th Battalion described the struggle to reach the front line in his diary: 'I carried my rifle in my left hand, just holding it by the sling and trailing the butt through the mud. It was too much energy to carry it any other way. Knees were giving way and I was plodding on like in a dream . . . Of what use would I be to fight to-night. My body was in a wretched state of weakness.'

In an effort to avoid a repeat of the previous night's debacle, the tanks had been ordered to be ready to advance by 3 am. That hour had come and gone, however, before the tanks even arrived. An order for machine-guns and artillery to cover the noise of the approaching tanks had been misinterpreted and the night was relatively quiet as the tanks approached, the noise from their belching engines drifting alarmingly across no man's land.

By 4.45 am only four of the tanks were in their correct positions—
the others had either broken down, got lost or became stuck in
the mud. Although without the tanks they had no way of getting
through the German wire, the troops advanced exactly on time.

The 4th Brigade, which had distinguished itself so well at
Gallipoli, set off into a hail of fire on the right of the advance.
Its men reached the German wire well ahead of any tanks. Major
Percy Black, who had been at Gallipoli and knew a thing or two
about tough fights, called to his men, 'Come on, boys, bugger the
tanks!' and began to hack through the wire. The Germans sent
up waves of flares, turning night into day, and poured machine-
gun and rifle fire into the Australians. Survivors later described a
swarm of fireflies buzzing around them as sparks from German
bullets fizzed off the wire.

In spite of the seemingly insurmountable obstacles, the 4th
Brigade fought its way through the wire and into the German
trenches. Then they did the impossible: they overcame the defenders
in both OG1 and OG2 and took their objectives. They began to
probe west, desperately trying to link up with the 12th Brigade.

The 12th was having a tough time. A communication mix-up
meant that they did not advance on time, instead waiting for the
tanks to pass them so that they could follow. Eventually a tank
lumbered up to their line, turned, and began firing its machine-
gun at them! After a chorus of shouts from the Australians a hatch
opened in the side of the tank and the head of a British officer
appeared, asking which troops they were, and could they please
direct him to the German lines. Duly instructed, the tank set off.
A few minutes later one of its crew came scampering back with
the news that it had been destroyed by a shell and he was the only
survivor. Another tank appeared, passed in front of the troops
and promptly broke down. Eventually the Australians decided to
advance without the tanks and set off at a run. By this stage it was
almost light and the 12th Brigade was badly cut up by machine-
gun fire. By the time they reached the wire their numbers had
been shattered, but the survivors grimly pushed on. One tank
had actually succeeded in breaking down the wire, and the 12th

Brigade poured through the gap. Machine-gun fire was furious. One group of 50 men made a charge for the German second line—only 10 men survived the rush. A lieutenant in the 46th Battalion called for all unwounded men in his company to follow him as he advanced, and only one man replied. Nevertheless, the 12th Brigade pushed on and after several hours of tough fighting had a toehold in the German lines.

By now the Germans were regrouping and beginning to counterattack. Severe bomb fights broke out along the German lines. The Australians sent up emergency flares, asking for artillery support to suppress the German machine-guns. Behind the Australian lines the gunners were unsure exactly where the Australians were, so held their fire. When they eventually did fire, their shells landed on their own men. The German artillery was better organised and began pummelling no man's land. The chance for reinforcements to reach the forward Australian troops was lost.

Unsupported, low on ammunition and losing men by the minute, the Australians began to fall back. Some battalions ordered a retreat through the hail of fire, but others fought on. Eventually the Germans flooded back into their trenches and captured scores of Australians at the point of the bayonet.

On 12 April, with the survivors back in their original positions and the Hindenburg Line still firmly in German hands, a tally was taken. The two brigades had lost 3300 men between them, including 1170 men taken prisoner: the largest number of Australians captured during a single engagement in the war. Many of the AIF's bravest leaders, including Percy Black, were dead. To call the First Battle of Bullecourt a debacle would be an insult to debacles. British army instructors later used this battle as an example of how *not* to plan an attack.

Gough may have lacked many things, but the ability to look on the bright side was not one of them. He told the 4th Division that he was 'satisfied that the effect upon the whole situation by the Anzac attack has been of great assistance'. Suggesting that the carnage at Bullecourt was somehow of 'great assistance' to British Army morale was like trying to cheer up a man who had just lost an arm by pointing out he won't have to clip his fingernails anymore.

Keen to demonstrate that the loss of half a division wasn't enough to spoil a good idea, Gough planned a second attack. In May the British were having another dig near Arras, and this time the scale was huge. Fourteen divisions would advance on a front of 25 kilometres, an assault as large as the First Battle of the Somme in July 1916. Apparently believing that surprise didn't play much of a role in modern warfare, Gough decided to throw his Australians in at Bullecourt once again.

There were a few important changes to the plan this time. Two brigades from the Australian 2nd Division (the 5th and 6th) would lead the attack on the Hindenburg Line, again supported on the left by the tireless British 62nd Division. Once again the British would attack Bullecourt and they had requested 10 tanks to help in this endeavour. Records don't reveal the nature of the response when the Australians were offered the assistance of tanks, but it was probably short and to the point. This time the Australians would attack without the dubious support of the tanks and instead rely on a traditional creeping artillery barrage and the massed fire of 96 Vickers machine-guns: more than the AIF had ever used in a divisional attack.

The failure of the first attack at Bullecourt was still fresh in the 2nd Division's minds and they determined to eliminate chance from the plan as much as they could. They located a similar piece of terrain to the Bullecourt battlefield near the town of Favreuil and constructed a full-size replica of the attack area, with tape and wire marking out villages, roads, trenches and barbed wire entanglements. Men with flags simulated the position of the creeping barrage. For several days the brigades practised the assault, the training culminating in a full night-time dress rehearsal. Details were important. At one stage a senior officer noticed the loud flapping of the men's bayonet scabbards against their thighs as they advanced. In response, the scabbards were securely tied down during the actual attack.

The attack was launched in the early hours of 3 May and started well. The 5th and 6th brigades were tasked with capturing OG1 and OG2 in short order and pushing on to take several villages beyond. The supporting artillery barrage made the job of breaking into the German lines easier than on 11 April, but the Germans quickly recovered and began pouring reinforcements into the lines. Second Bullecourt soon became a siege, with the Australians desperate to cling on to the small piece of German territory they had secured, and the Germans attempting to bomb the Diggers to oblivion.

On the right, the 5th Brigade had run into heavy fire and their attack began to break up. Reinforcing battalions rushed forward but the position was perilous. The 5th Brigade fell back, leaving the right of the Australian line exposed, and it was only through desperate defence that the Australians weren't driven completely out of the German lines. By the evening on 3 May the Australians were spread out thinly in the German lines, with a narrow avenue across no man's land the only means of reinforcements and ammunition reaching the fighting men. Isolated parties had even advanced beyond the German lines. One group from the 24th Battalion under Captain Gordon Maxfield had held a dangerously exposed position near an intersection called Six Crossroads throughout the day. A strong German force was seen assembling for a counterattack. They swept forward, Maxfield's position was swallowed up and he and his men were never seen again.

The Germans launched a series of violent counterattacks in an effort to retake their lines. On 4 May the exhausted companies of the 2nd Division began to be relieved by the 1st Division. The 1st Battalion, stalwarts of the tough fighting at Gallipoli, marched into 'some of the heaviest fighting that the Battalion experienced throughout its career', according to the unit's Official History. It goes on to describe the inferno faced by the men over the next few days:

There were continual bombing attacks and counter-attacks . . . There was a fierce enemy attack with Flammenwerfer [flame throwers], but Captain Somerset jumped out of the trench, hurling bombs, and they departed thoroughly, leaving five of their companions dead. All the time there was a heavy rain of shells and sniping and bombing went on without intermission.

On 6 May the Germans began to bomb back along OG1 from the right, forcing the Australians back as they went. Every available man was thrown into the defence but the situation seemed hopeless. A fierce bomb fight broke out and the main group of Germans, about 80 strong, forced their way forward along the trench. Suddenly the Australians saw a lone figure spring from their part of the trench and run across the open towards the Germans, hurling bombs as he went. They recognised him as George 'Snowy' Howell, a corporal from the 1st Battalion. Howell soon set the attacking Germans to flight and ran along the top of the trench, pelting them with bombs and stabbing down at them with his bayonet. Before long he was caught by fire and fell wounded into the trench. His bravery had broken the shackles, however, and the Australians swarmed back along the trench, eventually retaking it after a tough fight. Howell survived and was awarded the Victoria Cross.

Fighting in the rest of the Arras sector had died down, so the struggle at Bullecourt grabbed the attention of the entire British Army. Casualties were heavy and a procession of wounded men were stretchered across no man's land and to aid posts in the rear. The fighting had reached an uneasy stalemate. The Australians had advanced as far as they could and the Germans did not have the strength to evict them from their lines. For the time being both sides abandoned the attack and contented themselves with pounding each other with high explosives. By 10 May the 1st and 2nd divisions were exhausted and the 5th Division was brought into the line.

The 5th was a good unit but had not fully recovered from the mauling it received at Fromelles in July the previous year. Fortunately, after a week of continuous fighting, the Germans were as worn out as the Australians and the conflict began to die down. The British rolled the dice one last time and sent units forward to secure the small corner of Bullecourt village still in German hands. The Australian 58th and 60th battalions were assigned to support the attack by advancing along OG1 and OG2 and overcoming a number of German strongpoints on the way.

Rupert Moon was a lieutenant in the 58th Battalion, a slight 24-year-old who was quietly considered by his superiors to be too lacking in self-confidence to be an effective leader. Over the next few hours he would prove them wrong. His task was to lead a small party to attack a German concrete shelter between the two trench lines. He had only advanced a short distance when he was wounded and his men faltered. Moon rallied his men by calling out, 'Come on boys, don't turn me down,' and charged at the German position. After a short fight the Germans fled and Moon led his men in hot pursuit. He leaped among the Germans in a sunken road and emptied his rifle into the fleeing men. The clear thinkers among them realised Moon was alone and flung bombs at him; he escaped by the skin of his teeth after one of his men shot the leading German bomber. Moon ordered the Australians to shower the Germans with grenades and then dived back into the sunken road. He saw a mass of Germans rushing into some dugouts, and by ordering his men to fire on the entrances, convinced the Germans to surrender. Two officers and 184 men emerged and were taken prisoner, more than had been captured by the entire 2nd Division in the opening three days of the battle. Moon crept to the bank of the road and peered over, looking for the next objective. A rifle cracked and he fell back, shot in the face. He sat in the sunken road, blood and sweat pouring from his face, joking with his men that he had been wounded three times and not one of them was serious enough to have him sent back to England. Not surprisingly, Moon was awarded the Victoria Cross.

The fighting around Bullecourt spluttered on for another five days but the battle was effectively over. On 17 May the Germans gave up trying to retake their old lines and withdrew. Once again they had seen the tough fighting abilities of the Australians close up, and had high praise for them. German

Crown Prince Rupprecht wrote in his diary on 5 May that 'according to unanimous descriptions from the front, the English troops show themselves far less tough to repulse than formerly, with the exception of the Canadians and Australians, who are on all sides praised for their bravery and skill in making use of the ground.'

The two battles of Bullecourt marked the end of a bloody chapter in AIF history. Even though they shook the faith of the Australians in their British commanders, this was their last attack of the war where the objectives were unimportant or the planning inadequate. The Australians had matured as a fighting force and would now be used as crack assault troops by their British commanders, in attacks that had been well devised and would be well led. The Second Battle of Bullecourt had cost the Australians 7000 men but it closed a door on the dark days of Fromelles, Pozières and Flers.

BULLECOURT TOUR

The Bullecourt battlefield is deceptive; except for a few memorials there's nothing to indicate the historic importance of the site or the carnage that occurred here. This is a fairly easy walk and should take about two hours to complete. It can be driven in about an hour. It visits three memorials and the sites of two Victoria Cross actions.

Park next to the church in the centre of Bullecourt [1]. Facing the street is a memorial to the divisions that took part in the two great battles, the Australian 1st, 2nd, 4th and 5th, and the British 7th, 58th and 62nd. The focal point is a bronze sculpture of a First World War slouch hat. Not far from the slouch hat memorial, facing the carpark, a rusted old section of tank track is rather unceremoniously displayed on the ground. This is probably as fitting a memorial as the tanks deserve at Bullecourt, although their pathetic performance was not the fault of the tank crews—they did as much in the attack as their lumbering machines

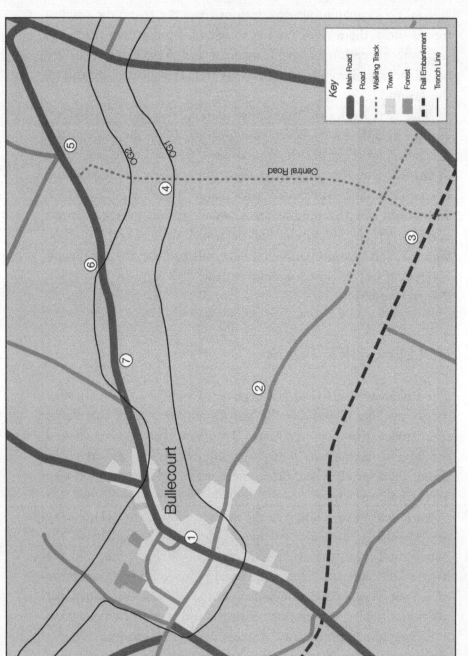

Key

Main Road
Road
Walking Track
Town
Forest
Rail Embankment
Trench Line

Bullecourt

Central Road

OG2

OG1

Battles of Bullecourt

allowed—but the appalling planning and misplaced faith in the tanks by the British commanders.

Leave the church, turn left and follow the road to the next intersection on your left. Follow this road out of town until it becomes sunken [2]. This is the section of road that was discovered by Captain Jacka in his reconnaissance of the battlefield and the starting point for most of the Australian troops in both battles. They advanced from here and crossed the field to your left, towards the Hindenburg Line. In the distance the flags in the Australian Memorial Park mark the site of the two lines of German trenches attacked by the Australians.

Continue along the sunken road to a crossroads with a farm track. This track is Central Road, a key landmark on the battlefield. Australians advanced on either side in both battles. During the First Battle, the depression on the left of the road was used by a tank as cover to advance all the way to the German trenches—one of the few to make it that far. It became tangled in the German wire while trying to cross the first trench and came under heavy machine-gun, shell and grenade fire while it struggled to break free. It was eventually hit by a shell and destroyed. Only three members of the crew survived. Another tank attempting to use the road as cover was hit by a shell just past the intersection and burst into flames. During the Second Battle, the 2nd Division's Pioneers dug a communication trench more than a kilometre long along the edge of Central Road, and from this time the road became known as Pioneer Trench.

Turn right at the crossroads and follow the track a short distance until you reach a scrub-covered embankment. This is the old railway line [3] that served as a jumping off point for the Australian troops in both battles, and the site of numerous headquarters and support positions during the attacks. Explore the embankment on either side of Central Road to find the remains of dugouts, as well as relics from the fighting.

Return along Central Road and pass through the crossroads. (If driving, continue along the sunken road until the next intersection, turn left and drive into Riencourt. Turn left in

the village and follow the road until it meets the far end of
Central Road, signposted on the left as 'Six Crossroads'.) As you
follow Central Road, you are walking in the footsteps of the
Australian troops during the two great battles. During the First
Battle the 46th and 48th battalions advanced on your left and
the 14th and 16th advanced on your right. In the Second Battle
the 21st, 22nd, 23rd and 24th battalions advanced on your left,
with the 17th, 18th, 19th and 20th on your right. In both battles
the troops advanced under fire from the moment they left the
sunken road until they came to OG1, the first German trench.

Today it is difficult to pinpoint the exact location where
OG1 crossed Central Road, but it is approximately one kilometre
from the crossroads [4]. This is where Corporal Snowy Howell
launched his one-man bombing assault against the Germans on
6 May. He leaped from OG1 on the left of Central Road, crossed
it and began hurling Mills bombs among Germans in the trench on
the right of the road. He was wounded and fell into OG1 a short
distance from Central Road.

George 'Snowy' Howell grew up in Sydney and worked as
a builder until he enlisted in 1915. He joined the 1st Battalion
at Gallipoli late in the campaign and travelled with it to France
in March 1916. He was wounded at Pozières in 1916 and a
month before his VC exploit received the Military Medal while
leading a bombing party at Demicourt. The wounds he received
at Bullecourt were severe and he was eventually repatriated to
Australia. After the war he worked on the advertising staff of
the *Bulletin*, but rejoined the army at the outbreak of the Second
World War and served with the US Sea Transport Service in the
Philippines. He died in Western Australia on Christmas Eve, 1964,
aged 71.

Continue along Central Road for another 200 metres. This is
the approximate point where the second German trench, OG2,
crossed the road. A short distance further the road curves left
and joins a sealed road. The curve is a recent diversion; Central
Road originally ran straight on and met several other roads at the

intersection known as Six Crossroads. Turn right and walk along the sealed road for a short distance until a signpost on your right indicates you have reached Six Crossroads [5]. This is the scene of Captain Maxfield's heroic defence of the second objective against overwhelming odds during the Second Battle. Maxfield and his small group lined the bank of a tramline about 150 metres into the field in front of you (i.e., north of the crossroads), facing Riencourt. Ostrich Avenue, a German communication trench captured by the Australians, ran north–south to the right of the crossroads.

Return along the road and continue past the intersection with Central Road until you reach a small cross set on a stone plinth high on the right bank [6]. This memorial marks the approximate location where OG2 crossed the road before looping around the rear of the village, and commemorates the 2423 Australians killed in the fighting who have no known grave. The cross has been embellished by private plaques, one of which reads:

IN MEMORY OF
ALL MY MATES KILLED IN ACTION
LEST WE FORGET
R.M. GUNN 4TH AIF

Private Ronald Gunn was a Gallipoli veteran who served in the 13th Field Ambulance of the 4th Division. He received a special mention in divisional orders for bravery during the first three weeks of the Gallipoli campaign and was wounded at Messines in 1917. He fell ill with dysentery and was returned to Australia in 1918.

Another plaque remembers Major Percy Black and was erected by his family from Victoria.

Continue along the road until you reach a park on your left. This is the Australian Memorial Park [7], opened in 1993 on ground between the German trenches, OG1 and OG2. The focal point of the park is a magnificent bronze statue of a Digger in full kit, looking out across the battlefield. It is a work by Melbourne sculptor Peter Corlett, the same artist who sculpted the 'Cobbers' statue at Fromelles, and is designed to complement both the Fromelles statue and the Digger sculpture on the 2nd Division Memorial at Mont St Quentin. The inscription on the base of the statue reads:

> Sacred to the memory of the 10,000 members of the Australian Imperial Force who were killed and wounded in the two battles of Bullecourt, April–May 1917, and to the Australian dead and their comrades in arms who lie here forever in the soil of France. 'Lest we Forget'

By looking across the fields from between the trees at the rear of the park, you are seeing the Bullecourt battlefield from the German perspective. On a clear day the tree-lined railway embankment where the Australian attack began is visible in the distance. Near the entrance to the park is a Bastiaan plaque detailing the Australian involvement in both battles at Bullecourt.

Leave the park and turn left. In the fields to the left of the road, just before the intersection with a track on the right, is the site where Lieutenant Rupert Moon won the Victoria Cross. He attacked from roughly the site of the Australian Memorial Park and led his men across the field parallel to the road, in the same direction you are walking. This is the road he leaped into during his bomb fight with the Germans. The dugouts where he helped capture 186 Germans were in this same stretch of road.

Rupert Moon came from Gippsland in Victoria and worked for the National Bank in Melbourne until his enlistment in the Light Horse at the outbreak of war. He served with the Light Horse throughout the Gallipoli campaign, transferred to the infantry and was commissioned as a 2nd Lieutenant of the 58th Battalion in 1916. He recovered from his Bullecourt wounds and returned to Australia in June 1919 with the rank of captain. He worked as an accountant for many years and died in 1986, aged 94.

Continue along this road as it leads back into Bullecourt and your car. Before leaving Bullecourt, visit the excellent museum located in the Rue d'Arras.

OTHER SITES OF INTEREST

Bapaume

The town of Bapaume was an alluring objective for British forces during the Somme fighting. It was as important a support base for the Germans as Albert was for the British. In yet another example of the hopeless optimism that characterised the First Battle of the Somme, Bapaume was the ultimate objective for British troops in the opening days of the attack. If they'd gotten there it would have been a good effort—Bapaume was 15 kilometres behind the German lines. As it happened, the Germans in Bapaume didn't need to panic; the British were mown down by German fire on the first day and didn't get anywhere near the town.

Even after the Battle of the Somme had dragged on for four months and exhausted all involved, Bapaume wasn't in any danger. The British had got 10 kilometres closer to the town, but the arrival of winter signalled the end of their advance.

Bapaume eventually did fall into British hands but it was gifted rather than taken. During their withdrawal to the Hindenburg Line in March 1917, the Germans abandoned the town and British troops occupied it almost unopposed. Patrols from the Australian 30th Battalion were the first to enter the town on 17 March. Lieutenant Arthur White was the first man to set foot in the place after actually racing one of his NCOs for the honour.

Even though Allied soldiers had marched into Bapaume instead of capturing it, the town had been such an important objective they were delighted to finally be there. There wasn't much to explore. The Germans had systematically destroyed most of the houses and the whole town was on fire. The only buildings in sound condition surrounded the main square, the town hall being the most prominent of these. Australian engineers searched the building and found that the Germans had planted a mine there, intended to destroy the building, but it had failed to explode. On the night of 25 March an undiscovered second mine exploded in the town hall and shattered the building. Thirty Australians and two French deputies were trapped in the rubble and only six men were pulled out alive.

Other booby traps were found in houses throughout Bapaume, and the Australian soldiers considered this high treachery on the part of the Germans. As Charles Bean noted in the *Official History*, this was hard to understand: the Australians had left similar booby traps behind for the Turks to discover when they abandoned their trenches at Gallipoli.

Over the next few months Bapaume was used as a forward base and British and Australian troops advanced from it as they moved to attack the Hindenburg Line.

Directions

Bapaume is a large town 19 kilometres north-east of Albert on the dead straight D929. The rebuilt town hall is in the centre, facing the main square. A monument on its wall commemorates the two Frenchmen killed in the mine blast but doesn't mention the 24 Australians who also died. A Franco-Prussian War statue stands on the square. Its base stood here during the war and was badly knocked around by shellfire. Australian soldiers who first arrived in the town scratched their names into the stone, and the marks are still faintly discernible.

Wellington Quarries (Carrière Wellington), Arras

For centuries chalk quarries beneath Arras had been used to supply stone for the town's buildings and roads—in 1917, during the height of the Battle of Arras, British troops found an ingenious new use for the network of caves and tunnels. In addition to providing shelter for Allied troops, the quarries were expanded to enable underground access to the enemy's trenches. More than 500 miners were brought in from New Zealand, most of them drawn directly from coal and goldfields. They worked tirelessly in appalling conditions alongside British tunnellers to dig more than 20 kilometres of tunnels, and paid a high price for their hard work—more than 200 tunnellers were killed or wounded while working on the quarries. In the end the underground network could shelter more than 20 000 men and was used to great effect to launch attacks on the German defences. The tunnellers named individual shafts and galleries after their home towns—Auckland, Wellington, Nelson, Blenheim, Christchurch and Dunedin for the New Zealanders, and Glasgow, Edinburgh, Crewe and London for the British. During the Second World War the tunnels were used as air raid shelters and in 2008, a section of the Wellington Quarry was opened as a museum. Today the museum is a highlight of a visit to the Western Front, and demonstrates in stark detail the claustrophobia and terror of the underground war.

Directions
The Wellington Quarries (Carrière Wellington in French) are located south of the centre of Arras, on the Rue Arthur Deletoille.

Vimy Ridge Canadian Memorial

Vimy Ridge was the most important German defensive position in the Arras sector. The ridge dominated the surrounding Douai plain and the Germans had strongly fortified it. By 1917, 200 000 French and German troops had fallen trying to gain control of the ridge—now it was Canada's turn. Four Canadian Divisions attacked Vimy Ridge on 9 April 1917, storming their way up the slope. They overcame row after row of German trenches, hacked their way through wire, tussled hand-to-hand with the German defenders and assaulted machine-gun posts. By the time their Australian comrades were launching the suicidal assault on Bullecourt two days later, the ridge was securely in Canadian hands. It was a magnificent achievement and the only significant success of the early part of the Battle of Arras. But the victory came at a high price. More than 10 000 Canadians were killed or wounded and four Victoria Crosses were won. Brigadier General Alexander Ross, a Canadian battalion commander, said of the battle: '. . . in those few minutes I witnessed the birth of a nation.'

In 1922 France gave 400 hectares of land on Vimy Ridge to Canada as the site for a national memorial. Work began in 1925 and the memorial was unveiled in 1936. There is no doubt that the Canadian memorials are among the most impressive on the Western Front, and Vimy Ridge is the best of the lot. A massive stone base supports two 27-metre pylons that soar skyward from the highest point of the ridge. Twenty sculpted figures on the memorial represent mourning and triumph. The most moving of these is a hooded woman resting her chin in her hand. She represents a young Canada, mourning her 66 000 lost sons. The names of 11 285 Canadians who were killed in France and have no known grave are carved onto the walls of the memorial. In a park next to it, a well-preserved trench system is well worth exploring.

Canada and Australia shared a special bond during the Great War. They were both young dominions of England who rushed to join the European war. In 1918 they both spearheaded the Advance to Victory which ultimately ended the war. And throughout the war they paid a similar price in lost youth. The sentiments expressed by the Vimy Ridge Memorial will resonate with Australian visitors.

Directions
The village of Vimy is 40 kilometres north of Bapaume. The Vimy Ridge Memorial dominates the surrounding plain and can be seen from all approaches. It is signposted in the village.

CEMETERIES NEAR THE HINDENBURG LINE

Most of the Australians buried in this area were killed in the two great battles of Bullecourt and in fighting in the nearby outpost villages. Most of the important cemeteries are listed in the Hindenburg Line Outpost Villages chapter, but there are a few others that are worth seeing.

Bapaume Australian Cemetery

This cemetery was started by the 3rd Australian Casualty Clearing Station after the Germans had withdrawn from Bapaume in March 1917. It was mostly used to bury men who died of wounds following the Australian attacks on the Hindenburg Line outpost villages and at Bullecourt, between March and June 1917. When fighting returned to this area in April and May 1918, the cemetery was used to bury 23 German soldiers. Today Bapaume Australian Cemetery contains 83 Commonwealth graves, of which 74 are Australian, all of them identified.

The senior Australian buried here is Captain Melville Hughes, a brave doctor with the 5th Division Medical Corps. He was killed by a shell while attending to wounded at his dressing station at Beugny on 20 March 1917 (grave A.1).

Several of the men buried here, including Private Alexander Gunn of the 6th Battalion (grave A.27) and Private Albert Scott of the 5th Battalion (grave A.28), were killed in the mine explosion that destroyed Bapaume town hall (see pages 307–308).

Directions
Bapaume Australian Cemetery is on a side street near the centre of Bapaume. Drive through Bapaume in the direction of Péronne and the cemetery is signposted before leaving the town. It can be difficult to find but is located behind the park that features a reclining statue of Abel Guidet, the mayor of Bapaume during the Second World War who was executed by the Nazis for supporting the French Resistance.

Beaumetz Cross Roads Cemetery: see Hindenburg Line Outpost Villages tour (page 280).

HAC Cemetery, Ecoust-St-Mein
HAC (Honourable Artillery Company) Cemetery was started by the British 7th Division soon after the capture of Ecoust in April

1917. Today the cemetery is yet another in this area swelled by Australian dead from the two battles of Bullecourt.

The first Australian burials were made here after the German counterattack at Lagnicourt on 15 April when 12 gunners were buried in Plot I, Row A. The majority of Australian graves, however, were brought in after the war from the surrounding Hindenburg Line battlefields. Today the cemetery contains nearly 2000 graves, 176 of which are Australian. Considering the horrific fighting at Bullecourt, it is not surprising that 111 of the Australian graves are unidentified.

The most senior Australian buried here is Captain Louis Smith of the 51st Battalion, who was killed in the attack on Noreuil on 2 April 1917 (grave II.E.3).

Also buried here is Signaller Percy Gray MM of the 27th Battalion. Gray had won his Military Medal at Warlencourt in March 1917 for carrying messages back to headquarters under heavy fire. His recommendation reports that he was 'unconcerned under the most concentrated fire and behaved with the utmost courage and coolness'. He was killed on 24 April 1917 (grave VII.G.1).

Directions
Ecoust-St-Mein is two kilometres south-west of Bullecourt on the road to Bapaume. HAC Cemetery is a kilometre south of the village.

Hermies British Cemetery, Louverval Military Cemetery, Morchies Australian Cemetery, Noreuil Australian Cemetery: see Hindenburg Line Outpost Villages tour (page 275).

Quéant Road Cemetery, Buissy

This large cemetery was started by British units in the last weeks of the war but was greatly enlarged after the Armistice when graves were brought in from the Bullecourt and Arras battlefields. Today the cemetery contains 2377 graves, and Australia is all too well represented: 995 of the graves are Australian, with 696 of them unidentified. The majority of these men were killed at Bullecourt in April or May 1917.

The most notable Australian buried here is Captain Percy Cherry VC of the 26th Battalion, hero of Pozières and Lagnicourt (see pages 281–282). Cherry is buried in grave VIII.C.10.

Another interesting grave belongs to Sergeant John White of the 22nd Battalion, killed at Bullecourt on 3 May 1917. It is interesting because Sergeant White's body wasn't discovered until 1993—76 years after his death. He was identified and interred in Quéant Road Cemetery in the presence of his daughter and other members of his family (grave VIII.B.28a).

A fine young leader is also buried here. Major Ben Leane, second in command of the 48th Battalion, was from a family of highly decorated officers—his brother Ray was the commanding officer of the 48th Battalion and his cousin Allan was a captain in the same unit. The men referred to the 48th as the Joan of Arc Battalion because it was 'made of all Leanes' ('Maid of Orleans'). Ben Leane was killed by a shell during the aborted launch of the First Battle of Bullecourt on 10 April 1917 (grave I.C.1). His cousin Allan was wounded by a grenade at Bullecourt the next day and was captured by the Germans. He died in a German hospital on 2 May 1917 and has no known grave.

Directions
Quéant is a village five kilometres south-east of Bullecourt. The cemetery is on the left of the D14, about two kilometres from Quéant in the direction of Buissy.

Vaulx Australian Field Ambulance Cemetery, Vaulx Hill Cemetery: see Hindenburg Line Outpost Villages tour (page 275).

Part V

The Aisne

The *département* of the Aisne became prominent in Australian military history during the Advance to Victory, the 100-day Allied assault that pushed the Germans out of France and Belgium and ended the war. Australian and Canadian troops spearheaded the advance and were responsible for liberating scores of villages across the region.

The advance forced the Germans back from the positions they had gained during their Spring Offensive of 1918, and across the old 1916 battlefields of the Somme. With unrelenting pressure the Allies continued to drive the Germans back until they neared the Hindenburg Line: the German line that the Allies had captured with so much bloodshed in 1917. The Germans, determined that this would be their last stand, occupied the line much as they had a year earlier, with their main force in the line itself and forward troops occupying a line of outpost villages. Once again, the Australians found themselves assaulting the Hindenburg Line outpost villages, but this time things would be different.

In 1918, unlike the previous year, the Germans didn't have time to prepare elaborate defences along the Hindenburg Line. By the time they fell back to this point they had been in disarray for over a month. Their troops were exhausted after waging a fighting retreat for several weeks and there were few fresh troops to relieve them. Communication and supply lines were strained.

The Australian troops who faced them were in much the same condition. By the fifth year of the war the AIF was a diminished force and new recruits from Australia had dried up. The Australians had been continually engaged since 8 August. The memories of their bloody assaults on the Hindenburg Line in 1917 were still fresh, and now they were called on to do it again.

In early September the Australians began assaulting the outpost villages and liberating them one by one. The Aisne had not seen much of the war and the landscape was green and almost untouched by shelling. Veterans of this fighting spoke for years afterwards of a strange mix of excitement and tension: excitement that the war was obviously in its closing stages and tension that they would be killed before it was over. Many of them also considered this period their hardest slog of the war: non-stop advances, little time to sleep and eat, facing an enemy who was tired but still keen to put up a fight.

By mid-September the Australians had overcome the outpost villages and were facing the Hindenburg Line itself. In another series of tough fights, they broke through and doggedly pushed the Germans back. By October the Hindenburg Line was safely in Allied hands and the Germans had dug in on their next defensive position, the Beaurevoir Line. By this late stage Germany's political leaders were wrangling over the terms of an Armistice, but the fighting on the ground was as tough as ever. The Australians continued to advance, and continued to die.

On 5 October the Australians took part in their last attack of the war, an advance against the village of Montbrehain. It was a strategically unimportant place, but the Australians were ordered to take it nonetheless. The AIF's final act was one of its most impressive. A ludicrously under-strength force captured the village and took 400 German prisoners. The following day the AIF was withdrawn from the fighting. The war ended five weeks later.

The Aisne is as important as any of the Western Front sectors, but it is often overlooked by battlefield visitors. Don't make the same mistake. Many Diggers considered this the scene of their greatest hardship, and hundreds of their mates lie buried in the region's cemeteries. Half a day spent driving through the Aisne villages and exploring the region's small, picturesque cemeteries can be one of the most rewarding experiences of a Western Front tour.

13

Battle of Montbrehain, 5 October 1918

Montbrehain was a dominant obstacle, located on a high plateau with excellent views of the surrounding countryside. The Australians were so worn out by early October that Prime Minister Billy Hughes had ordered they be withdrawn from the line. But on 4 October the 2nd Division learned that their relief, the II American Corps, had been delayed by a day. Instead of a bath and a warm meal behind the lines, 5 October would bring yet another opportunity to attack, and this one was going to be tough.

The British 46th Division had captured Montbrehain on 3 October, only to be driven out by fierce German counterattacks. Now the Australian 2nd Division was called on to finish the job. The 21st and 24th battalions were selected for the attack as they were considered fresh, having seen little or no recent action. (By this stage of the war, 'fresh' was a relative term. The two battalions between them had less than 500 men, about a quarter of their full strength.) To bolster their numbers the 2nd Pioneer Battalion would assault with them. The Pioneers, although more accustomed to trench digging than close combat, had been trained as infantry and were well capable of fighting, but they had been used sparingly in this role in the past.

The attack would be uphill from the village of Ramicourt, the two infantry battalions driving through Montbrehain and the Pioneers wheeling south to cover the advance. It was the sort of attack the Australians dreaded. The 1916 battles had taught them that driving a narrow bulge into the German front line was a bad idea: if enemy artillery remained unsuppressed, it could rain fire on the attackers from three directions. Nevertheless, the Australians were in high spirits. B Company of the 24th sang this little ditty the night before the attack:

> A takes the right flank
> D takes the left flank
> But we'll be in Montbrehain before you . . .

The attack turned out to be one of the Australians' greatest of the war. On the misty morning of 5 October, the battalions advanced up the slope towards the village, covering 500 metres of fire-swept ground. As they went, they scrambled through barbed wire entanglements, captured trenches, cleared dugouts and repeatedly assaulted machine-gun positions, 'riding them down in a manner which delighted our men', according to the 24th Battalion's diary. B Company of the 24th faced ferocious fire north-west of the village and was struggling to make ground until Lieutenant George Ingram led a charge against a German strongpoint in a quarry. He leaped among the Germans and killed without discretion, overcoming the garrison almost single-handedly. Forty machine-guns and more than 60 men were captured. He then went forward alone to reconnoitre and, after hearing a commotion, his men found him in the cellar of a ruined house, keeping a watchful eye on 30 Germans he had just captured. Ingram had shot a machine-gunner who was firing from the cellar and then smashed his way into the house, menacing the Germans into surrendering. He was awarded the VC, Australia's last of the war.

By this and other spirited actions the Australians captured Montbrehain by 9 am and then held it for the rest of the day against determined German counterattacks. By 5 pm the village was secure. The Australians were greeted warmly by dozens of French villagers who had remained in their homes through the thick of the fighting. That night the Australians were relieved and sent to the rear for their well-deserved rest. They were still there when the Armistice was signed five weeks later.

The capture of Montbrehain was a magnificent achievement. Through sheer reckless determination the bedraggled Australians had wrenched an important defensive position from the Germans and taken almost 400 prisoners. But many questioned the necessity of the attack. Charles Bean, the official historian, said it appeared to have been carried out simply to keep the troops occupied until they were due to be withdrawn the next day. It cost the 2nd Division more than 30 officers and 400 men, some of whom had served with the AIF since Gallipoli.

MONTBREHAIN TOUR

This is an essential tour, partly because the ground it covers gives an excellent impression of the battle, but also because of the special place Montbrehain holds in the history of the AIF. It was action that even today is controversial. Inescapable questions linger over the battle. Was it necessary? Should the Australians have been involved? Was it worth losing so many men—men who were supposed to be on their way to the rear for a much-needed rest? Remember them as you walk the fields of Montbrehain.

The tour is not difficult, with few uphill sections, and can be walked in about three hours. It can also be driven (with slight modification) in about an hour, but some of the smaller tracks may be impassable to vehicles in the wetter months.

Montbrehain is located in the *département* of the Aisne, about 40 minutes from Péronne. The tour begins at the village church,

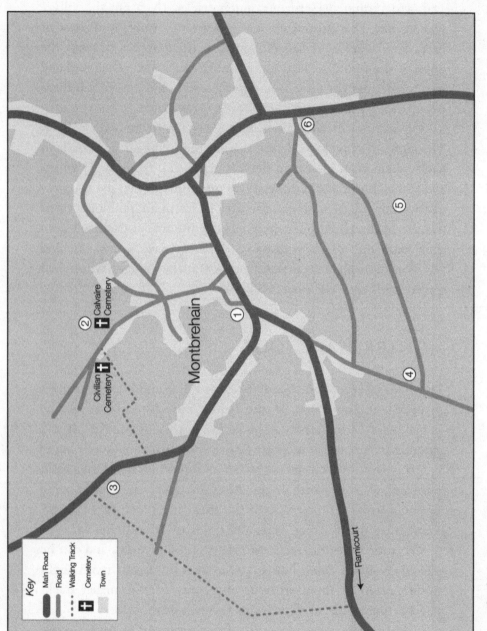

Montbrehain

near the centre of town. Park at the church **[1]** and then turn left onto the main road which heads north out of the village.

Follow this road until you reach Calvaire Cemetery **[2]** on your right. Of the 71 graves, 48 are Australian, including seven that are unidentified. From the cemetery, much of the ground captured by the 24th Battalion, to the north and north-east of the village, can be seen.

Buried here is Captain Harry Fletcher (grave A.11), who enlisted in the 24th Battalion as a private with his good friend Austin Mahony in 1915. Both men served at Gallipoli and both were promoted through the course of the war to captain. During the attack on Montbrehain both Fletcher and Mahony commanded companies of the 24th Battalion and led with skill and courage. Fletcher was killed during the initial assault on the village by a shell aimed at a tank he was directing. Mahony was prominent during the consolidation of the village, until hit in the head by machine-gun fire. He died of his wounds on 9 October and is buried in Tincourt New British Cemetery.

A number of decorated Australians lie in Calvaire Cemetery, including Sergeant Reginald Davies DCM, French Médaille Militaire (17th Battalion, grave B.23), Corporal Ernest Ford DCM (24th Battalion, grave A.18), Sergeant Eric Read MM, French Croix de Guerre (2nd Pioneers, grave B.10) and Private John Blankenberg MM (24th Battalion, grave A.10). Although he had won his Military Medal earlier in 1918, Blankenberg still had ample reserves of fighting spirit at Montbrehain. At one stage of the attack Blankenberg's platoon commander was pushing through a hedge and actually hit his helmet on the muzzle of a German machine-gun on the other side. Blankenberg shot the entire gun crew for being 'cowards'. He was killed later in the day.

Leave the cemetery and cross the road towards the civilian cemetery. (If driving, return along the road to the church and then turn right onto Rue de l'Abbaye.) Just before the cemetery is a farm track leading to the left. Follow this track along the edge of the field and turn right at the intersection of another track. Follow this a short way. Turn left at the next track and follow it to a sealed road, the Rue de l'Abbaye. Turn right into the Rue de l'Abbaye and follow it out of town. Soon the road curves left at a small farmhouse. In the field in front of the house is a large, rough depression. This is the quarry [3] that was captured by Lieutenant Ingram. The Australians advanced towards the quarry from the far side: it is easy to see the protection it afforded the German defenders and what a monumental accomplishment its capture was.

Ingram was tall and he was burly, the archetypal Anzac. He had enlisted in 1914 and served in New Guinea with the Australian Naval and Military Expeditionary Force before joining the 24th Battalion in France as a corporal in January 1917. He won the Military Medal at Bapaume in March 1917 and was commissioned as a 2nd lieutenant in June 1918. After the war he served on the permanent guard of Melbourne's Shrine of Remembrance and enlisted in the Royal Australian Engineers during the Second World War before retiring in 1944. He died in 1961, aged 72.

If driving, return to the village along Rue de l'Abbaye and turn right into Rue de La Haut, then continue the tour from point 4. If walking, turn left into a farm track just beyond the farmhouse near the quarry. The 24th Battalion advanced on both sides of this road towards the quarry during the opening stages of the attack. After one kilometre, at the intersection of several farm tracks, turn left on the sunken straight track that heads directly towards a tall rail silo (ignoring the track that follows a winding course through the field in front of you). The straight track is the remains of the old railway line that ran south of Montbrehain. The Australians began their attack in the fields to your right and attacked towards the village across the railway line (from your right to left). Follow the old rail line until it curves to the right around the silo and joins the sealed Ramicourt–Montbrehain road, at about the point where the Australians assembled to begin the attack. Turn left. As you follow this road into Montbrehain you are walking in the footsteps of the advancing Australians, with the 21st Battalion and 2nd Pioneers on your right, and the 24th Battalion on your left. The uphill slope leaves little doubt as to the difficult task faced by the attackers. Once back in the village, turn right into the Rue de La Haut.

Follow Rue de La Haut until it becomes a farm track. As the 21st Battalion advanced towards the village from the fields in front of you, they came under heavy fire from two quarries on either side of the road, the larger of which can still be seen on the left [4]. The Australians flung themselves down and, under the cover of fire from Lewis light machine-guns, advanced in rushes. As they closed on the quarries the Germans surrendered and eight machine-guns were captured.

Turn left onto a track just past the quarry. This is a continuation of the old rail line. (If driving, note that the track is rough but should be passable to vehicles in fine weather. Alternatively, return along the Rue de La Haut, turn right onto the Rue Charles De Gaulle and then right again on the Rue de Verdun. Follow it until a residential street joins it on the right, then park and continue the tour from point 6.) Follow this track through a crossroads and past another large quarry on your right. Ahead the track curves left. This is the point where, in 1918, two rail lines converged, the second running along an embankment diagonally across the field to your right [5]. Along this stretch of embankment (which has unfortunately disappeared) one of the greatest unrewarded actions of the war occurred. The 2nd Pioneers, advancing south of the village, had fought hard and overcome several German strongpoints. Two machine-guns from the 6th Machine Gun Company were attached to the Pioneers and were commanded by Lieutenant Norman Wilkinson. As the Pioneers advanced towards the railway they were met by ferocious machine-gun fire. Wilkinson crept along the embankment and was amazed to find himself facing about 100 Germans and several machine-guns. He called his guns up and they fired into the massed Germans, killing 30, wounding 50 and destroying 14 machine-guns. A captured German told the Australians that they were sick of the war and would not have fought at all had they known they were facing Australians. Wilkinson's outstanding action is well documented in the Australian *Official History*; why he was not decorated is a mystery.

Continue along the track until it enters the village and becomes sealed. Further along the street, the house at number 1 is the old railway station **[6]**. The platform has been enclosed by a brick wall, but its sloping roof makes its former identity unmistakable. The pharmacy across the road is housed in the former hotel. The first Australians to reach the station during the advance found it piled high with German stores, ammunition and, much to the delight of the troops, several barrels of beer. A group of French women and children emerged from a nearby cellar and were so excited to see the Australians it was difficult to get away from them. After the fighting died down the Australians returned and were given coffee and milk by the villagers.

Turn left at the intersection at the end of the street, then take the left fork towards the centre of the village. The next street on the left leads back to the church and your car.

Before leaving Montbrehain you may wish to drive to High Tree Cemetery, east of the village (see page 337).

OTHER SITES OF INTEREST IN THE AISNE

4th Division Memorial, Bellenglise

In September 1918 the 4th Division joined a joint British and American attack on the Hindenburg Line near the village of Bellenglise. They didn't know it at the time, but this was to be their last action of the First World War. By this stage the 4th was a hardened unit and its battalions performed exceptionally well. The 48th Battalion returned from the fight with so many prisoners that a senior officer was determined to find out how so few Australians could have captured so many Germans. 'The Australians are so brave,' a German battalion commander told him, 'and so quick that it is impossible to stop them.'

After the war the division was spoilt for choice as to where to place its memorial. In the end it settled on the heights overlooking Bellenglise, as this was the site of its last fight of the war and symbolised its service across all the battlefields of the Western Front.

In some ways it was an odd choice, considering how much the division had achieved and sacrificed at the great battles at Pozières, Bullecourt and Passchendaele. Even though the division was proud of its achievements at Bellenglise, it hadn't spent much time there, certainly not enough to form a strong association with the town. But the 4th Division had been on a long journey, one that had begun at Pozières in 1916, and it felt that the last stop was as fitting a place as any to honour its members.

The memorial is the standard stone obelisk and records the division's battle honours as: Somme, Pozières, Bullecourt, Messines, Ypres, Menin Road, Polygon Wood, Passchendaele (spelt 'Passechendaele' on the memorial), Arras, Ancre, Villers-Bretonneux, Hamel, Amiens, Albert, Hindenburg Line and Epehy. It's certainly an impressive list. The 4th was arguably the toughest division in the AIF.

The 4th Division memorial (along with the other four divisional memorials) is one of the most important places of remembrance for Australians on the Western Front but it is isolated and rarely visited. Honour the memory of the Diggers by stopping to see it.

Directions
Bellenglise is 25 kilometres east of Péronne and can be reached via the town of Vermand. The memorial is located off a back road behind some farm buildings and is signposted in the village. In 1998 a memorial plaque was unveiled on the wall of the *mairie* (town hall) proclaiming in French and English 'We do not forget Australia.'

Le Verguier—Gerald Sexton VC and James Woods VC

The final attack on the Hindenburg Line began on 18 September, with Australian and American divisions advancing on its outposts on a wide front. Over the next few days the Australians advanced more swiftly and aggressively than they had in any other battle of the war, taking all their objectives along with 4300 prisoners and dozens of machine-guns. They suffered more than a thousand casualties but this was considered a fair price for the crippling blow they had inflicted on the Germans.

On the left of the 4th Division, the 4th Brigade faced the formidable obstacle of Le Verguier, a fortified village packed with Germans. The 13th Battalion was ordered to swing south of the town but they were hit by shells from their own artillery soon after starting and lost several men. As they pushed on they came under heavy fire from a number of German machine-gun posts. Two were captured by Sergeant Gerald Sexton, who blasted them from close range with his Lewis gun. After passing south of Le Verguier, the 13th spotted a German field gun on a far bank preparing to fire on them. Sexton charged towards the gun and shot the crew, before attacking another post and killing a trench mortar crew. He returned to the bank and fired into several dugout entrances, forcefully convincing more than 30 Germans to surrender. Almost single-handedly, Sexton had captured the headquarters of the line battalion of the German 58th Infantry Regiment. Later in the day the advance continued and Sexton led his men in attacks on several German machine-gun posts that threatened the advance. All in all it was a good day's work for the young Victorian and he received the Victoria Cross.

Gerald Sexton was one of hundreds of men who served in the AIF under a false name, but he was the only one to be caught out by the award of a Victoria Cross. His real name was Maurice Buckley, the name under which he had originally enlisted in the 13th Light Horse in 1914. His service records with this unit have been lost, but we know that he returned to Australia and was discharged in September 1915. He re-enlisted in May 1916, this time under his mother's maiden name of Sexton. 'Gerald' was the name of his brother who had died of illness in a training camp in 1915.

Sexton was wounded at the Battle of Hamel in July 1918 and won the Distinguished Conduct Medal for engaging enemy machine-guns with his Lewis gun during the advance on 8 August.

After he won the VC, he was allowed to serve under his real name. He returned to rural Victoria in 1919, but just over a year later he fell off a horse and was badly injured. He died a few days later. Ten Victoria Cross winners served as pallbearers at his funeral.

The other notable act of valour at Le Verguier occurred when the 48th Battalion advanced from east of the town during the last phase of the attack. The British troops on the right flank had not reached their objective, but resolutely insisted they had. To find out for certain, four men from the 48th were ordered to patrol the ground ahead and report back. The patrol found that a junction of two trenches was strongly held by the Germans and a request was sent back for support troops to come up and attack it. One member of the patrol, Private James Woods, grew impatient at the delay and convinced his three mates to join him in an attack on the post. Such an impetuous stroke had no chance of success but, miraculously, Woods' small group reached the German trench with only one man slightly wounded. Woods killed one of the Germans and the rest—about 30 men—fled, leaving behind six machine-guns. The Germans had no intention of giving up an important position to a handful of impudent Aussies, however, and they counterattacked in strength. Woods climbed onto the parapet of the trench and lay there lobbing bombs at the Germans. His mates kept the supply of bombs coming and Woods was able to break up the German advance. Reinforcing Australian troops arrived to find the trench virtually deserted of Germans and were easily able to consolidate the position. Not surprisingly Woods was awarded the Victoria Cross. It was the first awarded to a member of the 48th Battalion, in the unit's last fight of the war.

Woods had been working as a vigneron in Western Australia when war broke out and immediately tried to enlist. He was rejected for being too short and was not able to join the AIF until manpower shortages forced an easing of the height restriction in 1916. He served with the 48th Battalion from September 1917 until the end of the war. He returned to Australia in 1919 and lived happily with his wife and six children in Perth until his death in 1963. He was 72.

Directions

Le Verguier is 16 kilometres east of Péronne. Leave Le Verguier heading south on the D31. Immediately after leaving the village you are in the sector captured by the 13th Battalion. They passed from right to left across the road and dug in east of the village. Gerald Sexton won his VC during this advance.

James Woods won his Victoria Cross during the 48th Battalion's advance east of Le Verguier towards the St Quentin Canal. Unfortunately the A26 motorway now cuts across the area like a scar and has destroyed much of the ground captured in the advance. By heading south-east out of Le Verguier and then following the D31 to Bellenglise you are driving along the southern flank of the Australian advance. Woods won his VC in the fields to the north.

Hindenburg Line—Blair Wark VC and John Ryan VC

On 29 September the Australians and Americans renewed the attack on the Hindenburg Line and broke through. Over the next few days they advanced well beyond it.

In the early stages the 32nd Battalion advanced from near Bellicourt under a screen of fog and smoke from the British barrage. The battalion's temporary commander, Major Blair Wark, was a brilliant young officer and led the men in several attacks on German machine-gun posts. As they advanced Wark came across 200 leaderless Americans wandering aimlessly across his front and ordered them to join his advance. His force cleared several German machine-gun posts as it moved forward and eventually realised that the American troops on their right had not reached their objectives. Wark decided to take on their job as well as his own and advanced south of Nauroy, taking 40 prisoners from the outskirts of the village. Wark could not see any friendly forces around him but decided to push on as far as he could. Several machine- and field gun crews fired until the 32nd were upon them and then surrendered. Wark and his men eventually met up with some British troops and dug in. Later that day the Germans counterattacked but were beaten off by the 32nd and 31st battalions, plus the British troops. The following day the 32nd Battalion advanced again, eventually digging in north of Joncourt. The day after that they captured Joncourt itself. The battalion had played an important role in the successful attack on the Hindenburg Line and this was entirely due to the brilliant leadership of Major Wark. He was awarded the Victoria Cross.

Blair Wark enlisted in August 1915 and was originally posted to the 30th Battalion. He served with that unit in the terrible fighting at Fromelles and, like most other officers that day, was wounded. After his return from hospital he transferred to the 32nd Battalion and received the Distinguished Service Order for repelling three counterattacks at Polygon Wood in September 1917. He was appointed second in command of the battalion in 1918 and was Mentioned in Despatches in June. His commanding officer referred to him as 'brave to the point of recklessness'. He returned to Australia in 1919 and worked in Sydney until the outbreak of the Second World War. He joined the 1st Battalion as second in command and became temporary commander in 1940. He died suddenly at Puckapunyal training camp in 1941 and was buried in Sydney with full military honours. He was 46.

On 30 September the Australians continued their assault on the Hindenburg Line, with the 5th Division launching a flanking attack near Bellicourt. The supporting artillery barrage was thin, and ferocious fights broke out at isolated German machine-gun posts scattered across the countryside. The 55th Battalion had taken ground but were forced to take cover in a German trench under a hurricane of fire. The Germans launched a counterattack and were driving the Australians back when Private John Ryan organised a small party and led a bombing attack against them. By the time the Australians were close enough to go in with the bayonet only four of them were unwounded but, under Ryan's direction, they killed the first three Germans they met. Ryan charged at the rest, throwing bombs as he went, but was hit in the shoulder. His action had unsettled the Germans, however, and they abandoned the trench, suffering heavy casualties from Australian fire as they withdrew across the open. Due to Ryan's audacious attack, the rest of the battalion was able to reoccupy the trench and continue on to their objective. Ryan received the Victoria Cross.

John Ryan was working as a labourer in Wagga Wagga, New South Wales, when he enlisted in late 1915. He joined the 55th Battalion in France in September 1916 and served with them until he was wounded in his VC action. He returned to Australia in 1919 but not much is known about his movements after the war. Like many of his comrades he struggled to fit back into civilian life and suffered from poor health and depression. In 1941 he was admitted to the Royal Melbourne Hospital with pneumonia, and died there soon after. He was 51. Major Blair Wark, who had won the VC at the same time and same place, died two weeks later.

Directions

The Australian attack on the Hindenburg Line was launched on a wide front stretching for about three kilometres from Bony to Bellicourt. Blair Wark won his VC by leading the 32nd Battalion on a long advance from just north of the St Quentin Tunnel entrance at Bellicourt, west of Nauroy and south to the road that heads north-east from la Baraque. John Ryan won his VC in the le Catelet Line east of Bellicourt. From the centre of Bellicourt drive east on the D93 (in the direction of Nauroy) and turn left at a crossroads before leaving the village. Follow this road past the chateau and on until you leave the village. Less than a kilometre after the crossroads is an intersection with a farm track on the left. Park your car and walk along this track until the bank disappears on your left. One hundred metres further on is the point where the le Catelet Line crossed the track. The trench ran north–south across these fields, and Ryan won his VC in the section of trench about 400 metres into the field to the north. Cabaret Wood Farm, a famous wartime landmark, is 400 metres south-east of where you are standing.

St Quentin Canal Tunnel, Bellicourt

The St Quentin Canal was built under orders of Napoleon in the 19th century and joins the Somme and Scheldt rivers. During the war the Germans incorporated this formidable obstacle into the defences of the Hindenburg Line. In order to break through the line the British had to cross the canal. The most obvious place to do this was where the canal ran underground along a five-kilometre tunnel between Bellicourt and Vendhuile.

During the attack on the Hindenburg Line on 29 September, the Australian 3rd and 5th divisions were ordered to capture the canal in conjunction with the American 27th and 30th divisions. But the attack did not go according to plan. The American troops were inexperienced and struggled to take their objectives. In the north the Australians, who were supposed to be following the attack, joined the fight and the advance became a series of brief but savage tussles for German trenches and strongpoints. At one stage Captain Hubert Wilkins, an Australian official photographer, came forward to photograph the advance and found a group of Americans calmly sitting in a captured German trench, cleaning their weapons. Wilkins walked further along the trench and, no doubt to his surprise, ran into a group of Germans lobbing hand grenades towards the Americans. Wilkins ran back to the Americans to warn them of the impending attack. They were totally unaware, believing that the grenade explosions they could hear were just ordinary shellbursts. Wilkins ordered them to line the parapet of the trench and with three shots they killed one German and scattered the rest.

Further south the Americans did better and the Australian 5th Division was able to advance and capture Bellicourt, while American units cleared the southern entrance to the St Quentin Tunnel on their right. Australian units who explored the tunnel found that the Germans had moored barges inside it and used it to shelter troops. They had also planted explosives at intervals for most of its length, intending to destroy it, but these were disarmed by Australian engineers.

Directions

Bellicourt is 22 kilometres east of Péronne. The St Quentin Tunnel at Bellicourt remains much as the Americans and Australians found it in 1918. The tunnel entrance is one kilometre south of the village. A path meanders down the hill to it, passing several German bunkers in the foliage. In 1918 Arthur Streeton, then an official war artist, made several watercolour sketches of the tunnel entrance from this path. After visiting the tunnel, stop at Bellicourt British Cemetery in the village (see pages 336–337). In February 2006 the remains of an Australian soldier were found near the Hindenburg Line at Bellicourt.

Estrées—Joe Maxwell VC

The village of Estrées came to prominence in October 1918, directly after the capture of Bellicourt in late September. With the Hindenburg Line secured, the 2nd Division was called forward to attack yet another German defensive line, the Beaurevoir Line, which ran past Estrées. It wasn't known at the time, but the 2nd Division's attacks between 3 and 5 October would be the last Australian actions of the war.

On 3 October the 17th, 18th and 19th battalions advanced towards the Beaurevoir Line east of Estrées. They immediately came under heavy fire and were having a hard time breaking into the German trenches. At several points during the advance Lieutenant Joe Maxwell of the 18th Battalion braved this onslaught to attack German machine-gun posts. His most remarkable feat of the day came when a captured German told him that some comrades in the next post wanted to surrender but were afraid to give themselves up. Maxwell and two other Australians entered the post but were immediately surrounded by about 20 men and taken prisoner. Just then a heavy British bombardment descended on the post and the Germans were momentarily distracted. Maxwell drew a spare revolver he kept in his gas mask pack and shot two of the Germans, before scarpering with his mates back to the Australian line. The 2nd Division successfully captured the Beaurevoir Line and Maxwell was awarded the Victoria Cross.

Joe Maxwell finished the war as one of the most famous members of the AIF. He was the second most decorated Australian after Harry Murray (see **Gueudecourt**, pages 182–183) and had immense personal charm. He had enlisted in 1915 and arrived in Gallipoli in time for the bitter fighting of the August offensives. He was a natural soldier and was quickly promoted through the ranks. At Ypres in 1917 he was a company sergeant major and won the Distinguished Conduct Medal for leading men under fire during the attack near Westhoek. In March 1918, then a lieutenant, he received the Military Cross while leading a patrol near Ploegsteert Wood. In August 1918 his company was advancing near Rainecourt into heavy fire behind a tank, which was soon hit by a shell. Maxwell jumped onto the burning machine and yanked open the hatch, dragging the crew out and leading them to safety moments before the tank exploded. He then rejoined his company and led them to the objective. For this sterling effort he received a bar to his Military Cross. In just over a year, Joe Maxwell had won the VC, DCM, MC & Bar.

After the war Joe Maxwell returned to Australia and worked in a variety of jobs around New South Wales and Canberra. At the start of the Second World War he tried to enlist but was rejected as too old; in response, he travelled to Queensland and successfully enlisted under an alias. His true identity was soon discovered and he was posted to a training battalion. Joe Maxwell died in Sydney in 1967, aged 71.

Directions

Estrées is 25 kilometres east of Péronne. The Hindenburg Line trenches ran immediately east of the village but modern development has encroached on the site. On 3 October 1918 the 18th Battalion attacked slightly south of the main road through the village, the D932. Follow this road to the eastern edge of the village and turn right onto a farm track at a small crucifix. After 200 metres you will reach the approximate position of the Hindenburg Line trenches and the site of Joe Maxwell's VC action.

CEMETERIES IN THE AISNE

Australian forces were prominent during the Allied sweep across the Aisne in the second half of 1918 and their sacrifice is chronicled in nearly every cemetery in the area. This is a lovely part of rural France and most of the military cemeteries here are small and intimate. Nearly every village you visit will have a small plot containing at least a handful of Australian graves. They are all worth visiting, but the following are some with special significance for Australian visitors.

Bellicourt British Cemetery

Bellicourt British Cemetery was begun soon after the town of Bellicourt fell to the Allies in October 1918. At the time of the Armistice the cemetery only contained 73 graves, but it was greatly enlarged by the concentration of graves from isolated plots and smaller cemeteries in the area. It now contains 1204 burials, of which 307 are Australian. Most of these men were killed during the Australian advance in September 1918 and 46 of them are unidentified.

Buried here is one of the AIF's outstanding young leaders. Captain James Sullivan was commander of the famous 'brewery' company of the 21st Battalion, named after the period of time it spent billeted in the brewery at Querrieu in early 1918. Sullivan had won the Military Medal at Gallipoli and two Military Crosses in 1918. He was killed by a shell at the start of the advance on Montbrehain, 5 October 1918—Australia's last day of combat in the war (grave VI.S.7).

Also buried here is Captain Arthur Rogers MC, a company commander in the 32nd Battalion. Rogers served under Major Blair Wark in the action that earned Wark the Victoria Cross (see pages 330–331). During the 32nd's long advance, Wark ordered Rogers to lead a tank and a company into the southern part of Nauroy and secure the village. The tank was soon hit by artillery fire and Rogers was shot and killed, but the company cleared the southern half of the village and took 40 prisoners. Rogers had won the Military Cross for his work during the Australian advance in August, only three weeks before his death (grave II.C.9).

Directions

Bellicourt is 22 kilometres east of Péronne. The cemetery is on the D331 (the road from Péronne), on the west side of the village.

Calvaire Cemetery, Montbrehain: see Montbrehain tour (page 337).

High Tree Cemetery, Montbrehain

This is one of three military cemeteries in and around the village of Montbrehain, the scene of Australia's last battle of the First World War. High Tree Cemetery is small and isolated, containing only 48 graves. Four of the men who lie here are Australian, but only two of them could be identified. They are Privates Charles Bateman and Joseph Taylor, both of the 2nd Pioneers. Pause for a moment in front of Private Taylor's grave. This is the most easterly Australian grave on Australia's last battlefield of the war. Symbolically the AIF's long journey, which began on the shores of Gallipoli, ended here. Private Taylor's grave is as appropriate a place as any to remember four years of sacrifice and 61 000 Australians who never came home.

Directions

Montbrehain is 38 kilometres east of Péronne. High Tree Cemetery is a kilometre east of the village on the D705 to Fresnoy-le-Grand. The cemetery is hidden from view along a farm track. Montbrehain is rarely visited by Australians, or anyone else for that matter. Even those who do come this far don't usually make it to High Tree Cemetery. Spend a few moments here to honour the Diggers who fell in the AIF's last fight of the war.

Jeancourt Communal Cemetery Extension

The Australian 2nd Battalion entered Jeancourt on the night of 10 September 1918. They found the town deserted but heard a column of Germans approaching and lay in ambush. As soon as the Germans appeared the Australians opened fire and shattered the column, with very heavy loss according to the German unit history.

Jeancourt had been a German hospital base earlier in the war and both the Germans and the British used the extension to the communal cemetery to bury their dead. Further Commonwealth graves were added after the Armistice. Today there are 492 Commonwealth and 168 German burials in the cemetery. Australian graves number 114, with all but 16 identified. These Australians were all killed during the advance in September 1918.

The most senior Australian buried here is Captain Robert Young of the 3rd Field Ambulance, who was killed when a shell landed in his dugout at the regimental aid post at Jeancourt on 18 September 1918 (grave III.B.3).

Directions
Jeancourt is 15 kilometres east of Péronne. The cemetery is signposted in the village.

Prospect Hill Cemetery, Gouy

This cemetery was made in October 1918 and contains the graves of men killed in the immediate area. It was slightly enlarged after the Armistice when isolated bodies were brought in from the surrounding fields. Today the cemetery contains 538 graves, of which 77 are Australian. Eleven of these are unidentified.

This is an interesting cemetery because all Australian graves except one belong to men killed in October 1918, in the very last days of Australia's involvement in the war.

The most senior Australian buried here is Captain William Braithwaite MC of the 22nd Battalion, who was killed attacking a machine-gun post near Estrées on 3 October 1918. He had won his Military Cross at Bullecourt in May 1917 (grave IV.D.17).

The inscription on his headstone reads: 'His last words were, as he fell, "Go on C Company"'. Prospect Cemetery includes dozens of interesting headstones from a range of units such as the Australian Flying Corps, the Royal Flying Corps (and its successor, the Royal Airforce—including burials from both World Wars), the Tank Corps and even an Army chaplain. The good work done by Australian troops in 1918 is demonstrated by the large number of Australians buried in this cemetery who had received bravery awards.

Directions

The village of Gouy is 27 kilometres east of Péronne, next to the larger centre of le Catelet. The cemetery is less than two kilometres east of Gouy on the road to Beaurevoir.

Somme American Cemetery, Bony

In spite of the name, this large cemetery is located in the Aisne, and is the final resting place for 1844 Americans killed fighting in the area. Like all American military cemeteries it is dramatic and impressive, with the graves in razor-straight rows separated into four large plots. A memorial records the names of 333 men missing from fighting in the region. Look for the graves of Pte Robert Blackwell, Cpl Thomas O'Shea and Lieutenant William Turner who all received the Medal of Honor, the highest bravery decoration a US soldier can receive. Also look for graves dated July 4 and September 29, 1918—these men were killed while fighting alongside Australian troops.

Directions

Somme American Cemetery is located south-west of the village of Bony on the D57.

Tincourt New British Cemetery

The village of Tincourt fell into British hands after the German withdrawal to the Hindenburg Line in March 1917 and became the site of several casualty clearing stations. The Germans recaptured it in 1918 and used the cemetery to bury their own dead until it was taken by the Allies for the last time in September 1918. Tincourt New British Cemetery was greatly enlarged after the Armistice, when graves were brought in from the surrounding battlefields. Technically the cemetery is in the *département* of the Somme, but because most of the 228 Australians who lie here were killed in fighting in the Aisne, I have included it in this section.

Tincourt is well known for its high number of Australian officer burials. It has even been claimed that this cemetery has the highest number of identified Australian officer graves on the Western Front, with 37 in total. While this is certainly a large number, it falls well short of the 68 Australian officers buried in Heath Cemetery, Harbonnières (see **Village Battles of 1918**, pages 235–237).

One of the great leaders of the AIF lies in Tincourt Cemetery. Captain Austin Mahony MC was a company commander in the 24th Battalion. He had enlisted as a private in 1915 with his good mate Harry Fletcher. Both men served at Gallipoli and were promoted through the ranks to captain. At Montbrehain on 5 October 1918 both men commanded companies in the 24th Battalion and both were hit during the advance. Fletcher was killed instantly and now lies in Calvaire Cemetery, Montbrehain. Mahony was severely wounded but hung on for four days. He died at Tincourt on 9 October (grave VII.A.20).

Also buried here is Captain Walter Hallahan of the 11th Battalion who was twice wounded and won the Military Medal at Gallipoli. At Pozières in 1916 he won the Military Cross for his excellent leadership during the opening days of the attack. He was killed during the advance to the Hindenburg Line on 18 September 1918 (grave V.E.6). Two of his brothers, Wendell and William, were killed in action in 1916.

The family of Private Joe Baxter, who lies in Tincourt Cemetery, could have been forgiven for thinking that he had done his bit long before the Great War even began. Baxter was originally from Scotland and had served in Egypt and the Nile from 1882 to 1885 and had been awarded the Egypt Medal with five clasps. He was also a veteran of the Boer War, where he again excelled and was awarded the Distinguished Conduct Medal. He was living in Australia during the First World War and enlisted in the AIF in 1917, even though he was 54 years old. He served with the 21st Battalion and was killed by a shell at Montbrehain on 5 October 1918, Australia's last fight of the war (grave X.C.19).

Directions
The village of Tincourt is seven kilometres east of Péronne. The cemetery is on the western edge of the village, on the D199.

Unicorn Cemetery, Vendhuile

The village of Vendhuile was captured by American and British units in September 1918. The cemetery was started soon after by the British 50th Division, who named it after their divisional emblem. It was enlarged after the Armistice, when graves were brought in from the surrounding 1918 battlefields as well as the nearby 1917 battlefield of Cambrai. Today the cemetery contains 1008 graves, 78 of which are Australian. All these men were killed in the Australian advance in the area in September and October 1918, and 18 of them could not be identified.

The most prominent Australian buried here is Corporal Lawrence Weathers of the 43rd Battalion, who won the Victoria Cross on 2 September, 1918 for capturing German machine-gun positions near Allaines (see pages 260–261). He was killed during the advance on the Beaurevoir Line on 29 September (grave III.C.5).

Directions
Vendhuile is 23 kilometres north-east of Péronne. Unicorn Cemetery is three kilometres south-west of the village on the D28 road to Lempire.

In Memoriam

In Memoriam notices first appeared in Australian newspapers during the Great War, as a means of helping families, and indeed the nation, come to terms with the loss of so many young men. They provide a unique insight into the crushing grief that enveloped Australia and is today, mercifully, difficult to fully comprehend.

The following notices originally appeared in metropolitan newspapers.

BAKER—In loving remembrance of our dear son and brother, Frederick James, of the 21st Batt., who died of wounds in France on October 6, 1918.

> Our loved one is sleeping his long last sleep,
> And his grave we may never see;
> But some gentle hand in that far distant land
> May plant a small flower for me.

Inserted by his loving mother and father, sisters and brothers.

The Argus, October 6th, 1919

BASS—Love's tribute to the memory of my dear husband, Sapper S. N. C. Bass, died of wounds received in action in France, Anzac morning, 1918. Remembered always by his loving wife, Lily.

Sydney Morning Herald, April 25th, 1938

BIRD—In loving memory of my dear father, Pte. C. Bird, killed in action, Mont St. Quentin, September 1, 1918.

> On Quentin's heights he fought and fell,
> Serving his God and country well.

Inserted by his loving son, Stan (recently returned).

Sydney Morning Herald, September 1st, 1919

BIRD—In loving memory of my dearly loved and only son, Pte. C. Bird (Charlie), 5th Batt., killed in action Mont St. Quentin, September 1, 1918.

> I little thought when we said good-bye
> We parted forever and you were to die.
> We'll meet again, my dearest son.

Inserted by his loving mother, A. Madden.

Sydney Morning Herald, September 1st, 1919

BLACK—In sad and loving memory of our dear son, James Frederick Black, killed in action, April 5, 1918, aged 20 years and 5 months.

> Could I, his mother, have clasped his hand,
> The son I loved so well,
> Or kissed his brow when death was near,
> And whispered, "My son, farewell."
> I seem to see his dear, sweet face,
> Through a mist of anxious tears;
> But a mother's part is a broken heart,
> And a burden of lonely years.

Inserted by his loving mother and father, and brothers, Babe and Norman Black.

Sydney Morning Herald, April 5th, 1919

[Many similar listings appear in 1919, indicating this was a standard verse suggested by the newspaper.]

BLAKE—Killed in action on 19 July, 1916 (previously reported missing). George Francis, No. 4737, late of 59th Bn, sailed only on March 7 of the same year.

> I have lost my soul's companion
> A life linked with my own
> Each day I miss his footsteps
> As I walk through life alone.

Inserted by his loving wife.

The Age, July 19th, 1917

BLAKE—In loving memory of George Francis, killed in France, 19 July, 1916.

30 long years. Ever remembered.

Inserted by Jean.

The Argus, July 19th, 1946

BRADLEY—In loving memory of our dear son and brother, Private Earnest William Bradley, killed in action, France, September 1, 1918.

No one knows the silent heartache,
Friends may think the wound is healed;
But they cannot see the sorrow,
Deep within our hearts concealed.

Inserted by his sorrowing mother and father, brothers and sisters.

Sydney Morning Herald, September 1st, 1919

BUTTERWORTH—In loving memory of my beloved brother, Rupert Godfrey, killed in action at Polygon Wood September 26, 1917.

The war, the cruel red war, took one,
He sleeps where brave men sleep;
He was the loved of all, yet none
O'er his grave may weep.

Inserted by his loving sister, Alice.

Sydney Morning Herald, September 26th, 1918

CROCKETT—In sad and loving memory of my dear son, Corporal W. Crockett, killed at Pozières, July 23, 1916, aged 18. Not forgetting his dear father, Sgt. W. J. Crockett, 56th Batt., wounded at Fleurbaix, died August 4, 1916.

We'll stem the storm, it won't be long.

Inserted by their loved ones at home, "Pozières", Tramway Street, Tempe.

Sydney Morning Herald, July 23rd, 1921

DAVIS—In sad and ever-loving memory of my darling Roy, Sergeant Roy B. Davis, 35th Batt., killed in action at Hamel, August 8, 1918, aged 24 years 11 months.

At the heavenly gates he will meet us
With the same sweet, loving smile,
For we are only parted dear,
Just for a little while.

Inserted by his ever-loving Eva and baby, Phyllis.

Sydney Morning Herald, August 8th, 1919

FLETCHER-MAHONY—In loving memory of my true friends, Captains Harry Fletcher and Austin Mahony, M.C., 24th Batt., who were killed in the battle of Montbrehain, 5th October, 1918, the last day's fighting of the A.I.F.

Lieutenant Leslie V. Starr, 24th Batt., abroad.

The Argus, October 6th, 1919

GEORGE—In everlasting memory of Roy (Snowy) George, killed in action, April 5, 1918, late 13th Battalion. Inserted by his comrade, Private Reg. Davis.

Sydney Morning Herald, April 5th, 1919

GILL—In loving memory of my dear husband, George Arthur Gill, No. 2908, 59th Batt., killed at Harbonnières on August 8, 1918. Inserted by his wife, Jessie J. Gill, and three little sons, George, James and David.

Sydney Morning Herald, August 8th, 1919

GILLESPIE–McMURTIE—In loving memory of my brother, Private Noel Gillespie, 7th Battn., who died of wounds in France, October 6, 1917; also my fiancé, Private Fred McMurtie, 38th Battn., killed in action at Passchendaele, October 12, 1917 (reported missing).

That which they had to give, they gave—their lives.

May Gillespie, District Hospital, Swan Hill.

The Argus, October 6th, 1919

GLASSINGTON—Died of wounds in France, April 6, 1918, in his 24th year, Private J. P. Glassington, dear loved husband of Myra, and father of little Jack and Millie.

Our home is always lonely,
Our hearts are always sad;
I miss my loving husband,
The children miss their dad.

Sydney Morning Herald, April 5th, 1919

GLAZEBROOK—In loving memory of our dearest sons, Pte. Harry, died of wounds, Pozières, August 8, 1916, 45th Batt; also Pte. Roy, killed in action, April 2, 1917, 56th Batt.

Our heroes.

Inserted by their loving mother and father.

Sydney Morning Herald, August 8th, 1919

HANRAHAN—In memory of our brother Denis, killed October 6th, 1917.

– Jack, Maggie and Jim.

The Age, October 6th, 1967

HITCHCOCK—In loving memory of my dear son, Albert, killed in action Passchendaele Ridge on October 12, 1917, aged 27 years.

> When all alone we sit and think,
> We seem to hear him say,
> "Keep up your heart, dear mother,
> "We will meet again some day."

Inserted by his loving mother, Annie Lamb, Cessnock.

Newcastle Morning Herald, October 12th, 1923

HOLLAND—In loving memory of my dear husband and our father, Lance-corporal J. P. Holland, who was killed at Pozières, between July 23-25, 1916. An Anzac.

> He gave his best—his life, his all.

Inserted by his loving wife, Jessie, and children, Jack and Eileen.

Sydney Morning Herald, July 23rd, 1921

[Jessie Holland also posted memorial notices for her husband on the anniversary of his death in 1926, 1936, 1946, 1956 and 1966. By 1956 Eileen was no longer included in the insertion line.]

JEFFRIES—Captain Clarence Smith, V.C. 12th October, 1917.

Newcastle Morning Herald, October 12th, 1923

JONES—In proud and loving memory of my dear son, Lance-Corporal W. T. Jones, 1579, 57th Battalion, late of the 8th, who was killed in action at Bullecourt, France, May 13, 1917.

> Our Anzac.

Inserted by his loving mother, Alice Jones.

The Argus, May 13th, 1918

LINFORD—In sad and loving memory of our dear son and brother, No. 3880, Private Charlie Henry Linford, 2nd Pioneer Battalion, killed in action on the 5th October, 1918, at Montbrehain.

> Our brave hero.
> When we see the boys returning
> Our hearts they throb with pain
> To think that you're not there, dear Charlie,
> And will never come again.

Inserted by his loving mother and father, sisters and brothers.

The Argus, October 6th, 1919

MACGREGOR—In everlasting memory of dear Alan, killed in action, September 26, 1917. Affectionate friend of Rubie Tripp.

Sydney Morning Herald, September 26th, 1918

MALONE—A tribute of love and remembrance of my dear husband, Private W. T. Malone, who died of wounds, Amiens, August 8, 1918.

Until the day breaks.

Inserted by his affectionate wife, Ethel.

Sydney Morning Herald, August 8th, 1919

MARLES—In ever loving memory of my dear husband and our daddy, Pte. Harry Marles, 54th Batt., killed in action near Péronne, September 1, 1918.

Too dearly loved to be forgotten.

Inserted by his loving wife, Celia, and children, Irene and Harry.

Sydney Morning Herald, September 1st, 1919

McDONALD—In fondest memory of Jack, killed October 12 (his 24th birthday), 1917.

Though lost to sight to memory ever dear.

Inserted by his loving sister, Mary.

Sydney Morning Herald, October 12th, 1937

MILLS—In loving memory of our beloved boy, Gunner Jack L. Mills, killed in France, September 26, 1916.

Inserted by his loving mother and brother, Claude.

Sydney Morning Herald, September 26th, 1918

NITCHIE—In loving memory of my dear daddy, Pte. J. L. Nitchie, killed in action, July 19, 1916, also my dear uncle, Pte. L. Nitchie, killed in action, August 4, 1916.

Though I am far away dear daddy,
And your grave I cannot see,
I am always thinking of you,
As you used to think of me.

Inserted by his loving daughter, little Ivy.

Geelong Advertiser, July 19th, 1920

OHLSEN (Axel Olaf), Anzac—A tribute to his loving memory, missing in France.

Those who think of him to-day
Are those who loved him best.

Inserted by his loving wife, Ada Ohlsen.

Sydney Morning Herald, April 25th, 1927

ORROCK—In proud but sad memory of our brave boys, Perce and Hal, who fell on the field of honour somewhere in France.

Oh, do not ask if we miss them,
Our noble lads.

Father, mother, sisters, and brother.

The Argus, April 22nd, 1918

OVERMAN—In loving memory of Private R. J. Overman, "Jock", 13th and 2nd Batts., died of wounds received while stretcher-bearing at Polygon Wood, September 26, 1917, aged 23. A re-enlisted Anzac.

Inserted by father, mother, brothers and sister.

Sydney Morning Herald, September 26th, 1918

PARTRIDGE—Memories of my dear husband and our dad, Sergeant C. Partridge, 1st Pioneers, died of wounds in France, April 24, 1916. Remembered by his loving wife and children.

Sydney Morning Herald, April 23rd, 1938

POLGLAZE—Charles, 2884. 59th Bn of Thornbury. K in A Fromelles, France, July 19, 1916. Remembered with respect. Bruce Jager.

Herald-Sun, July 19th, 1991

QUILL—In loving memory of my dear husband and my uncle, Private George Quill, 1st Batt., killed in action October 4, 1917.

Twenty years have passed,
But memories last forever.

Inserted by his loving Flo and niece, Gladys Burridge.

Sydney Morning Herald, October 4th, 1937

SOMERS—In loving memory of Corporal Egbert Somers, 37th Battalion, killed in action, Messines, 7th June, 1917, dearly loved only son of Arthur J. and M. Perry, aged 23 years.

He played the game.

Inserted by his loving parents and sisters.

The Argus, June 7th, 1918

THOMPSON—In loving memory of my dear sons and our brothers, George Frederick, killed in France April 11, 1917, aged 25 years; Wilmore Harry, killed August 4, 1916, aged 18 years.

Sadly missed.

Inserted by their loving mother, sisters, and brothers, and son, Georgie.

Sydney Morning Herald, April 11th, 1927

To the everlasting memory of all members of 1st Field Engineers, A.I.F., who made the supreme sacrifice during the Great War, 1914-18; also to those who have since passed on.

1st Field Engineers Association. S. Lalor. Hon. Secretary.

Sydney Morning Herald, April 25th, 1938

WALLIS—Dear old Lou (an Anzac). Lovingly remembered by Auntie Mag., Mrs. Grounds and family.

Sydney Morning Herald, September 1st, 1919

WEIR—To the memory of Private T. Weir, killed in action October 12, 1917.

Never forgotten.

Inserted by his widow, Louisa Weir, Dudley.

Newcastle Morning Herald, October 12th, 1923

WENSOR—My ever remembered chum, Pte. Eddie Wensor, 55th Batt., killed in action, Polygon Wood, September 26, 1917.

Pte Morris Shelton, 18th Batt. (returned wounded).

Sydney Morning Herald, September 26th, 1918

YOUNG—In sad and loving memory of our dear friend, Private Joseph Allen Young, killed in action, "somewhere in France", October 4, 1917.

Under the flag with the five-starred cross,
The pride of the southern seas,
He laid down his life in the deadly strife
To keep Australia free.

Inserted by his loving and best friends, L. R. and A. Gangell, Forcett.

Hobart Mercury, October 4th, 1918

Select Bibliography

This book was predominantly compiled using unit diaries, personal records, official communications and other primary sources in the Australian War Memorial archive. The following secondary sources were also used:

Bean, Charles, *Official History of Australia in the War of 1914–18,* vols I–VI, Angus & Robertson, Sydney, 1921–1942.
——*Anzac to Amiens,* Australian War Memorial, Canberra, 1961.
——*Gallipoli Mission,* ABC Books, Sydney, 1991.
——*Letters from France,* Cassell, 1917.
Beumelburg, Werner, *Schlachten des Weltkrieges,* vol 27, Stalling, Berlin, 1928.
Carlyon, Les, *Gallipoli,* Macmillan, Sydney, 2001.
Carthew, Noel, *Voices from the Trenches,* New Holland Publishers, Sydney, 2002.
Cave, Nigel, *Polygon Wood,* Leo Cooper, London, 1999.
——*Passchendaele,* Pen & Sword Books, Barnsley, UK, 2003.
Clark, Lloyd, *World War I,* Helicon, Abingdon, UK, 2001.
Cochrane, Peter, *The Western Front,* ABC Books, Sydney, 2004.
Coppard, George, *With a Machine Gun to Cambrai,* Cassell, London, 1999.
Corfield, Robin S, *Don't Forget Me, Cobber,* Corfield & Company, Rosanna, Vic., 2000.
Cutlack, FM, *Official History of Australia in the War of 1914–18,* vol. VIII: The Australian Flying Corps, Angus & Robertson, Sydney, 1923.
Edmonds, Charles (pseud. of Charles Carrington), *A Subaltern's War,* P. Davies, London, 1929.
Ferguson, Niall, *The Pity of War,* Penguin Books, London, 1999.

Fewster, Kevin (ed.), *Gallipoli Correspondent: The Frontline Diary of CEW Bean*, Allen & Unwin, Sydney, 1985.

Grant, Ian, *Jacka VC*, Macmillan, Sydney, 1989.

Green, FC, *The Fortieth: A Record of the 40th Battalion, AIF*, 40th Battalion Association, 1922.

Holt, Tonie & Valmai, *Major & Mrs Holt's Battlefield Guide to the Somme*, Leo Cooper, Barnsley, UK, 2000.

Keech, Graham, *Pozières*, Pen & Sword Books, Barnsley, UK, 1998.

Keegan, John, *The First World War*, Hutchinson, London, 2001.

Knyvett, R Hugh, *Over There with the Australians*, Scribners, New York, 1918.

Laffin, John, *A Guide to Australian Battlefields of the Western Front 1916–1918*, Kangaroo Press, Sydney, 1994.

——*Digging Up the Diggers' War*, Kangaroo Press, Sydney, 1993.

——*The Battle of Hamel*, Kangaroo Press, Sydney, 1999.

——*British Butchers and Bunglers of World War One*, Macmillan, Sydney, 1989.

——*Western Front 1917–1918*, Time Life Books, Sydney, 1988.

Middlebrook, Martin, *The First Day on the Somme*, Penguin Books, London, 2001.

Middlebrook, Martin & Mary, *The Somme Battlefields: A Comprehensive Guide from Crécy to the Two World Wars*, Penguin Books, London, 1994.

Oldham, Peter, *Messines Ridge*, Pen & Sword Books, Barnsley, UK, 2003.

——*Pillboxes on the Western Front*, Leo Cooper, Barnsley, UK, 1995.

Pedersen, Peter, *Fromelles*, Pen & Sword Books, Barnsley, UK, 2004.

——*Monash as Military Commander*, Melbourne University Press, 1985.

Pidgeon, Trevor, *Flers & Gueudecourt*, Pen & Sword Books, Barnsley, UK, 2002.

Reed, Paul, *Walking the Salient*, Pen & Sword Books, Barnsley, UK, 1999.

Rule, Edgar, *Jacka's Mob*, Military Melbourne, 1999.

Spagnoly, Tony & Smith, Ted, *The Anatomy of a Raid: The Australians at Celtic Wood*, Leo Cooper, Barnsley, 1998.

Steadman, Michael, *Advance to Victory 1918*, Pen & Sword Books, Barnsley, UK, 2001.

von Stosch, Albrecht, *Schlachten des Weltkrieges*, vol 21, Stalling, Berlin, 1927.

Wigmore, Lionel (ed.), *They Dared Mightily*, Australian War Memorial, Canberra, 1963.

Index